Eugen Wendler

The Political Economy of Friedrich List

Springer

Eugen Wendler
Reutlingen, Baden-Württemberg, Germany

ISSN 2662-6098 ISSN 2662-6101 (electronic)
Springer Studies in the History of Economic Thought
ISBN 978-3-031-24600-5 ISBN 978-3-031-24601-2 (eBook)
https://doi.org/10.1007/978-3-031-24601-2

The translation was done with the help of artificial intelligence (machine translation by the service https://www.DeepL.com). A subsequent human revision was done primarily in terms of content.
Translation from the German language edition: "Die Politische Ökonomie von Friedrich List" by Eugen Wendler, © The publisher 2020. Published by Springer Fachmedien Wiesbaden GmbH. All Rights Reserved.

This Springer imprint is published by the registered company Springer Nature Switzerland AG
The registered company address is: Gewerbestrasse 11, 6330 Cham, Switzerland

This book is dedicated to Ulrich Sihler, Product- and Marketing Manager for overseas markets with an automobile manufacturer in Stuttgart, for our close and long standing collaboration together with Reutlingen University, and the time-consuming content review and editing of the electronic translation.

Foreword by Prof. Dr. h.c. Erwin Teufel

Three monuments have been dedicated to Friedrich List: the first by his hometown of Reutlingen, the second by the first President of the Federal Republic of Germany, Theodor Heuss, in the third volume of his series *The Great Germans*, and the third by Professor Dr. Eugen Wendler, who has researched Friedrich List for more than 40 years and shared his findings in the books, *Friedrich List—an Economist with Vision and Social Responsibility* and *Friedrich List in the Age of Globalization*, as well as in many other books and publications. Prof. Wendler has become the foremost expert on Friedrich List.

Theodor Heuss wrote: "When the name of Friedrich List is mentioned, the Germans have a guilty conscience. They feel the tragedy connected with him was so possible only on German soil. It is an eternal indictment."

In 1803, the Holy Roman Empire of the German Nation came to an end in Regensburg in the never-ending Imperial Diet. This also ended the independence of the Free Imperial City of Reutlingen, which was incorporated into the State of Württemberg. Friedrich List, who was born in Reutlingen in 1789, also became a Württemberg citizen. However, he did not fit into an absolute monarchy. Even at a young age he was a person who was enthusiastic about freedom and human rights, and he fought for citizen participation in public affairs, for free trade between the German territorial states, a trade and crafts association as the first representation of the interests of German merchants, and for free speech in everyday life and in the chamber of deputies.

List traced the struggle for these liberties to the examples of the French Revolution and the United States of North America and was himself a pioneer of human rights and a fighter for freedom of speech, commerce, and competition. He was an expert in national economics, a scholar of distinction, a practitioner of great vision, an extraordinary personality.

As a public civil servant, he failed because obedience and a subservient mentality were not part of his character. He was far ahead of his time—a prophet. However, the prophet often counts for nothing in his fatherland. He was best understood in his native city, where he was elected a Deputy to the Württemberg Chamber of Deputies. However, as he was not quite thirty years old, the mandate had to be withdrawn from him. Only in the following special election was he successful. Most regrettably, after only a short time, he ended up not in government but at the Hohenasperg prison. Dismissed prematurely, List had to emigrate to the USA because "the homeland wanted to be rid of him", as Theodor Heuss put it. Although he was successful in the United States and became an advisor to the President, he returned to Europe and became a renowned railway pioneer. Yet his life ended tragically.

Prof. Wendler and others have made clear how relevant List's ideas still are today. The "social market economy" with free competition within a regulatory framework set by parliament is based on List's ideas. "The measure of the economy is the human being," says Wilhelm Röpke. This sentence could also have come from Friedrich List. Today, List would remark, "the degree and outcome of politics, the economy and society is driven by man's own initiative, responsibility to help, freedom of opinion and research for the benefit of all mankind. Friedrich List was both a citizen of his homeland and a citizen of the world. Theodor Heuss called him "the envoy of the German future". Eugen Wendler honors him as a "mastermind of the social market economy."

Baden-Württemberg, Germany

Prof. Dr. h.c. Erwin Teufel
Prime Minister (ret.) of the State
of Baden-Württemberg, Germany

Preface

For 50 years now, I have devoted myself to researching the life and work of the German national economist Friedrich List (1789–1846). At present, his classic works of political economy are largely forgotten and unknown, both nationally and internationally, although to paraphrase a German advertising slogan, in my estimation, "he has never been more valuable than today!" In the face of the current daunting global challenges, economics, especially political economy, is desperately seeking ideological systems and alternatives. To this end, Friedrich List's Economic Theory can offer valuable methods and guidelines. In this respect, I am pleased for every reader who picks up this book, studies it, and finds creative suggestions, perhaps also answers to guide his own opinions as well as systemic approaches to solving upcoming national and international problems in economy and society.

In the 1970s, the famous Report to the Club of Rome, *The Limits to Growth*, made a great impression on me and prompted me to look outside mainstream economics for viable and convincing ideological approaches that could point the way to the future. On the basis of my own understanding and thoughts, I endeavoured to convey to my students a somewhat different view of global challenges with corresponding approaches to solving them. In this respect, the academic debate with Friedrich List was an inexhaustible treasure trove for me. If I had not consistently found new sources of his writings at home and abroad, such a long study of this classic of national economics would have been inconceivable. For this, I neither received research funds nor was I supported by academic staff, financing all of my research myself before and during my retirement. I only received translation help from a few foreign students, some of whom also brought me valuable sources from their study semesters abroad.

From 1972 until my retirement, I was Professor of International Marketing, Consumer Behavior and Communication at Reutlingen University. In 1992, I founded "The Friedrich List Institute for Historical and Contemporary Economic Studies" at the University and directed it until 2012. For my research, I have been awarded the State Prize for Local Research of Baden-Württemberg, the Medal of Merit of the City of Reutlingen and Reutlingen University, the Federal Cross of Merit as well as the List Medal of the Chamber of Industry and Commerce and the Citizen's

Medal of the City of Reutlingen. I also received an Honorary Diploma from Reading, Pennsylvania, Reutlingen's American partner city.

As a result of my intensive study of Friedrich List, I have come to the conclusion that he should not only be seen as a notable German pioneer of national economics in the nineteenth century but that it is not presumptuous to place him in the illustrious ranks of Adam Smith (1723–1790), Karl Marx (1818–1883), and Deng Xiaoping (1904–1997) because, including List, these four protagonists founded their own economic system. Smith stands for capitalism and free trade, List for temporary protectionism and social market economy, Marx for socialism and communism, and Deng Xiaoping for state capitalism. Basically, Smith's doctrine is rooted in the second half of the eighteenth century and Marx's in the nineteenth century, while List's ideology points equally to the twentieth and twenty first centuries, as is the case with Deng Xiaoping.

In the course of my List research efforts, I have written 25 monographs and a large number of journalistic and scholarly essays on this brilliant and much-revered economist. My most important discovery was the finding of List's lost second Paris Prize Competition pamphlet of 1837, which I located in 1983 in the archives of the "Institut de France" in Paris. In the past 10 years, I have been privileged to publish an 12-Volume scholarly series on Friedrich List with the renowned scientific publisher SpringerGabler in Wiesbaden.

The first volume is entitled *Friedrich List (1789–1846)—A Visionary Economist with Social Responsibility*. The focus is on List's enigmatic biography. This book has also been translated into Chinese.

For the present book the most important passages from Volume VIII, *The Political Economy of Friedrich List* and Volume XI: *The Way of Thinking of Friedrich List: "Wider den Herrendünkel!!! in Economy and Society"*, have been fused together. In this way, a holistic presentation of his political economy is obtained. I am particularly grateful to the Springer publishing house in Heidelberg and especially to Dr. Johannes Glaeser.

In this respect, the inquisitive reader is offered a rich fund of thought-provoking ideas that appear very modern and can be applied to many current problems. From this, valuable food for thought can be derived for one's own positioning in the field of economics, and perspectives for the solution of current problems can be gained.

My special thanks go to the former Minister President of the State of Baden-Württemberg, Prof. Dr. h.c. Erwin Teufel, for his benevolent foreword.

I am very grateful to Ulrich Sihler for the critical review and editing of the electronic translation.

I thank the publisher for supporting this publication with such dedication and hope that the reader will reap a rich harvest from this work.

Reutlingen, Germany
June 2022

Eugen Wendler

Contents

Chapter 1
Biographical Outline of List's Life and Work

Friedrich List was born in 1789 in Reutlingen, which was still a free imperial city in southern Germany at that time.[1] He attended Latin school in his hometown until the age of 14. Then he completed an apprenticeship as a leather tanner in his father's business. Since this work did not suit him his parents sent him to Blaubeuren where he completed a second training for the middle civil service career in the town and district clerk's office. Here he became acquainted with the citizens grievances with the government administration, justice and finance in the Kingdom of Württemberg.

After this training and further practical activities List attended lectures at the University of Tübingen as a guest student and then as a law student before he was appointed as a government councillor in the Württemberg Ministry of the Interior in Stuttgart.

From 1811 to 1817, all of Europe, especially the German southwest, experienced famines of almost medieval proportions, so that many subjects from Württemberg emigrated to America. These citizens traveled to Heilbronn, where the Neckar River was navigable, then downstream by ship to the Rhine and then across the Atlantic to the New World. Since King Wilhelm I of Württemberg, who had only been on the throne for 5 months, was interested in the reasons why so many of his subjects were leaving their homeland, List was instructed to go to Heilbronn, Neckarsulm and Weinsberg on May 1, 1817, and ask the emigrants gathered there why they were leaving their homeland.

At that time he interviewed more than 200 emigrants, representing approximately 700–800 people. A few days later he sent the king a comprehensive report. It can be said that this was the first opinion poll ever conducted worldwide, with which the discipline of demoscopic research began.

Under the impression of the interviews, List immediately submitted the proposal to the Württemberg government that King Wilhelm I should find a "State Economic Faculty" at the State University in Tübingen, at which prospective higher administration officials would receive an academic education and be enabled to set early industrialization in motion in the poor and underdeveloped agricultural state of Württemberg and, above all, to remedy the administrative grievances.

E. Wendler, *The Political Economy of Friedrich List*, Springer Studies in the History of Economic Thought, https://doi.org/10.1007/978-3-031-24601-2_1

After some hesitation, the king approved this faculty for the winter semester of 1817/18, which became the first continuously existing faculty of economics at a German university, celebrating its 200th anniversary in 2017. Although List did not complete his academic studies, King Wilhelm I appointed him to one of the first three chairs of this faculty.

During this time the young professor married his wife Karoline, a widow who brought a son into the marriage. This union produced four biological children, three daughters and a son. Karoline was very loyal to her husband, despite all the adversities of his tragic life's journey, and was affectionately referred to by her husband as "the woman with heavenly gentleness."

With the founding of the "Staatswirtschaftliche Fakultät" (Faculty of Political Economy) at the University of Tübingen, List helped to broaden the scientific spectrum from the four classical disciplines of theology, philosophy, medicine and law to include political economy. This marked the beginning of institutional teaching and systematic research in economics.

List's academic career, however, was short-lived. During the Easter holidays of 1819, he undertook a trip to Frankfurt am Main. Since the Middle Ages, the famous trade fairs at which merchants from all German territorial states presented their wares have been held in the Main metropolis and Leipzig in spring and autumn. In Frankfurt, List met with the leaders of the merchants, who complained bitterly that the many customs borders between the 38 sovereign German states largely strangled trade and that the ponderous, predominantly handcrafted, locally manufactured goods were no longer competitive with the mass produced goods made in England and France with the help of early industrialization. Therefore, the merchants demanded the abolition of internal tariffs and the creation of an inner German economic union. List offered to write a petition within two days to the Federal Assembly meeting in Frankfurt, the loose representation of the interests of the German principalities and city states, in order to lend weight to the political demands of the merchants.

As the petition was well received and applauded, List, elated by his success, spontaneously founded the "Allgemeiner Deutscher Handels- und Gewerbsverein" (General German Trade and Industrial Association) in Frankfurt, which was to give the necessary weight to the demands raised in the petition. This was, if one disregards the medieval Hanseatic League, the first representation of the interests of German merchants.

However, the Württemberg sovereign felt ignored regarding this heavy-handed behavior, so List had to give up his teaching post under pressure from the king after his return to Tübingen. He then took over the management of the association as a consultant and endeavoured to convince the German courts of the necessity of a customs union and to make it clear to them that a renunciation of customs revenues would be more than compensated by the resulting economic growth. These activities are among List's most important political achievements because they laid the foundation for the political discourse surrounding Germany's economic and political unification process. The formation of extended customs territories and their merger to form the Zollverein of 1834 marked the first historic stage of this arduous unification process, which was then followed by political unification in 1871 with the founding of the German Empire. List deserves credit for striving for this unification process by peaceful means and for being aware that this could only be achieved through several intermediate political steps. This sequence of steps is analogous to the modern unification process in the EU.

In his function as an officer of the Handels und Gewerbsverein, List also edited the first trade journal for the representation of the interests of German merchants, "Das Organ für den deutschen Handels- und Fabrikantenstand" (The newsletter for the German Merchants and Manufacturers). During important delegation trips of the association to the Bavarian court in Munich and a stay of several months in Vienna, he undertook the laborious attempt to convince above all the Habsburg Emperor Franz I and the Austrian State Chancellor Prince von Metternich of the necessity of this customs union. While the delegation was granted two audiences by the Emperor, it was unable to get through to Metternich, who was to prove a "grand seigneur" of the "ancien regime" and a bitter enemy of List's liberal aspirations in the so-called Vormärz until 1848. From now on both the King of Württemberg and the Austrian State Chancellor became the fiercest opponents and adversaries of Friedrich List blocking any initiatives whenever possible.

In 1820, while working as a consultant, List was elected by the electors of his hometown Reutlingen as a member of the Württemberg state parliament. Immediately afterwards, in a sharply worded document, the so-called "Reutlinger Petition", which in reality had the character of an anonymous pamphlet, he criticized the inadequacies in Württemberg's administration, its legal system, legislation and financial management. His spirited treatise culminated in 40 individual demands which he intended to present to the government and parliament. Because of the sharply formulated preamble, however, he was expelled from parliament under pressure from the monarch after only two months of membership by 56 votes to 36 and sentenced by the criminal court in Esslingen to ten months of honorable imprisonment in a fortress.

This was the fateful time period of the "demagogue persecution". After the student Karl Sand had murdered the Russian State Councillor and comedy poet August v. Kotzebue, the Carlsbad Resolutions were passed under pressure from Metternich, which suppressed all liberal movements. All of List's pioneering initial and later efforts were also affected by this development.

Initially List tried to escape this politically devastating jail sentence by fleeing to neighboring countries, expecting an honorable rehabilitation there. He was granted temporary asylum in Strasbourg, Kehl and Aarau.

From his exile in Switzerland, he undertook an exploratory trip to Paris and London in 1823 to explore the chances of settling there and setting up a business. In Paris he met the famous freedom hero of the American struggle for independence, Marquis de Lafayette, who had been invited by the American government to make a triumphal tour of the Atlantic coastal states. Lafayette made List the honorable offer to accompany him on the trip. However, as his wife was not yet prepared to take on the uncertain fate in the New World, not the least because of their four underage children, List first traveled on to London. It was in the English metropolis that he first heard of railway transportation and immediately recognized the revolutionary potential inherent in this innovation. From there he returned to Aarau.

After an absence of two years he returned from Swiss exile to Württemberg trusting in the king's mercy but was immediately arrested and taken to Hohenasperg, the Württemberg state prison, to serve his sentence. Only when he promised to emigrate to America permanently was he released early, after two-thirds of the prison sentence had been served.

List came to the New World in 1825 as a political emigrant where he first tried his hand at farming before taking over as the editor of a German language weekly newspaper, the "Readinger Adler", in the state of Pennsylvania. Here he discovered a large anthracite coal deposit in the area of the Blue Mountains, a part of the Appalachian mountain range. List founded one of the first railway companies in the USA with his American business partner, Dr. Isaac Hiester, to exploit this deposit. In a planning and construction period of only four years, the two succeeded in completing this 22.5 mile (36 km) long line in November 1831 under unimaginable technical and financial difficulties. A raging mountain river had to be conquered and 17 bridges had to be built. The locomotives ordered in England were delivered in the winter of 1832/33 and put into service in the spring, three years prior to the inauguration of the first German railway line "Nuremberg-Fürth", which was only 6 km long and ran on level terrain.

The railway designed and built by List was the third railway line in the entire United States and one of the first ten in the world. Friedrich List thus became a renowned railway pioneer and the first mobility economist who, against all obstacles and fears, recognized the revolutionary significance of this new mode of transport and communication. From the very beginning List foresaw and considered the manifold effects that steam navigation, railways and telegraphy would have on the state and social fabric as well as the economic and political development not only within the individual nation states but also with respect to international trade.

After his return from American exile List benefited from the experience he had gained and became one of the most renowned railway pioneers in Germany. He also used the American model to study the conflict between English style economic liberalism and the protective tariff policies of countries that were economically underdeveloped. In doing so he was inspired by the ideas of the first American Secretary of Commerce, Alexander Hamilton, who introduced the infant-industry argument into political economy. This argumentation was published in List's first writing on trade policy, "Outlines of American Political Economy".

While achieving prestige and prosperity in the United States, homesickness and family motives drove him to return to Germany. So it was very convenient for him that the American President Andrew Jackson, who List had actively supported in his election campaign and was granted American citizenship in 1830, appointed him American Consul for Hamburg, then for the Grand Duchy of Baden and finally for the Kingdom of Saxony. Sadly, he was unable to perform these functions, or only to a very limited extent, because of the icy disapproval that the one-time political prisoner still faced, especially from the king of Württemberg and the Habsburg Chancellor v. Metternich. Instead List fought with all his physical, psychological and financial strength for the construction of a German railway network. His untiring efforts were mainly directed towards the construction of the first German long distance railway, the so-called Saxon railway from "Leipzig to Dresden" as well as the Baden railway from "Mannheim to Basel", but without finding the hoped for employment in either project.

These and other misfortunes prompted him to move to Paris in September 1837, where he hoped to have better prospects of making a decent living. There he participated in two prestigious contests of the French Academy of Sciences which, due to the tremendous time pressure and his flawed French, were not successful but nevertheless count among List's most important literary works. The two submitted milestone publications were titled "Le système naturel d'économie politique" ("The Natural System of Political Economy") and "Le monde marche" ("The World Moves").

In addition, List continued his rich journalistic work in the French metropolis, which included some 700 articles. In the course of his life he was a publisher or editor of approximately 10 newspapers and authored essays in numerous other publications at home and abroad. He earned his not exactly lavish livelihood with the fees from these publications.

After his return to Germany he dedicated himself to the construction of the Thuringian railway. Although the professional success he longed for was denied him here as well, the law faculty of the University of Jena honored his dedicated efforts for the railway system by awarding him an honorary doctorate of the law faculty. Interestingly, half a year before Karl Marx, who was 26 years younger, was awarded a doctorate by the philosophy faculty of this university. Thus, the two most important German classic works of political economy in the nineteenth century were awarded doctoral degrees by the University of Jena almost simultaneously.

List then moved to what was to be his last home in Augsburg. Here he completed his main economic work, "The National System of Political Economy", which is one of the classics in the field of economics and is ranked by John Carter and Percy H. Muir among the approximately 460 books that have moved the world in the 500 year history of printing. The work has been translated into numerous foreign languages and has had a lasting effect on the reception of List in many parts of the world, continuing to inspire its readers to this day.

Important journeys followed to Belgium, Austria-Hungary and England, from which List hoped to achieve the professional breakthrough. In London he submitted a proposal to the government of a German-English trade agreement that would help Germany achieve political unification and England to maintain its economic supremacy. The English Prime Minister Robert Peel and the leader of the opposition Lord Palmerston, regrettably, gave him the cold shoulder and demanded that List first see to it that free trade be introduced in the German territorial states and then throughout the country so that English mass produced goods could be exported there without difficulty. Only when this non-negotiable prerequisite was fulfilled could, at some point, the discussion regarding political unification be started.

The overwhelming opposition to his person and his farsighted ideas finally triumphed over List's seemingly inexhaustible reserves of strength. Mental and physical illness and financial hardship worsened his situation to such an extent that, hopeless and in deep despair, he put an end to his life in the Austrian border town of Kufstein on November 30, 1846.

Remarkable is the legacy that Friedrich List left behind, his understanding of global economics and politics as the basis of his visionary thinking, all of which are very applicable to the challenges that humankind faces today, 175 years after his death.

Note

1. Wendler, E.: Friedrich List (1789–1846)—A Visionary Economist with Social Responsibility, Heidelberg 2014.

Chapter 2
The Systematic Positioning of List's Economic Theory

2.1 The Almost Forgotten German Classic Writings on Political Economy

In 1903 Max Höltzel introduces the essay "*On Friedrich List*" with the following words: "There are very few people who have been of such great importance for trade and industry, transport and economics in theory and practice who have had such a profound effect as Friedrich List. Rarely, too, has a person had to face so many detractors in his lifetime. The shortsightedness and pure antagonism of his contemporaries regrettably succeeded only too well in diminishing List's significant contributions and undermining an appreciation of his life's work even after his death." That is why List's name is still far too little known "both in the circles of national economy and among historians as well as in general education". One can add that even today not much has changed. According to Höltzel, "it may generally be taken for granted that the ideas which Friedrich List wrote down in his major works have strongly influenced not only the teachers of economics in recent times but also, for example, Prince Bismarck".

List was not a limited and one-sided champion of a "national protective tariff policy". Instead he foresaw the great struggle of the world powers regarding the distribution of spheres of interest around the globe which was only just beginning at that time. This at a time when almost none of his contemporaries understood this development. List had even predicted very accurately the domination of English as the world language, an almost unimaginable insight at that time. That is why Höltzel (1903) refers to him as "a giant with economic foresight".[1]

On Karl Marx, Höltzel comments, "the economic dogmas and slogans from Karl Marx could hardly have exerted such a hypnotic influence on the younger generation and especially on the masses if German economic understanding had been able to comprehend the basic economics of Friedrich List earlier and more completely". List was "a god-blessed genius…for where we stand today with our struggles and interests (at the start of the twentieth century), Friedrich List already stood in the first

E. Wendler, *The Political Economy of Friedrich List*, Springer Studies in the History of Economic Thought, https://doi.org/10.1007/978-3-031-24601-2_2

half of the previous century (1789–1846) with his keen intellectual gaze: a lonely man, an adult among children."

An Austrian history publication by A. Reschauer in 1876 titled, "*The Viennese Revolution of 1848*", contains one of List's earliest political tributes, quoting his visionary words: "Germany - in science and art, in literature and morals, a star of the first magnitude among the nations of the earth. Germany is destined by her natural resources, by the efficiency of her peoples and by a wise commercial policy, to become the richest country on the European continent. Germany, with its unity and internal development is destined to become the primary guarantor of European peace—Germany! Long live our great and glorious, our common and beloved fatherland!"[2] How these words contrast with the further course of history, where it is very clear what crimes the Kaiserreich and National Socialism brought upon the world and Germany in the twentieth century and how long it took the involved countries to recover from both.

In discussions with younger Germans and foreign colleagues one notices that they have dealt intensively with the works of Anglo-American economists, especially the Nobel Prize winners, and are very well informed about Karl Marx. At the same time they know little or nothing about Friedrich List. When an article on List does appear or a lecture is held on his life the author or speaker is by and large content with repeating List's biographical career and the stereotypical comment that he was the intellectual father of protectionism. In the face of global free trade his ideas had become obsolete. Consequently, the quintessence of List's economic thought is rarely reviewed and certainly not answered adequately. In the process it is overlooked that the historical dispute of free trade versus protectionism is basically outdated. For example, if one compares Monaco with North Korea the classic contrast between free trade and protectionism is clear. However, in regard to almost all other countries, there is a varying degree of economic liberalism with more or less strong protectionist regulations and prohibitions. The latter, of course, are not limited to tariff barriers to trade. Since List's lifetime, innumerable new forms of non-tariff barriers and state support measures have been implemented and continue to be developed by countries, in various combinations and intensity. Examples are numerous, to name just a few:

- the obligation to declare the ingredients of products
- setting of technological standards for imported goods
- certification and approval regulations (ISO and other standards)
- incentives and subsidies through tax legislation
- foreign trade regulations and import bans
- the legal obligation to set up joint ventures and other forms of cooperation when setting up a business locally
- occupational health and safety laws
- social standards such as minimum wages and weekly working hours
- legal regulations on environmental and consumer protection.

So-called "free trade agreements" or intergovernmental trade treaties are not exempt from such regulations. Basically international trade policy is only about defining the corresponding free spaces in foreign trade and making these as large as possible to approach, as close as possible, the free trade idea. This is the subject of much debate and argument at every trade conference, at every G20 summit, at the WTO (World Trade Organization) and at countless other international institutions and meetings.

In many cases the terms "free trade" and "protectionism" are also used as ideological weapons to characterize one's own "open" position and perspective in comparison to other countries. Many governments propagate free trade even though they pursue a rather restrictive, that is protectionist foreign trade policy compared to others, such as China. It's all a question of who and how it is defined.

When protectionism is mentioned in connection with Friedrich List it is usually overlooked that he clearly wanted it to be understood as a temporary protective tariff in the sense of the infant-industry theory, enabling underdeveloped countries the chance to develop certain industries to make them internationally competitive. Often forgotten is that the leading European industrial nations such as England, Germany as well as the USA, realized their rapid industrial growth in the second half of the nineteenth century with the help of protectionist measures. A similar development occurred after World War II with the Japanese government policy of the MITI (Ministry of International Trade and Industry), as well as that of South Korea. At present the Chinese government, for example, follows these principles despite its accession to the WTO.

In this respect, there is no basis for viewing Donald Trump's protectionist policies during his term in office as a renaissance of Friedrich List. The American President used import tariffs as punitive measures (penalties) to basically turn back the clock, reviving non-competitive, rusty industries while relaxing environmental protection. This is a very different approach to that of List.

Another argument repeatedly heard against List is the absurd accusation that he preached German imperialism and nationalism and thus even provided the theoretical economic and geopolitical justification for national socialism. Two examples clearly illustrate why such accusations are unfounded.

In 2009, Rüdiger Gerlach published his history thesis, "*Imperialist and Colonialist Thought in the Political Economy of Friedrich List*",[3] at the FU Berlin. The definition of "imperialism" refers to the efforts of a state or its political leadership to gain economic and political influence in other countries or among other peoples in the sense of domination, which can extend to subjugation (occupation) and incorporation into its own state system. The term was coined in the sixteenth century and at that time was seen negatively since it was based on military power and despotism, as opposed to the rule of law.

The fundamental criticism of Gerlach's "research results" is that key terms used in his argumentation are not explained or only insufficiently in some footnotes. On such a weak foundation, it leads to contradictions in the thesis set up in the book's title. While the author criticizes List's theories for having been improperly interpreted and instrumentalized in the Wilhelmine era (e.g., by Ludwig Sevin) and the National Socialist era (e.g., by Friedrich Lenz), the author is continually caught up with contradictions and inadequate interpretations to substantiate his own theses.

Gerlach bases his remarks on what he refers to as the "expansionist thinking" of Friedrich List without providing an understanding of what he means with this term. Is it economic growth, the political union of the states of the Zollverein, European integration, geopolitical conquests (such as the expansion of the English colonial empire), or something else? The author cites Jürgen Osterhammel and equates "expansion" with "imperialism", by this he means "the intensification of European expansion in the era of high imperialism." Gerlach claims that "List's scientific imperialism was received with great interest in high-imperialist Germany" and that "the late renaissance of his expansionist ideas" served as an impetus for scholars to examine his national economic writings with regard to the history of imperialistic thought. At the same time Gerlach criticizes the corresponding research deficit, which he seeks to eliminate with his so-called "investigation".

Gerlach concedes that the hypothesis formulated in the introduction to his analysis that List "completed the transformation from the theoretician of free trade imperialism to the mastermind of high imperialism" can be shared "only to a limited extent." To save his chain of argumentation the author brings the concept of "objectivist imperialism" into the discussion, but immediately concedes that for List the guiding principle of his economic theory was international trade and not conquest. A little later Gerlach contradicts himself again believing that he can discern in List's world view "the highly imperialist expansion of his thought". In doing so he overlooks that he has become entangled in a tautology. The author comes to the conclusion, "List did not know an aggressive nationalism or even racism in the sense of high imperialism", but then maintains that "List became an important theorist of political imperialism on an economic basis" and in looking back, List made "a contribution to the development of high-imperialist thought." This does not fit to Gerlach's clear statement, "List personally cannot be called a high imperialist."

Generally such a contradictory treatise does not deserve a scholarly rebuttal but the title of Gerlach's analysis demands such a critical review. The author's thesis that List's idea of integration in the sense of a "cosmopolitan confederation of world states" (a tautology that is linguistically incorrect) gave rise to an "informal imperialism", whereby it again remains Gerlach's secret what is meant here.

A similarly questionable book titled, "*The Tainted Source - The Undemocratic Origins of the European Idea*", was published by John Laughland in 1997.[4] In the third chapter the author discusses Friedrich List, lumping him together with the national socialists and fascists. He makes the sacrilegious but futile attempt to give his economic and geopolitical ideas a totalitarian and chauvinistic veneer. The former British Prime Minister Edward Heath has criticized this book "as an absurd and vile distortion of the past and present."

In sum, these arguments and others, such as the realization that Friedrich List's economic theories cannot be represented mathematically, may have individually or jointly contributed to the reality that he hardly experiences any lasting significance in current economic theory, at most playing a certain, but only marginal role in the historic treatment of protectionism.

2.2 Marx, Smith—or List?

Under this title, Michael Lind, the editor of "*Harpers' Magazine*", published a provocative essay in "*The Nation*" magazine in October 1998, comparing the political economy promoted by Friedrich List in relation to Karl Marx and Adam Smith's these political economy heavyweights, the most important passages are quoted.[5] (Fig. 2.1).

"More than 150 years ago, a German thinker foresaw the problems of uninhibited free trade in a global economy of developed and undeveloped nations (…). It is important to recall that socialism and classic liberalism are only two of three rival traditions of political economy that emerged in the first half of the nineteenth century. The three traditions are symbolized by Karl Marx, Adam Smith and Friedrich List (…). It was List who taught the Germans and later the Japanese to follow the nineteenth-century American example of using tariffs and other industrial policies to promote the industrialization of their nations. As Chalmers Johnson and James

Fig. 2.1 Friedrich List versus Adam Smith

Fallows have observed, this long-neglected figure had more influence on the development of industrial civilization in Europe and East Asia than either Marx or Smith (…).

List was an American citizen, a German patriot and universalist who believed in the ultimate harmony of national interests (…). List was a liberal and a democrat who admired the United States and Britain and wanted the extension of representative government, civil liberty and the rule of law to accompany the industrial revolution.

He would have been appalled by the authoritarian modernization of Bismarck's Germany and Meiji Japan, shocked by Hitler—and delighted to see his dream of a United States of Germany finally realized by today's Federal Republic (…).

According to List, 'cosmopolitan economics—or universal free trade between all the countries in the world—is only in the very earliest stage of development' (…). Although 'perpetual peace and universal free trade are both desirable and necessary', List observed that 'nations have not yet attained a state of political and social development which would make such a reform possible' (…). Developing countries had to protect their infant industries until they caught up. At that point, the newly developed countries should phase out protectionism and move toward free trade with the already developed countries.(…)".

"If he were alive today, List would oppose institutions like the World Trade Organization on the grounds that the time is not yet ripe for global free trade. He would oppose the International Monetary Fund for trying to force all developed countries to adopt an often inappropriate neoliberal economic model. List would disapprove of treaties like NAFTA that deprive poor countries like Mexico the needed flexibility to shape their development rather than turning them into low-wage assembly sites for affluent countries (in this case primarily the economic merger of the United States and Canada)..."

"If the 19th century saw a debate among Smithians, Marxists and Listians, the 20th century between Smithians and Marxists, then the 21st century should see a debate between Smithians and Listians. It will be a discussion between those who want laissez-faire global capitalism now and those who envision a social market version of global capitalism as the negotiated results of generations of different national and regional development paths. Smithians believe that global market integration will produce national and regional development, Listians believe that global market integration should follow national and regional development. Smithians want a global market by the year 2000 or 2020 at the latest; Listians are willing to postpone the completely integrated global market until 2200 or perhaps 3000. What's the hurry? Better to take it slow and do it right."

In their compendium published in 1967 under the title "*Printing and the Mind of Man*", John Carter and Percy H. Muir selected on the order of 460 outstanding works of Western intellectual history. Among these "books that move the world", as titled in the German edition, Friedrich List's main work "*Das Nationale System der Politischen Ökonomie*" is Number 311. The book caused a great sensation when it was first published. "For seventy years the advocates of protective tariffs in Germany, Great Britain, and the United States used it as their gospel."[6] List's "National System"

Chapter 7
The Morning Star of Civil Liberty

7.1 Natural and Civil Liberty

As already mentioned, Friedrich List was born with the philosophy of the Enlightenment and the slogans of the French Revolution so the concept of freedom also plays a central role in his thoughts and actions. This is already clear from his credo, "through prosperity to freedom". List distinguished between natural and civil freedom. The latter he also called reasonable, useful and lawful liberty, to which he contrasted unlawful or harmful liberty.[1,2]

By natural liberty, he understood the boundless scope of action of individuals in a wild, uncultivated society, as he found among the Indians during his exile in the United States. In the 6th Letter of his *Outlines of American Political Economy*, he mentions Native Americans at one point, saying, "individuals without the rules of the community are savages, and the principle of letting the individual have his way is especially true among the Indians". He could have said something similar about other nomadic tribes, but they all have fixed rules in their social behavior, without which a community cannot exist and survive. Nevertheless, such tribes possess a great deal of natural freedom in that they can move about without restriction in a vast territory and need only defend it against external enemies.

In such tribal structures, however, natural freedom in reality leads to mutual violations of rights and miserable self-preservation because each individual must sacrifice as much of his personal freedom and submit to the community as is necessary for the good of the tribe as a whole and as has been handed down in the traditional pecking order. In this way, the productive power of the individual is weakened to the extent that he must surrender his natural freedom to the community (Fig. 7.1).

From this, Friedrich List derived the conclusion, "the strictest despotism is also the weakest and most untenable government, for the power of all is dead, concentrated only in one. This is, as it were, the nominal number in front of a quantity of zeros; it counts for much as long as it stands there, but if it is struck out, the nominal value of all the other characters dwindles away into a manifold nothingness".

E. Wendler, *The Political Economy of Friedrich List*, Springer Studies in the History of Economic Thought, https://doi.org/10.1007/978-3-031-24601-2_7

Fig. 7.1 Caricature of police power in the Vormärz; from: Bauernfeld, C: Die Republik der Thiere, Vienna 1848; Collection E. Wendler

One criticism of this conclusion is that List has overlooked the ancient advanced civilizations, such as Babylon, Egypt, Persia, India, Japan, China, Indonesia, Mexico and Peru, to name but a few examples, not to mention later despotic and authoritarian systems, first and foremost the Third Reich. In many cases these civilizsziond cannot be denied an enormous boost in economic and cultural development because these examples were essentially historical precursors to state capitalism as practiced today in China and to some extent in Russia, producing leading achievements in certain economic sectors. The same is true of North Korea, but only in terms of missile production and its overall military power.

On the other hand, List criticized the English school of political economy. This school knew no difference between industrialized nations with a higher level of development and those that were at a lower level. Everywhere, the school wanted to exclude the influence of state power according to the principle: "Laissez faire, laissez aller". In any case, the greater the scope of action of individuals, the better they would be able to produce and increase their wealth. The falsity of this thesis is shown by the reality that according to this doctrine, savage peoples must be the most productive and richest on earth because there is practically no state power there.

In agrarian societies limited to working the land, on the other hand, "mental inertia, physical awkwardness, clinging to old habits, customs and techniques, lack of education and freedom" prevailed. The striving for constant improvement of intellectual as well as material goods, for competition and freedom, on the other hand, could only develop in a manufacturing and commercial state. Anyone who doubts this should take a look at the former free imperial cities as an example, which benefited from the blessings of freedom for centuries and can be regarded as a model of "high national strength".

For List, other models for the development of civil liberty were England, Switzerland, and the United States. In England, he argues, civil liberty developed earlier than elsewhere because there the divergent interests of monarchy, aristocracy, and democracy were united in a reasonable compromise. Similarly, the security of person and property in confederacy would have produced a large measure of civil liberty and spurred the spirit of enterprise. Where the barren soil had not been sufficient to support a livelihood, he said, many Swiss had emigrated but had often "returned under the open skies of their mountains" with the wealth they had acquired abroad, thus contributing significantly to the prosperity of their country. List praised the United States above all for its liberal democratic constitution.

According to List, freedom and industry are inseparable companions. If industry is established somewhere, freedom must follow on its heels, and vice versa. The establishment of industry will not be long in coming where the flag of freedom is planted. The examples of China and Russia show how the growing prosperity and ideological influence of the West via social media also inspires liberal aspirations, which are brutally suppressed by the state apparatus. We are seeing something similar in present day Belarus and Kazakhstan.

Reasonable freedom is the basic prerequisite for all physical and spiritual developments of man. Just as the spirit is depressed by the prohibitions and bonds limiting speech, prosperity is reduced when limits are imposed on production and the prohibition of material goods. In view of the freedom movement that arose from the French Revolution, List spoke of the "morning star" and the "palladium" of civil liberty. This, he argued, consisted of the fact that the state must grant every individual unimpeded access to his or her "individual welfare" insofar as it does not conflict with the common good. This is because freedom, education, patriotism and welfare were the cornerstones of bourgeois society. It is the blessing of freedom that man's innate striving for dominion is ennobled by it and that strength is gained by the power of the spirit and of truth.

7.2 The Oppression of Württemberg's Subjects in the First Third of the Nineteenth Century

On the one hand, List said that it seemed to him that Württemberg had been chosen as a model of civil liberty above all other German states. On the other hand, he lamented the still existing excessive oppression of citizens by administrative bureaucracy and state agencies. His praise resulted from the relatively liberal constitution introduced under King Wilhelm I in 1817, which undoubtedly also pointed the way for other constitutions in the German territorial states. His criticism was based primarily on the emigrant survey he conducted in Heilbronn, Weinsberg and Neckarsulm in the first days of May 1817,[3] which three years later formed the empirical basis for his notorious "Reutlingen Petition".

Statements from those surveyed, among the many collected and extensively noted by List, generally came from participants who represented a group who wished to emigrate or whose complaint was also approvingly confirmed by others. Often, the speakers were fathers of families with many children who were particularly concerned about their welfare. For example, an emigrant complained that he had been oppressed beyond measure by the mayor of his municipality because he was not able to perform services for the royal hunt, as he had contracted severe frostbite on his feet during the Russian campaign during the Napoleonic Wars. In addition, he complained that the Schultheiss and the town councillor were cousins and they were related to all the other magistrates. He said that during the famine years, he lost all his property. During the tax assessment, they had even assessed the value of the clothes he wore on his body (Fig. 7.2).

Another emigrant expressed himself disparagingly about the lawlessness, the high taxes and the personal enrichment of the town clerk/controller. The mayor had threatened him with pressure from the the tax collector. From the authorities, one hears nothing else but insults and foul language.

Fig. 7.2 "Off to America"—Emigration in the first half of the nineteenth century

Another criticized the fact that a dam had been commissioned by the lord but this had not been made known beforehand. Since there had been no invitation to tender, the contract had been awarded to a favorite, and he himself had no chance to competitively bid.

One emigrant substantiated this complaint, stating that the same reasons compelled him to emigrate. Whoever could not pay would have to perform the hardest labor. He reckoned that he would face great dangers by emigrating. Indeed, it was possible that he would be treated like a serf in the USA, but the pressure and hardship could certainly not be greater there.

Another father of a family, like so many others, stated that he had to leave his beloved homeland because of the poor earnings, the great inflation and the hungry mouths of his children and had no support from anywhere.

Another was so enraged by a debt collector that he sold his property. One was not even allowed to fetch leaves from the forests on the part of the forestry office, which is why there is a lack of manure everywhere. The forester does not release any wood, which is why one has to fetch it from the forest on one's own and is severely punished if one is caught doing so. Another forester demanded that storm wood be removed from the forest paths in forced labor without being allowed to take any of it with him.

Others complained that one was not allowed to speak about the many abuses. If one is summoned by an official, one is threatened with huge negative publicity, heavy fines and shorter or longer prison sentences. Several interviewees stated on record that they were forced to emigrate because of the injustice they had suffered, describing the clerks as crooks who had people locked up until they turned black. One poor man complained that he could not sue the town head because he himself was an "inferior" citizen, and some criticized the widespread fraud of local government heads.

Due to a maid's affair with an unmarried youth, her brother-in-law was brought before the town office who urged that she be removed from her employer's house and brought home. When the homeowner refused to comply with this demand because he wanted to keep the maid, he had to pay a heavy fine. He was also threatened with imprisonment. Finally, the maid was taken away by the police.

Many citizens were afraid to share their bitter experiences with the authorities during the emigrant survey because they feared serious consequences. The situation was so bad that they would rather be slaves in America than citizens and subjects in Württemberg.

A father of a family reported that for two weeks he had no bread, wood or money for his children. In his distress, he went into the forest and fetched wood. On the way back, the hunter's son confronted him and physically attacked him. He threw him to the ground and hit him in the face so that he bled. Therefore, he had defend himself and now had to fear punishment and the confiscation of his only cow.

Another reported that he fed on frozen potatoes that had remained in the fields the previous year and on all kinds of herbs that he could not even melt because he lacked lard. This statement was also confirmed by other people who wanted to emigrate. Another agreed, saying that he would rather emigrate than be considered a rebel.

One would not get justice anywhere if one complained. The lords would not even allow the common people to rake leaf litter in the forests, and of course no chance of collecting wood. In many cases, the wild boars would devastate the fields without any compensation. It is grotesque that the hogs of the nobleman are allowed to upturn the fields, but the ordinary citizen is not even allowed to collect leaf litter. Not having this material they would have to get rid of the cattle. In addition, they would have to pay road tolls even where there were no roads at all. In sum, one should not complain, because then one would immediately be accused of being a rebel.

Many of the interviewees stated that the authorities ordered them to work in public service many days a year, which endangered their livelihood. The scribal system also swallowed up high taxes. The scribal fees are unduly high, so the scribes become richer than the king. "If one asks for anything, he is considered a rebel and if one opens his mouth, he is imprisoned". One gets no support anywhere because the government employees are related to each other and defend each other.

In his final analysis of the survey results, Friedrich List concludes that the main cause of emigration is the lack of civil freedom. As a secondary cause, he considers the enthusiasm of religious groups, "which drives the sects of separatists and pietists to leave their fatherland. This he considers secondary, because the desire of many Württembergers to sectarianism is due to the lack of civil liberty". In addition, he wanted to note that some emigrants stated that their local government heads had urged them to emigrate since they wanted to acquire their property cheaply and get rid of disagreeable persons. List added that he found these statements very credible.

In the preamble of the *Reutlingen Petition*[4] List then ruthlessly exposed all these grievances and summarized:

> A superficial glance at the internal conditions in Württemberg must convince the impartial observer that the legislation and administration suffer from fundamental defects which consume the vitality of the land and destroy civil liberties. A world of officials, separated from the people, poured out over the whole country, concentrated in the ministries, unacquainted with the needs of the people and the conditions of civil life, circling in an endless system of forms, asserts the monopoly of public administration, fighting against every influence of the citizen, as if it were dangerous to the state, elevating its system of forms and caste prejudices to the highest state wisdom (activity). The officials are closely allied among themselves through the bonds of kinship, of common interests, of equal education and of equal levels of prejudice. Wherever one looks, nothing but councillors, officials, chancelleries, clerks, and supporting registries, file cabinets, official uniforms, and employee luxuries all the way down to the servant.
>
> On the other hand, the worthlessness of the harvested fruits, the stagnation of the trades, the fall in the prices of goods, complaints about the lack of money and taxes, tax extortionists, bitter complaints about dishonest magistrates, violent officials, secret reports, lack of impartiality of the superiors, in sum, misery and distress everywhere.
>
> Nowhere honorable efforts, nowhere income, nowhere cheerfulness, but left alone in the service mayhem.
>
> The administrative authorities lacking knowledge of trade, commerce and agriculture and, even worse, without respect for the inquiring citizens, bent on administrative forms and obsolete or inappropriate bureaucratic laws, mostly only hindering rather than promoting national industry.

> The administration of justice is costly, weary and endless, not helpful, and lacking all documentation and sound legislation. It is often administered by men who, instead of drawing from the pure and fresh fountain of sound reason and practical life, bring up their wisdom from a world long since submerged.
>
> The finance organization, at last, with its high internal costs due to a bloated and disproportional administration, impeding traffic, hampering industry, unhelpful in collection, lacking equal treatment when paying, everything without plan and state-economic principles. This is a brief but faithful outline of the administration.

To add a positive touch, List writes, "far from reproaching the present government for what the errors of centuries have inflicted upon the citizen, we rather recognise with heartfelt gratitude that our good King, through the Constitution, has given us the prospect of a better future that he has founded institutions without which we could not even raise our voices above the prevailing weaknesses. Duty to ourselves and to the fatherland demanded the frank confession that a constitution could only be of value to the citizen insofar as it brought about laws and administrative institutions which granted him freedom and prosperity. That we could therefore only measure the goodness of the work of which we had such high hopes by the decisions which the Chamber of Deputies would take in agreement with the government. Wherefore, noble deputies of the people, we beseech and adjure you, in whose hands the destiny of the country now rests, by all that is sacred to you, mindful of your great profession, to bring unhesitatingly before the throne the grievances of the people, and their ardent desire for notable relief, and for institutions which will afford them the full enjoyment of civil liberty."

If one compares this sharply formulated preamble with the results of the emigrant survey, one can see for oneself that it was by no means exaggerated, but only unsparingly calls the grievances by their names and how unjust Friedrich List must have felt the disastrous consequences of these sentences throughout his life.

7.3 Citizen Versus Master Conceit

In his work, "*Die Ackerverfassung, die Zwergwirtschaft und die Auswanderung* (The farm constitution, the dwarf economy and emigration)," List states, "As long as the body politic is constructed wrongly from the ground up, even the most powerful remedies become poison to it. (One is reminded here of the Third Reich). However, the representative state can only be efficiently constructed from the ground up by providing it with a proper number of fully fledged citizens."[5]

In his so-called second Paris Prize Competition pamphlet, List states: "We are citizens of the state before we are citizens of the world. Our efforts and our abilities are consecrated to the civilization, prosperity, glory, and security of our nation. We strive to the same end for mankind".

"Now one no longer speaks of the misera contribuens plebs (the rule of the nobility), now one speaks of citizens of the state".[6] And in the preface to the "*National System*", he expresses himself as to how in the future the national unity of Germany should be constructed: "No well-thinking and sensible person will further demand in Germany any other national unity than that which guarantees to each individual state and tribe of the people independence, free movement, and effectiveness in its particular circle, and subordinates it to the general will only in relation to the national interests and national purposes (Fig. 7.3)".[7]

Surely this is a clear commitment to the federal state!

In the introduction to his teaching at the Lehrverein in Aarau, List exhorted his audience to perceive their role as citizens of a free republic: "You all live in free states. Already as citizens of a republic, the fatherland demands of you that you contribute as much as possible to the public welfare in your district. You will speak, write and act for the common good as members of your community, your district, as cantonal citizens and Swiss. Your profession, whether that of doctor, lawyer, clergyman, or youth teacher, will give you incomparably more opportunity and weight than some other individuals to assert your insights among your fellow citizens. You will thereby infinitely increase the intellectual power of your fatherland, for in republics it is not only important that the state possesses citizens who assist it in word and deed; it

Fig. 7.3 Varnish monkeys; caricature by E. v. Bauernfeld; in: Die Republik der Thiere, Vienna 1848; collection E. Wendler

is important to it, if only for the sake of obedience and public tranquillity, that the citizens see the reasons on which the laws, the public institutions and measures are based; for only this conviction is the guarantor of internal tranquillity for it,—not armed power!".

> Only after the human spirit had risen above childhood did it, recognizing the nature of society, approach more or less the rule of law. However, at first this was only possible in small states, where the people could exercise their rights in real assemblies. This kind of rule of law was called a republic, with which it was also associated the concept of a democratic appointment of the regency.[8]

Despite his stormy life, List had a deep unfulfilled longing for peace, security and family happiness. He would have preferred an estate where he could have lived a carefree life with his family. In his courting letter to his future wife Karoline of January 14, 1818, he revealed what was in his heart and described his character traits, "his inner self drove him to fight for truth and justice. He loves his fatherland perhaps more than his own happiness. The stupidity and malice of his contemporaries and the widespread crookedness had given him reason enough to follow petty selfish intentions, although he had always been concerned only with the common good. He was a born republican, he said, who longed to get away from everyday people and clung with all his soul to the memory of his youth, convinced of the value of man and the full freedom of citizens. He saw the arrogance of the lord, which finds its honor only in the service of the lord and looks down on the citizen and the peasant as lowly beings. Nature has given him a heart that is sensitive to the beautiful, the good and the noble, to joy and pain, to gentle sensation and music but also to fiery passion, where his good intention, his honor, and his human dignity are misjudged. Never could he be angry and hate where he found commonality of soul, but even his enemies could be reconciled to him if they wished to approach him."[9] If others, like the active participants in the French Revolution, aimed at the destruction of the nobility, List merely wished to eliminate their harmful intentions. The nobility, he argued, should enjoy no privileges over the commoners. If the nobility was an essential element of national liberty, he said, it must be recognized that they must be incorporated into a free, capable, educated, and commercial democracy. "Such a nobility, in league with the bourgeois interests of agriculture, industry, and commerce, will reform the bureaucracy and keep it in proper bounds".

Edgar Salin adds: "In this sense, he spoke, wrote, and acted cunningly, and no sensible and well-meaning person could reproach him with anything other than that which he later reproached himself with. Namely, that he got up and made a noise while the sleepers of the house were all still sleeping soundly, so that it was not to be wondered that they became angry with him and mistreated him" (Fig. 7.4).[10]

7.4 Through Prosperity to Freedom

List repeatedly referred to the importance of entrepreneurship for economic development. In this, he said, much depended on the use of the most favorable moment,

Fig. 7.4 Predatory cats and hyenas among the high nobility of the Habsburg Monarchy; Karikatur by E. v. Bauernfeld; in: Die Republik der Thiere, Vienna 1848; Collection E. Wendler

"he who cannot do as he pleases loses the favor of the moment".[11] In this context, he disagreed with the thesis that a temporary protective tariff system leads to the formation of monopolies. In reality, he said, it offers domestic entrepreneurs the opportunity to invest their capital, entrepreneurship and labor in new, hitherto unknown branches of production, thus "awakening dormant and idle productive forces", and bringing in foreign capital, both material and intellectual, from other countries.

According to List, the basis of civil liberty is human and civil rights, which are enshrined in the constitution of a democratic state. Among these, the most important rights were listed, counting the expression of opinion as "the most beautiful prerogative of a free citizen", freedom of the press as "the sun of political life", the inviolability of the person in honor, body and life, the openness of the courts and the introduction of jury trials, "the freedom of belief and the unrestricted exercise thereof", the free choice of education, freedom of travel, establishment of a business and trade at home and abroad, freedom of trade within the country except for monopolies, the guarantee of parental rights in the education of children, and the "canonization of the mail", i.e., the preservation of the secrecy of the mail.

These rights were matched by corresponding duties and burdens. The duties of citizens included the right of the municipality or the state to call upon citizens to perform services for the common good (e.g., in the event of natural disasters, the restoration of peace and order or in the event of national defense). However, such burdens had to be distributed fairly and there should be no privileges or special rights for individual strata of the population.

In his critique of the draft constitution, List expressed the relationship between the rights and duties in a liberal-democratic state and the individuals forming it or their association in corporations in the following legal terms, "the subject, that is, the single individual or corporation, has the right to apply as much in the state as he is able to do without violating the overall purpose, and the duty to sacrifice as much of his civil liberty and individual powers as the overall good requires".

On the other hand, the state has the right to limit or concentrate the power of the individual to the extent that the overall good requires it. The state has the duty not only to let the individual work freely to the extent that his work does not contradict the state purpose but also to support it with the overall power of the nation so that it is not disturbed in its effectiveness.[12]

In this context, List also advocated the abolition of torture and other so-called "embarrassing interrogation methods". On the other hand, he said, every citizen was obliged to constitutional obedience. In the event of any expropriation of land, e.g., for road and railway construction, the owners would have to be adequately compensated.

In his 1819 manuscript "*Staatskunde und Staatspraxis*," List succinctly noted, "in some countries the constitution of the state is founded on the rights of man; in others, such as Turkey, the word is not even known".[13] And in his two major economic works, he condensed human rights into his motto: "Et la patrie, et l'humanité!".

7.5 Freedom of Trade and Free Trade

Friedrich List always stressed the importance of distinguishing between freedom of trade and free trade. He understood the term freedom of trade to mean the unlimited exchange of goods in domestic trade and free trade to mean the exchange of goods free of duties and taxes in international trade. In this connection, he remarked that wherever freedom of trade came into question, one came up against a confusion of terms caused by the word "freedom", which had already led to great errors. One speaks of freedom of trade as of religious or civil freedom. The friends and spokesmen of freedom consider themselves obliged to defend freedom in all its forms, which is why general freedom of trade has become so popular, without any distinction being made between internal trade and international trade, although the two are vastly different.[14]

However, any restrictions on internal trade are only exceptional in nature.

While in some cases, such as the ban on trade in toxic substances, weapons and ammunition, free trade could have a negative impact on the freedom of citizens, it could also have a positive impact on the less privileged.

Indeed, it is quite possible that international trade freedom will lead to servitude and total oppression of the countries affected by it.

On the domestic markets, therefore, free trade and free competition should in principle be realized as far as possible. Only for private monopolies and under certain circumstances would this not apply.

The more international trade benefited from the new means of transport and communication, and the more foreign trade extended to the whole globe, the industrially highly developed states endeavoured "with irresistible force" to extend their productive powers to the less developed countries. In this respect, the theory, i.e., Adam Smith, was based on a true idea that should not be misjudged. However, the theory had assumed an ideal state as truly existing, namely, the existence of the universal union or universal confederation of nations and of perpetual peace, and derived from this the great advantages of freedom of trade. In this way, however, cause and effect were confused.

In contrast, in the case of already united provinces and states, there was a uniform legal system based on the existing national peace, where the basic prerequisite for freedom of trade was given.

In view of the whole range of states with completely different levels of development, general freedom of trade would not lead to an universal republic but to universal subservience and total dependence of the less advanced states on the supremacy of the leading industrial, commercial and maritime powers. If, on the other hand, several states are at a similar level of development, freedom of trade would bring great advantages to all concerned, as is the case, for example, with the EU.

For countries lagging behind, i.e., less developed countries, on the other hand, a protective system was appropriate. From this point of view, national economics appeared as a science that, taking into account existing interests and individual conditions, taught nations in what way each country could reach a higher level of economic and political development. To this end List advocated, among other things, the so-called infant-industry argument, i.e., temporary protective tariffs and import restrictions for the development of national key technologies until they become competitive in international markets.

7.6 Concluding Remarks

In his wonderful and timeless speech on the occasion of the 100th anniversary of Friedrich List's death on 30. November 1946, Theodor Heuss drew the conclusion that, "List was a transitory phenomenon in his own time, which he interpreted, and at the same time the herald and messenger of the future for his (own) present (time). Cosmopolitanism and nation-state and then perhaps cosmopolitanism again? We do not know. However, the sharp antithesis does not seem justified to us; through him both flow in a wonderful way. The basic imperial elements of democratism live as a legacy, and this too, no disempowerment of civic life by the state, but always a strengthening of the community out of the forces of civic freedom, which was never in question for List. It alone was the air in which he wanted to and could live".

Then, Heuss continues: "List stood in his time and yet also against it as the explorer and advocate of the future. Researchers will find in List's works for a long time to come very attractive tasks that have not been exhausted. Analysing this List in his time or in his gratifying and dismaying prophecy will remain a useful and fruitful business".[15]

I have made this equally wise prediction of Theodor Heuss my own in my efforts in List research and have made it the guiding maxim of my actions for 50 years. This field has often been very difficult and laborious to work, but it has indeed borne rich fruit.

Notes

1. List, F. (1817): Staatskunde und Staatspraxis; in: W. I/1, p. 308 ff.
2. Ibid, p. 231 ff.
3. Moltmann, G: (1979): Aufbruch nach Amerika, Stuttgart und Tübingen.
4. List, F. (1820/21): The Reutlingen petition; in: W. I/2, p. 68.4 f.
5. Ders (1842). The arable constitution, the dwarf economy, and emigration; in: W. V, P. 449.
6. Ibid, p. 471.
7. Ders. (1841): The National System of Political Economy, W. VI; p. 38.
8. Ders (1817): Staatskunde und Staatspraxis, W. I/1, p. 370.
9. Wendler, E. (1996): "The bond of eternal love" -.
   Clara Schumann's correspondence with Emilie and Elise List, Stuttgart, p. 453.
10. Ders: Tagebücher, W. VIII, p. 11.
11. Ders: Tagebücher, W. VIII, p. 11.
12. List, F. (1816): Critique of the draft constitution; in: W I/1, P. 210.
13. Ibid, p. 436.
14. Ders: The national system of political economy; in: W. VI, pp. 69 f, 168–171.
15. Heuss, T. (1946): Der Reutlinger Friedrich List, Stuttgart und Tübingen 1946, p. 28.

Chapter 8
War and Peace

8.1 The So-Called "Martial Law"

In his "*Encyclopaedia of Political Science*", Friedrich List counted the so-called law of war as part of the practical law of nations and states.[1] It was pointless to distinguish between lawful and unlawful wars, as was done in theory. The practice, he said, was to wage wars to harm others if one expected to gain advantages from them. In this connection, he criticized the Swiss publicist Emmerich v. Vattel, who held that wars were generally declared only after careful consideration, when the state concerned had become convinced that it was justified in doing so. This might be true for the Confederation at large but not for the rest of the world. List held, on the other hand, that law is always on the side of the stronger. Although there was a sacredly held law not to open hostilities without a declaration of war, such an omission was held to be on the side of the stronger.

In the literature, the conquest of peoples had been put into a system, as if people could be conquered in any other way than through civilization and the establishment of their civil liberties. In reality, the violence of arms also sanctifies unlawful conquest.

Peace and friendship are made for eternity, and no thought is given to the possibility of a time limit. Such insights serve to underline the necessity of the union of independent states, which is called the "European system of states", the "European equilibrium" or the "system of the papal sea". In this respect, it seems grotesque that in the European treaties one basically assumed the eternal duration of membership and hardly provided for and agreed upon the voluntary and certainly not the compulsory exit by contract.

We have seen the difficulties that arise from this with Brexit, and how to deal with the recalcitrant member states Hungary and Poland, for example, is rather unclear.

On the other hand, Friedrich List clearly rejected the utopia of eternal peace. This was nothing other than a moral apostle stating the correct proposition that the moral law forbids killing one's brother, and war is impermissible under all circumstances. Just as Christ had already taught that one must also offer the other cheek to the

E. Wendler, *The Political Economy of Friedrich List*, Springer Studies in the History of Economic Thought, https://doi.org/10.1007/978-3-031-24601-2_8

one who slapped us on the cheek. If all nations were to once follow this teaching, the human race would undoubtedly be in very good shape. However, under present conditions, what would the people think of a statesman who responds to a declaration of war with principles of morality?[2]

8.2 The Utopia of Eternal Peace

In his first Paris Prize competition pamphlet, List takes up the utopia of perpetual peace in connection with Adam Smith's cosmopolitan economics and postulates that to realize the prosperity of every nation in particular and of all mankind in general, nothing else is necessary than perpetual peace, i.e., the cessation of all hostilities from nation to nation as they are carried out by laws or with arms in hand. That is an alliance of nations under a common legislation for all mankind or, as Jean-Baptiste Say had demanded, "a republic of the globe".[3] One could think here of the League of Nations or the United Nations.

However, the nations do not yet form this "republic of the globe". What is called international law is for the time being only the embryo of a future state of law. Reason should guide the nations and their interests should advise them to renounce their natural jealousy and ill-will, telling them that war between nations is as foolish as it is cruel, as is the duel between individuals. It should teach that the eternal peace and freedom of trade of nations are capable of raising them to the highest level of wealth and power. Albeit, the time has not yet come when the lamb can lie down in safety by the lion's side.

Even in the most enlightened nations there are only a few individuals who have understood the necessity and usefulness of such a state of affairs, and in such countries the political and social conditions are not yet sufficiently prepared for such a reform. Moreover, civilized and cultured nations cannot dispense with the protection of arms and with war so long as there are existing powers which, instead of aiming at the prosperity of the human race, direct their ambition to the conquest and enslavement of other nations and their peoples.

Similar to international law, social economy or perfect freedom of trade between all the nations of the globe is only an embryo. Nations can only approach this desired state step by step if their national interests are not harmed but, on the contrary, favored. The political economy commands that every nation strive for the highest level of independence, civilization and prosperity, taking all measures necessary to ward off any external attack against its economic and political situation, whether by commercial or armed means, and to promote its development. To this end, it was above all necessary to strengthen and develop the national economic power.[4]

The less each individual is restricted in his striving for personal welfare, and the greater the number and the wealth of those with whom he can enter into free interaction and competition, and the greater the space in which he can develop his individual activity, the easier it will be for him to use the qualities bestowed on him by birth, his acquired knowledge and abilities, and the natural forces at his command, to increase his own prosperity.

It is indisputable that the idea of a universal confederation and of eternal peace is commanded by reason as well as by religion. If the duel between individuals is already contrary to reason, how much more must it be the duel between nations? The proofs The cultural history of mankind proves that a social economy, based on the reasonableness of the union of all men under the rights of law, makes the most (common) sense. History teaches that where individuals are in a state of war, the prosperity of men is at its lowest level and that it increases in the same proportion as the unions and cooperation of men increase. List called this insight the "law of the union of forces" or the "confederation of productive forces".

If the nature of things is powerful enough to extend unification to hundreds of millions of people in one nation, it should also be considered powerful enough to contemplate the unification of all nations as a visionary, if utopian, goal. If the human mind is capable of comprehending the advantages of such great unifications, it should also be trusted to comprehend the advantages of unifying the whole human race. There were already many signs pointing to this necessity, for example, the progress in the sciences and arts, the manifold technical inventions, industrialization and the establishment of democratic state structures, as well as the variety and improvement of the means of transport and communication.

The more industrialization expanded and the more evenly it spread across the globe, the less war would be possible in the future. Conversely, the same forces that have hitherto served primarily for production will, in the event of war, also be used for destruction. Two nations of equal industrial strength would be able to inflict greater damage on each other in a week than they would be able to repair in a human age.

In the governments of the great powers (meaning above all the parliaments), Europe already possesses the prototype of a future national congress. Europe would one day experience a government that would gradually loosen the trade restrictions that it had so artificially managed to put on itself. Apparently, there was already an effort to settle national differences by means of negotiations and signed agreements and not to obtain justice by force of arms. The more this realization progressed that the civilization of underdeveloped peoples, torn apart by internal anarchy and badly governed, was a common task that could only be solved by negotiation, the less danger there would be of war.

If a country is no longer sufficient to feed the population, the hungry will try to seek out more distant countries where they can find work. If in a country the well educated are unable to find adequate employment, they will also seek to emigrate to countries where there is a demand for such skilled labor. In this respect, Adam Smith's free trade school is based on a reasonable idea. This, however, had assumed a state of affairs lying far in the future and probably even utopian, where the existence of universal union and perpetual peace is given and deriving thereof the great advantages of free trade. A stable peace, or at least an unstable peace, exists between the already united provinces and states, and it is from this constellation that the commercial union has arisen.

History shows that political unification has always preceded trade unification. There is not a single example where this process has been reversed (with the EU there is now such an example, which also shows the whole problem). In the existing world situation, general freedom of trade does not lead to an universal republic but to the universal subservience of the less advanced nations under the supremacy of the powerful. The reasons that support this prediction are very strong and, in List's view, irrefutable.

When one considers that machines will probably soon be invented whose destructive power will have as immense an effect as the new means of transport have on the mobility of men and for the transportation of goods. Consequently a single machine, controlled with boldness and skill, may be capable of destroying whole army corps and fleets. One cannot close one's mind to the idea that war between civilized nations would end quickly and permanently and that a time would come when war would only be fought between civilized and underdeveloped nations because there would be no doubt about the outcome of battles. So that eventually the time would come when war would become impossible.[5] (one thinks here of the current so-called proxy wars in the Middle East including the Arabian Peninsula).

In the sense of international cooperation, if a pirate can make entire seas unsafe with the help of a single steamship and a single destroyer, nations would have to come to an understanding and work together to protect the seas. In this way, in connection with water transportation, List foresaw the danger of air piracy and terrorism and the resulting need for international cooperation in this fight against terrorism.[6]

8.3 List's Utopia Concerning the Military Deterrence of Railways

In the second Paris Prize competition, Chapter XIV is devoted to the effects of the new means of transport on war and army command. Nowhere else did Friedrich List make such miscalculations in his visions and forecasts as his expectation that railways have a deterrent effect on warfare. In reality, exactly the opposite happened because the material battles as well as the entire war economy, for example, in the Franco-Prussian War and especially in the first and second World Wars, were not least due to the railways. World War I and II were only made possible and truly fuelled by the railways.

In contrast, List expressed the conviction, "a developed railway system, traversing the entire territory of a nation, must be in the eyes of every thinking man a wonderful machinery for concentrating the unifying forces of the nation, i.e., the confederation of productive forces in an almost ideal manner and for giving them a deterrent effect. In time of war, it would be possible, with the aid of the railways, to move forces in the shortest possible time to the place where they were urgently needed. Artillery could just as easily be deployed and ammunition and food depots created and supplied at the front. (there were, after all, no planes, missiles or drones yet to destroy supply lines).

Troops would be spared tiring journeys, so they could be transported to theaters of war rested, likewise, the wounded and sick could be quickly taken from the war zone and transported behind the front for medical care and recovery."

The railroad was primarily useful for the defense and less useful for the attacker because the latter could only advance via the few conquered rail routes, while the defender had the entire route network of his country at his disposal. In addition, fortresses could be built along railway lines to make it more difficult for the enemy to advance, or if necessary, railway lines and especially bridges, could be blown up to repel the enemy. In other words, railways could turn the entire national territory of a country into a huge fortress.

The immeasurable advantage of the railways was ultimately to prevent wars of aggression and to turn them increasingly into border wars. Experience has shown that border wars are military conflicts without meaning and purpose. (examples are the unnatural border between India and Pakistan or the hermetically sealed demarcation line between North and South Korea).

Eventually, as List prophesized, the nations of the European continent will come to understand that the wisest decision is to live in peace and friendship and to listen only to the counsel of justice and reason when differences of opinion arise. In this way, he said, the railroad, which was at first an instrument for containing and shortening war, would eventually become a machine which would kill war and therefore be of immeasurable advantage to all. The second generation would no longer destroy what the first had built so that the third would have to start rebuilding all over again, but each generation would continue the work of civilization and national wealth and pass it on to the next.

It was therefore indispensable to make use of this new invention and to use it not only in the interest of trade and industry but also for one's own security and independence. Every new mile of railroad possessed by a nation gave it military supremacy. Even in peacetime, he said, railroads offered enormous advantages in military terms. such as the transfer of regiments from one garrison to another, for carrying out military exercises, or the local inspection of units by the ministry. From this, in the course of time, it was to be expected that standing armies would become superfluous and that citizens would keep arms in their homes, as was the practice in Switzerland. In this way, the soldier would "unite the character of the citizen with that of the military".[7] This formulation is strongly reminiscent of the credo of the German Bundeswehr: "Citizen in uniform".

One might smile at the naivety that was List's inspiration for these ideas. However, one should give him credit for having sensed and foreseen the impending danger of wars of extermination like no one else in his time. As far as the European continent is concerned, after all, there had to be two world wars and a whole series of smaller border and civil conflicts before List's fears and visions, it is to be hoped, permanently prevailed and the European Union becomes the garat for lasting peace.

In a short speech at the ceremony marking the refounding of the List Society in Reutlingen in 1955, the then President of the Federal Republic of Germany, Theodor Heuss, referred explicitly to List's utopian vision of avoiding war through the railways and made the following statement on the subject: "If I may speak personally, one of the strongest impressions I have ever had is when I discovered a work by Friedrich List that appeared quite casually, two memoranda that he sent to the 'Topgraphisches Institut' (topographical institute) in Berlin, a military authority. He made it clear to the Prussian (authorities) that they had to take on the railways for military reasons, The strategic function of a railway system is described in detail, which is designed in such a way that the capital cannot be conquered. There are no longer any wartime marching troops, but in the early 1830s, in the case of List, the only way to go to war was by rail. There are also hospital trains. Bypass battles are fought by rail with the strange proposal offered to the military for their consideration: on the railways, the war will die. You see, a completely false prophecy in the final effect, but a great prophecy in the thinking through of the matter: the technical material about hospital trains, about the transport of artillery, about the supply of horse feed and so on, as if he had been in a military administration since time immemorial. Why am I talking about this? Because this has actually remained the strongest impression for myself: that of a concrete imagination and outrageous realism, as captured by the new things".[8]

8.4 The Outlawing of War

The more industrialization spreads across the globe and the greater the technological progress, the more costly and devastating war becomes. Not only could governments and nations no longer afford wars because they could no longer justify the sacrifices they caused, so that it became increasingly difficult to wage wars, and the time finally came when wars became such a nuisance that they became practically impossible. Therefore, civilized nations must renounce war and concentrate exclusively on improving the living conditions of their people.[9]

Likewise, steam navigation would lead to a revolution in naval warfare. The stronger the navy of the United States became, the closer the European naval powers should ally themselves to be the equal to the leading naval power. This was to be done until new inventions had "advanced thus far as to make naval warfare altogether a folly," and the leading powers united to maintain peace. Such a confederation of states would not come about, however, until the leading powers had arrived at a roughly equal degree of civilization, law, and power. However, List conceded, centuries "might easily elapse before that could happen".

In the present world situation, he said, every great country must strive to attain continued prosperity and independence by the development of its own forces. To this end List wanted to call out to the Germans, "consider your national advantages and abandon your national prejudices!".

In view of his visions, which were futuristic on the one hand and unrealistic on the other, it is easy to understand why Friedrich List travelled to England of his own accord in the last year of his life to propose a German-English alliance to the reigning government and opposition. He saw it as possible, among many other dangers, "that maritime traffic between England and Germany might be interrupted for a long time by naval warfare".

All these fears can be explained by List's "politics of the future," which he wanted to be understood as his legacy. In summary, "advances in the sciences, great inventions especially in machinery, and political and commercial changes will so alter future global realities that what might once have been considered wisdom will seem folly and fundamentally different from what might have seemed highly useful." This wise sentence could also stand for the geopolitical consequences of Russia's war of aggression against Ukraine.

8.5 Concluding Remarks

If one wants to properly understand and evaluate List's pacifist views, hopes and expectations, one should not overlook the casualties he or his family suffered due to military operations. When his brother Johannes, who was two years older, was to be drafted into the Württemberg military service in the Russian campaign under Napoleon in 1812, he wanted to be exempted, in accordance with the legal provisions, by being able to avoid the draft by marrying quickly as he had reached the age of 25. To do this, he needed a certificate from the conscription list from the military department of the state of Württemberg. Having obtained this certificate in Stuttgart, he rode back home as fast as he could but fell off his horse shortly before Reutlingen, dying a few days later from his severe injuries. This fatality soon led to the death of his heartbroken father and mother as well. These strokes of fate did not remain without consequences for Friedrich List's later thoughts and actions.

The far harder blow was the death of his only son Oskar, who, against his father's declared wishes, had been drawn to military service during his exile in Paris between 1837 and 1840. However, fearing a threat of war between France and Prussia, Oskar preferred to join the Foreign Legion in Algiers. After some time, he died of typhoid fever. How the news of his death was received by his parents is described by Clara Wieck, who was living with the List's at the time and who later became the wife of the composer Robert Schumann, in a letter to her beloved Robert dated 24. June 1839: "An hour before we were to leave the day before yesterday, the List's received the news that their son Oskar had died in Algiers. Fortunately, Mr. List was not there, so it was only gradually brought home to him. Oskar was a soldier there, but his father had not wanted him to be. You can imagine what I suffer now, to see the mother's pain, always calling for him and wringing her hands, and the father sunk in silent pain, with tears continually in his eyes".

Friedrich List never quite recovered from this blow. He could not bring himself to remain longer in the French capital and therefore returned to Saxony. "In later times he suddenly burst into tears when he thought of the fate of his only son. He made himself feel responsible for having let him go and regarded his sad lot as a consequence of his own adverse fortune".[10]

Notes

1. List, F. and W.S. (1843); in: Das Staats-Lexikon, Vol. I, Altona, pp. 644–649.
2. Ders (1841): The national system of political economy; in: W. VI, P. 452.
3. Ders (1817): Staatskunde und Staatspraxis Württembergs im Grundriss; in: W. I/1, p. 382. Ibid, p. 357.
4. Ders. and W. S. (1845): Africa; in: Das Staats-Lexikon, Vol. I, Altona, pp. 577–584.
5. Ders (1817): Emigrant survey; in: W. VIII, P. 106.
6. Ders (1817): Emigrant survey; in: W. VIII, P. 106.
7. Ders (1817): Critique of the Draft Constitution; in: W. I/1, pp. 205 and 210.
8. Ders (1817): Staatskunde und Staatspraxis Württembergs im Grundriss; in: W. I/1, P. 291.
9. Ders (1827): Outlines of American Political Economy; in: W. II, P. 124.
10. Ders (1841): The national system of political economy; in: W. VI, P. 413.

Chapter 9
Friedrich List's Understanding of Democracy

9.1 Democracy Under Threat

Contemporary politicians rightly keep reminding us what a great democracy is in our society and that it must always be protected and fought for anew. In the face of the coronavirus epidemic, we are witnessing how fragile our democracy is and how it is threatened by extreme groups, such as the cross-thinkers or the Pegida movement, who pretend to be the people but in reality represent only a minority that wants to impose its will on the majority, not to mention violent terrorists, hate preachers, conspiracy theorists, anti-Semites and race fanatics.

The European Union's community of values is based primarily on this common political principle. In this context, the liberal demands that found their lasting expression in the French Revolution, the Napoleonic wars of liberation and the revolutions of 1830 and 1848 play a prominent historical role. Nor should we forget the intellectual opinion leaders who championed the ideals associated with them through their literary and political struggles. Friedrich List was one of them.

In the time of absolutism, the concepts of "public" and "public opinion" played no role. The inhabitants of a country were subjects who had to obey and carry out the orders of the ruler. This only changed in the course of the Enlightenment, when the awakening middle classes began to demand their rights and democratic participation. In the 18th and the first half of the nineteenth centuries, the concept of the public primarily referred to the public hearing of court cases. In the course of the nineteenth century, the content of the term expanded to include all areas of social coexistence.

Historically, the public sphere is an invention of antiquity. The agora and the forum were places of assembly where the citizens of the Greek city states could voice their opinions and fight for the realization of their demands. Under the influence of the Enlightenment, the public sphere was rediscovered as a central democratic element. It then experienced its breakthrough through the French Revolution. This was also the intellectual breeding ground for Friedrich List.

Two hundred and thirty years after the outbreak of the French Revolution, the public sphere and democracy in despotically ruled countries are still red flags among

E. Wendler, *The Political Economy of Friedrich List*, Springer Studies in the History of Economic Thought, https://doi.org/10.1007/978-3-031-24601-2_9

those in power and are viewed and interpreted through their own ideological spectacles. One only has to think of Belarus, Russia or the People's Republic of China. In many other countries in Africa, Asia and South America, the respective constitution formally assures citizens that democracy and civil liberties will be upheld and that human rights will be respected. The stark reality, however, is anything but what has been set forth, and the right to freedom of expression cannot be exercised safely but is threatened with more or less severe repressive measures including intimidation, social exclusion, torture and other physical and psychological abuse, prison sentences, civil war, migration flight, and so on. One need only think of Poland, which is currently in the process of restricting the independence of judges and media diversity, of Lukashenko's forced landing of a passenger plane to arrest a critical opposition figure, of the murder of two disagreeable journalists in Slovakia or of a critical journalist in Malta, of discrimination against lesbians and gays in Hungary, the banning of liberal newspapers in Hong Kong, etc.

9.2 The Concept of the Public

Friedrich List already referred to the concept of the public sphere in his early writings. It had long been agreed that the French Revolution had not merely brought about the outbreak of brute force but also the awakening of the human spirit, which had felt constricted and oppressed previously. At the same time this brought about "the turning point of a transformation of political forms and the political spirit in Germany".[1]

The French Revolution taught Germany to develop the political demands of the Enlightenment in peaceful harmony, noting that, "like a morning star, Germany's political day shines ahead of other countries because the foundations for a good constitution are laid here, (namely) popular representation and public sphere." In this context, he criticized the Württemberg Minister of the Interior Paul Friedrich v. Maucler (1783–1859) and the President of the Württemberg Chamber of Deputies Jakob Friedrich Weishaar (1775–1834), who gave "twenty reasons why the public sphere is far more dangerous than useful."[2] In contrast, List regarded the public as "the sun of political life". "Where it does not shine, only poisonous plants flourish,"[3] of which, one might add, despotic rulers, such as Lukashenko in Belarus or the military junta in Myanmar and Venezuela, are justifiably afraid and therefore do everything they can to suppress any oppositional activity. List made it unmistakably clear that this would only be possible for a certain time period. At some point, he said, the pressure in the boiler would become so intense that it would explode and the people's resistance would break out in revolts and revolutions.

As a rule, such changes are bloodily put down by the rulers with the help of the military and the police apparatus or have to be fought for by the opposition at a high cost in terms of casualties. That is why German reunification is considered a shining exception with its peaceful revolution.

According to List, public communication forms the basis for the realization of the democratic principle. "Communication in legislation, (general) administration,

Fig. 9.1 Viennese police dogs keep the revolting people in check; caricature by E. v. Bauernfeld; in: Die Republik der Thiere, Vienna 1848; Collection E. Wendler

administration of justice, freedom of the press and ist guarantee by judicial courts—therein lies the basis of all and every good constitution of the state, call it what you will."[4] (Fig. 9.1).

The most important means of communication for the exchange of public opinion in List's time were printed matter, such as books, pamphlets and petitions, as well as press organs in the form of the pub and coffee house journals as well as local and regional newspapers. The latter were of particular importance to List in his capacity as editor, publisher, and co-publisher of some 10 newspapers, as well as his activities as a freelance journalist contributing articles to a whole series of other periodicals. With his more than 700 thematically wide ranging newspaper essays he became a notable pioneer of German journalism in the first half of the nineteenth century and an important protagonist in German economic journalism.

9.3 Freedom of Public Opinion

As a form of government for a political entity, be it the municipality, a state or country, List could only consider a representative system as one in which the citizens determine their delegates in a free and secret election. The freedom of public opinion was the basic prerequisite for this and without it a representative system or constitution cannot last with a despotic government. One thinks here of the Third Reich.

Freedom of political opinion entitled citizens to express their views and judgments on all matters affecting the policy without legal liability, noting, "against the phalanx of bogus civil service and learned hobby-horse theories, only the phalanx of common sense can help. "[5] "Then, the inhabitants of the imperial cities may appear at the Diet and declare what it means when the citizen may freely and unabashedly deliberate on public affairs, when he may give his opinion and censure what is to be censured. When he may come before his authorities without fear or trepidation to plead his cause and demand his right. When every word that displeases the official is not threatened with outrage and turret."[6]

Legal responsibility for an opinion was to be excluded because the judge lacked a corresponding basis for evaluation, whereby he could convince himself of the truth or falsity, the exaggeration or correctness of opinion, or of well-meaning or spiteful judgments. "For opinion is something purely subjective. "[7] Each one views the public state from his individual standpoint with the requirements, experiences, insights, and powers specific to himself. The judge could well pass judgement on a political opinion, but only a political and not a legal one. A judicial judgement would impose his individual standpoint, his individual demands on the public state, his individual experiences, insights and powers of understanding on the whole of society as a norm. This would give rise to the supreme lack of freedom of political opinion because no citizen would then be allowed to express his views on the public state without first asking the judge responsible for permission.

An exception only comes into consideration and can only be punished with a penalty if the expression of opinion is dishonoring according to moral principles or is to be regarded as a misdemeanor or crime. If this is not the case and a legal sentence is nevertheless pronounced, the infamy falls back on the judiciary. List summed this up with, "the Israelite gallows has become the holiest symbol of educated humanity through a single criminal tendency!"[8]

If a people are enlightened and educated, "they cannot make every screamer believe what that screamer has concocted in his burnt brain," but they are capable of forming a judgement about the screamers and putting them in their place as a minority.[9] "Free communication of thought is the most delicious right of a constitutional citizen."[10] So there will always be sectarian minorities who hold views different from those of the majority.

Citizens have the right not only to criticize the organs of the state and their representatives but also to accuse them and to bring them before a public court if they fail in their duties. If a country has a genuine democratic constitution and not merely a sham constitution, the principle applies everywhere that every citizen has the right to freedom of expression and that only the incitement to riot and indignation is punishable.[11]

It is the job of politicians to balance the conflicting demands of citizens and to bring them into harmony in the interest of the whole. The greater they succeed in placing their decisions above the views of special interests, the more public opinion will stand by them. In this way the politician would have to put their efforts first and foremost on economic development, especially on the promotion of manufactures and factories. For "manufacturers and factories, are the mothers and children of civil liberty, enlightenment, the arts and sciences, internal and external commerce, navigation and transportation improvements, civilization and political power." (Fig. 9.2).

Fig. 9.2 The press censorship of the Habsburg government; caricature by E. v. Bauernfeld, in Die Republik der Thiere, Vienna 1848; Collection E. Wendler

9.4 Scientific and Intellectual Freedom

List was aware of the great influence that science and the most prestigious and well-attended universities exert on the public opinion of present and future generations. For new discoveries and new theories to prevail, scientific and literary freedom had to be given. Only in the intellectual struggle of interests and talents and in the struggle for the inherent power of truth could the state of science develop further. This applied in particular to political economy, where it was important to grant the new theories "all possible freedom" so that they could spread and win over "intelligent public opinion".[12]

The progress "in connection with the freedom of the press promotes the sciences and arts, education and learning, and from this marriage spring in turn tremendous advances in industrial inventions, extraordinary improvements and discoveries in agriculture, in political enlightenment, in governments as well as in rulers. A new power arises, the power of the mind, with the desire that it should be endowed by freedom of opinion, speech, and the press, and that the state of law should in turn be fortified by public proceedings and the judgement of judges."[13]

"It is only in a democratic political system, in which the concentrated force of science, of the arts and of literature can be developed, and through the union of scientific, charitable, industrial, and commercial purpose, that a public opinion can be formed strong enough to assert itself in the face of physical force, and to conquer and preserve liberty for all, and to dictate to the administrators of power the direction which they must follow in order to bring about and consolidate the general prosperity of the nation.[14] The efforts expended on the pursuit of the fine arts and sciences afford man recreation, enliven his mind, educate his spirit, and beautify his life."[15]

The spiritual state of nations is a result of the accumulation of all the discoveries, inventions, improvements, and perfections of the efforts of all the generations that have lived before. These form the spiritual capital (capital of mind) of living mankind. Every nation is productive only in the proportion in which it is able to absorb the achievements of earlier generations and to increase them by its own acquisitions.[16]

According to List, human capital constitutes a nation's treasure chest, which can only be filled in the air of freedom. In his "*Outlines of American Political Economy*", he illustrated this thesis with a concrete example. The productive power of a nation, he argues, is determined mainly by the intellectual capacities and social circumstances of its people. List calls it intellectual capital (capital of mind). Suppose ten wool weavers in a country each possess $1000 of capital. They spin the wool with a spinning wheel with primitive tools, and have not mastered the art of dyeing. Each of them manufactures for himself, does all the work himself, and therefore produces no more than $1000 worth of cloth a year. Now suppose the ten weavers pool their capital and labor, invent a spinning machine and a better loom, become instructed in the art of dyeing, divide the work among themselves, and in this way are able to produce and sell fine cloth worth $10,000 a month. With the same total capital of $10,000 they can now, as a consequence of improved social and intellectual circumstances, or in other words, as a consequence of acquired mental capital, produce fine cloth to the value of $100,000. In the same way, a whole nation, by improving its social and intellectual conditions, could increase its productivity many times with a small amount of financial capital.[17]

9.5 Freedom of Speech and Press

According to List freedom of speech and of the press is the basic condition of all physical and intellectual human development. Therefore, this primal right must be a central component of every democratic constitution. Every human being has "a right to the undisturbed use of his reason, his talents, and in general his intellect, as well as the free use of his physical powers." "That writers should speak their convictions freely, they may be as foolish as they please, he said, was all right. Only against this should it be protested that if the minds of youth should be filled (with immorality), instead of teaching them how they might one day promote the welfare of their nation. For such a thing leads to evil and is indeed unlawful."[18]

However, just as the use of the physical strength of the individual is limited by the freedom and welfare of all other citizens, this also applies to the development of his intellectual powers. Through man's innate capacity for communication (speech, writing, printing, images), he could violate the rights of individuals or of the state by endangering the security of the person, of property, of human and civil dignity, or undermine the duty of the state to maintain law, order and morality. For either the freedom of speech or press, writing and printing relates to a fact or a judgement about a fact. In the case of public communication of a fact what matters is whether the fact is presented truthfully or falsely. Only in the latter case can the communicator be punished according to the nature of his guilt, his evil intent and the harm inflicted.[19] In the present day this also applies to fake news.

The inferences and judgement about a fact may not be punishable even if incorrect conclusions are drawn from it or the presumed negative effects are exaggerated. Only where there is bad faith could an expression of opinion be punishable (e.g., denial of the Holocaust). An opinion referring to a fact, on the other hand, could never be legally challenged. This is also true when a reviewer "judges a work to be stupid, shallow or harmful". Such a judgement, if consistently carried out, would soon lead to the point where in the end, all judgement on actions and research of the human mind would have to cease. Incidentally, it was quite indifferent whether the justly criticized person was of high or low standing and whether he belonged to the class of civil servants or private citizens. The civil servant is subject to public judgement on assuming his office and is free to withdraw from public judgement by resigning his office; even members of the government were not exempt from this.

9.6 The Establishment of Jury Courts

Jury courts, also known as courts of lay assessors, are courts in which jurors or lay assessors are fully or partially involved in reaching a verdict. These are not lawyers but elected citizens who have to, above all, judge on the factual situation of the case, while the judge has to examine the legal situation. From 1848 onwards, there were such jury courts in various German territorial states which were established as a result of the March Revolution. The National Assembly in the Paulskirche made such courts compulsory for press offenses as well as for serious criminal cases and all political offenses.

The importance of this topic for Friedrich List is shown by the fact that his first independent writing is devoted to this problem. In 1822, the French author Etienne Aignan published a book under the title "*Histoire du Jury*". During his first exile in Strasbourg, List translated this writing into German with the help of his French teacher Karl Flachsland and published it in March 1823 under the title "*Die Geschichte des Jury*" with the Heidelberg bookstore C. F. Winter on commission. This writing was intended as the first volume of a whole series of further treatises to which List gave the meaningful name "Themis". Themis, a figure of Greek mythology, was for a time the owner of the Delphic Oracle and left it to Apollo when Zeus raised her to be his wife. She was worshipped alongside Zeus as the goddess of custom and order, as well as the representative of divine law, especially the right of hospitality. Therefore, it is easy to understand why List invoked this very legendary figure. However, despite the "divine protection", this series of writings, which was followed only by a second volume, met with little success.[20]

Etienne Aignan (1773–1824) was a French translator and writer. He was 16 years old when the French Revolution broke out. He was imprisoned in Paris from 1793 to 1795. After his release, he worked on a career as a writer, writing plays and translating some from English. He made a name for himself by translating Homer's Iliad, an as a result he was admitted to the Académie Française. Until his early death at the age of 51, he published a number of historical treatises on legal matters, his writing on the history of jury courts becoming most well known. Between 1822 and 1829, it was printed in 14 editions in French and Latin.

The word "jury" comes from the English legal system and refers to the entirety of the jury in a criminal trial. The writing was dedicated to none other than Marquis de Lafayette, who was to take on special significance for List at the beginning of his exile in the USA. From the "Announcement" of Themis, the fundamental idea of the series is summarized, "no false national pride in our days keeps people from letting foreign experience serve as a lesson and from taking in institutions tried abroad". As list adds programmatically in the Preface, "my eyes are fixed on Europe."

The question now arises as to why List of all people translated this work into German. There are two reasons for this. First, the French edition was a contribution to a prize question at the University of Tübingen, which List was familiar with, and second, this topic corresponded to his own ideas and political position. At first, he thought of writing the history of the jury itself to win the "Palm" prize of the

University of Tübingen. In his estimation, the separation of powers, the prestige and effectiveness of popular representation and the independence of the courts in the German territorial states existed only on paper. Without jury courts and public trials, there would be no independence of the judiciary and without this no guarantee of constitutional rights.

"Personal interest, prejudice of class, old fixed notions, learned trade guild spirit, arrogance and conceit in the judiciary were opposed to the cause of liberty and truth", commented List. It was time, "to close the insatiable maw of arbitrary justice." Instead, List called for clarity of terms and speech, a correct understanding of the nature of things and of man, and, above all, a sense of truth and the human good. These, he said, "were the cornerstones of civil liberty and by which philanthropists shine beyond their age and earn immortal merit, while the misty castles of the sophists (here, pseudo wisdom) dissolve into dust with the first rays of the sun". List, however, since he was not a legal scholar, lost the desire for such a project. He "did not feel strong enough to argue against the heroes of the German erudition (scholarly circlesa)."

9.7 Opinion Poll

According to Wikipedia, "the first documented opinion poll was conducted in 1824 by the local newspaper in Harrisburg". It asked who would become the next American president in the 1824 U.S. election. Fiftynine percent said Andrew Jackson would win. While Jackson received the most votes, the majority of the Electoral College voted differently, which is why John Quincy Adams became the 6th President of the United States of America. The twentieth century then saw the development of methods for representative polls, most popularized in the 1930s by George Gallup.

In Germany, the study "*Die Arbeitslosen von Marienthal*" (The Unemployed of Marienthal), from 1933 is considered a milestone of demoscopic market research. Elisabeth Noelle-Neumann, who founded the "Institut für Demoskopie" (Institute for Opinion Research, the first of its kind in Germany) in Allensbach on Lake Constance with her husband Peter Neumann on 16. June 1948, is regarded as the pioneer of German opinion research. Despite E. Noelle-Neumann's National Socialist past and involvement, the institute developed into a household name in business, politics and journalism under her leadership. The Institute received its first major commission from the Ministry of Economics under Ludwig Erhard. It was to determine how the Deutschmark, introduced with the currency reform on 20. June 1948, was received by the West German population and whether the new currency was generally trusted.

Today, opinion research is a natural part of the social sciences. In Germany the Ifo Business Climate Index, the ZDF Political Barometer, customer satisfaction surveys or the Allensbach Advertising Media Analysis, are a few examples that come to mind.

Already 130 years before the foundation of the "Institute for Demoscopy in Allensbach" and seven years before the opinion poll in Harrisburg, List conducted the first opinion poll in Germany on behalf of King Wilhelm I of Württemberg, which thus became the first opinion poll worldwide. On 29. April 1817, Friedrich List, then an accountant with the Ministry of the Interior, received instructions from the Minister of the Interior, Karl Friedrich Freiherr v. Kerner (1775–1840), by express order of the King, to go to Heilbronn, Weinsberg and Neckarsulm on 01. May 1817, to question the emigrants gathered there about their reasons for leaving the state of Württemberg and, if possible, to dissuade them from their plans by providing appropriate information. His Majesty expected a report as soon as possible based on those questioned to understand the reasons behind their planned emigration and how the government can reduce or eliminate this movement through appropriate measures.

List conscientiously undertook this task by interviewing 200 individual emigrants as well as two citizen delegations that represented 700–800 family members and friends willing to emigrate. In a protocol of sixty printed pages, he summarized the results of his questioning. This is, as mentioned, the oldest known demoscopic survey in the world, 130 years before opinion research took root in Germany.

Günter Moltmann, who first published this protocol in his book, "*Aufbruch nach Amerika*" (Departure to America) in 1979, praises List´s work as "an unusually valuable historical source". In the way List conducted the interview, the commentary and criticism of the circumstances, a "part of his personality" is also reflected, as he was able to approach and solve such a task with the help of his scientific and political talent.[21]

9.8 Concluding Remarks

The ideas widely scattered throughout Friedrich List's oeuvre and brought together in a mosaic picture here for the first time show that his economic understanding and literary works are based on a solid democratic foundation. This was often overlooked in the past when, for example, in Russia under S. J. Witte or in List's reception in the former East Germany the focus was placed only on List as a railway pioneer or, as is currently the case in the People's Republic of China, the development of national productive forces in lagging developing countries. List's democratic legacy, his advocacy of human rights and the social aspects of his economic theory were more or less strongly excluded or neglected for ideological reasons. This includes, of course, the period of National Socialism where Friedrich List's democratic self-image and world view do not fit at all. That is why all attempts to place him in the sphere of this heresy were completely absurd.

Notes

1. List, F. (1818): Staatskunde und Staatspraxis; in: W. I/1, P. 286 f.
2. Idem (1822): The struggle for the Württemberg constitution; in: W. I/1, P. 42.

3. Idem (1819): An die Wahlmänner von Reutlingen; in: W I/2, P. 680.
4. Idem (1841): The national system of political economy; in: W. VI, P. 104.
5. Idem (1843): On state science, state service, and freedom of the mind in Germany; in: W. VII, P. 137.
6. Idem (1817): Critique of the draft constitution; in: W. I/1, P. 228.
7. Idem (1823): Articles of complaint; in: W. I/2, P. 777.
8. Ibid, p. 793.
9. Ibid, p. 815.
10. Idem (1821): Aktenstücke und Reflexionen über das politische und kriminelle Vergehen gegen den Professor List, Abgeordneter der Stadt Reutlingen; in: W. I/2, P. 1075.
11. Idem (1823): Themis II; in: W. I/2, P. 1091.
12. Idem (1843): Über Staatswissenschaft, Staatsdienerschaft und Freiheit des Geistes in Deutschland; in, W. VII, p. 138.
13. Idem (1842): The arable constitution, the dwarf economy, and emigration; in: W. V, P. 422.
14. Idem (1837): Le système naturel d'économie politique; in: W. IV, P. 272.
15. Idem (1834): Work; in: W. V, P. 44.
16. Idem (1827): Outlines of American Political Economy; in W. II, p. 119 f.
17. Ibid, P. 62 f.
18. Idem (1841): Das nationale System der politischen Ökonomie; in W. VI, p. 191.
19. Idem (1818): Staatskunde und Staatspraxis; in: W. I/1, p. 411 ff.
20. Wendler, E. (1984): The life and work of Friedrich List during his exile in Switzerland and his opinion of the Confederation.
21. Moltmann, G. (1979): Aufbruch nach Amerika, Tübingen, pp. 14 and 120 ff.

Chapter 10
Friedrich List's Opinion on Slavery

10.1 Fundamental Rejection

In a contribution to the first and second editions of the *Staatslexikon* of 1834 and 1845 on the keyword "work", Friedrich List took a fundamental stand on the physical oppression of man through enslaved dependence. In the state of nature, arduous physical labor appears to man everywhere as an evil. This submissive and servile position of children and women in patriarchal societies—slavery, the division of humans into castes, and the denial of privileges that were commonplace during serfdom in earlier times and up to the present are all included here. List described serfdom and slavery as the "curse of mankind".[1]

In Greek and Roman antiquity, slavery had taken the place of the caste system, in that each family had almost formed an autonomous, self-contained state with regard to the economy. The term "family" also included the number of slaves necessary for a complete household. In such a complete household, not only were all the necessary agricultural products produced but also all the farming implements and the usual clothing. Indeed, from Cicero's letters to Atticus, we know that some of the musicians, artists, scholars, and writers were also slaves. That under such conditions industrial production could not have the same influence on agriculture is self-evident. Cicero only wishes to remark that the production of such manorial goods as the wealthy Romans possessed depended only in the smallest part on the market because the greater part of them were produced and consumed by the common master's own slaves engaged in agriculture and trades. It is therefore easy to explain why these peoples did not attach the same importance to manufactures as is the case today.[2]

The Romans, and after them the Germans, inherited two remnants of that crude state: paternal authority over children and slavery.[3] However, the more bourgeois society strives to achieve a high moral state, the greater the tyrannical power of the father of the house is limited. In his submission to the Württemberg draft constitution, List called for "explicit provisions to secure the freedom and property of the individual, so in relation to personal liberty, the illegality of serfdom and slavery."[4]

E. Wendler, *The Political Economy of Friedrich List*, Springer Studies in the History of Economic Thought, https://doi.org/10.1007/978-3-031-24601-2_10

In another contribution for the *Staatslexikon* on the keyword "Africa" he lamented, "the slave trade continued with great insolence", especially by Portuguese, Spanish, French and American slave traders. It is true, he said, „that the number of slaves carried off to North and South America and the West Indies, which had formerly amounted to between 100,000 and 150,000 heads a year, has decreased. Nevertheless, it had not yet been possible to eradicate "this shameful traffic with the root".[5]

Because the evil of slavery still stood in the way of the spread and progress of civilization even in List's day, he called for its worldwide abolition so that the blessings of free and voluntary labor might prevail everywhere. This would promote the division of labor, improve machines and processes, and prepare people for the era when they would find the means to rid themselves of their oppressors, to buy themselves out of the grip of physical labor and to demand guarantees for the preservation of their rights.

In man's will to shift the burden of work, the curse pronounced on him at his expulsion from paradise, away from himself and onto others, List saw the source of all aspirations to dominion and privilege, of war and of hostilities between nations. Self-determined physical and mental labor, he argued, was the only reasonable, legitimate, safest, and most sustainable means for both individuals and entire nations to attain wealth and prosperity. Therefore, all social conditions that are not based on this foundation are opposed to the progressive enlightenment and improvement of people's living conditions.

The less time that the part of society which has to work physical labor has left for its own enjoyment, the greater the mainstream of labor will lose its elasticity and the more detrimental will be its influence on the general well-being. This can be seen most clearly in the state of the "slave states".

There was, however, a condition almost worse than slavery, namely, that in which the public payments and taxes were so oppressive that, even with excessive exertion, they left the free laborer no mental or bodily pleasures and were insufficient to keep him from starving. Such untenable social conditions not only crush the spirit but also gradually cripple the nation, resulting in famines, streams of migration at home, and mass emigration to other countries. List was inspired to these thoughts above all by his experiences during the emigrant survey in Heilbronn, Weinsberg and Neckarsulm in May 1817. The years of famine at that time, with the lack of food, work and general inflation, brought many subjects to such despair that they had no choice but to have left their homes and emigrated to the USA, the Balkans and Russia. The emigrants let List know that they expected no improvement and therefore preferred to be slaves in America rather than subjects in Württemberg. "Even if they saw death before them, they could not change their decision because they no longer wanted to live in such bleak conditions."[6]

These are the same motives that today lead millions of migrants to take the risk, despite all the dangers and insecurities, to flee to Europe or the USA as refugees in search of their fortune there.

Such degradation of the working classes, as List put it, also punished such countries in another way than by impoverishment and crippling. Nature had scattered the talents and aptitudes among men equally. If, for example, among 1000 physically working people, 10 are gifted above average, one may assume that among 9000 gainfully employed people, there are 90 more gifted. If all of them had a healthy and well-fed body and at least some intellectual education, it would be all the easier for the cleverer brains among the working class to work their way up to the position assigned to them by Creation, while under the pressure of excessive exertion and privation and for lack of intellectual stimulation they would not be able to develop their talents and might even become good-for-nothings and criminals out of aversion to an occupation unsuited to their intellectual powers. If one considers that the class of society destined for hard work is by far the most numerous in all countries, it explains why there is a great lack of talent in countries governed by despots because the elites emigrate and thus a vacuum is created in their own country.[7]

Physical labor, too, List said, is more or less of spiritual origin. "The more well-mannered and insightful a man is the more he has at heart the welfare of his relatives, the brighter he looks to the future, the more his powers have free scope to prepare his own future, the more he is assured of the fruits of his labor, and the more he holds to honor and external decency, so that the greater will be his efforts to acquire knowledge and skill and to produce values by means of his skill. Hence, he works more and better in free countries than in despotic and morally depraved ones; hence slave labor is the most expensive."

10.2 The Abolition of Slavery

Above this title can be placed the quotation by Friedrich Schiller from his poem "*The Words of Faith*", which List already mentioned in his criticism of the Württemberg draft constitution of 1817 and later used again:

> Before the slave - when he breaks the chain - Before the free citizen tremble not!

While the free citizen paid taxes and duties and served the common good, "the bonded servant could only sacrifice his blood and his life".[8] Therefore, List feared that a slave revolt or a sudden abolition of slavery could lead to bloody and social upheavals.

The sudden abolition of slavery in the South American and West Indian tropical countries showed that their economies were "immensely weakened and in the end even reduced to zero" This could be seen in the example of the Dominican Republic, whose economic strength declined sharply from year to year after the expulsion of the French and Spanish and was still declining. Experience had shown that the "free blacks continually sought to increase their daily wages" while limiting their work to the satisfaction of the most basic needs, so that the freedom they had gained initially benefited only idleness.

This phenomenon was also exemplified in Zimbabwe, when the government of the former English colony of Rhodesia expropriated the British farmers after independence and their properties were taken over by the local population. This abrupt change triggered a great economic crisis with an even greater impoverishment of the population than before the expropriation of the English landowners. Therefore, as early as 1817, List advocated "changing the name of slave to apprentice in the West Indian colonies."[9]

It is alleged that England, in promoting the emancipation of slaves in the North American slave states, is seeking to hang "a sword over the head" of the government there in that the more this emancipation spreads and creates a desire among the North American blacks to share in those liberties, the more threatening it will be to the Union. On the face of it, such a philanthropic experiment must appear nothing less than advantageous from the point of view of those in whose favor it is made out of general philanthropy."[10] On the one hand, slavery may be a general misfortune to a country, yet some people may make a very good living by the continuance of the slave trade and slavery. Nevertheless, he said, the question must be asked whether a sudden transition from slavery to freedom would not be more disadvantageous to the blacks at first than the preservation of the present condition.

Instead of an abrupt liberation of slaves, List argued for an orderly longer-term transition, wondering whether it would not be better to effect the transition from slavery to freedom by introducing "a mild serfdom"; that is, to grant the serfs a legal title to land and a fair share of the fruits of their labor, while the landlords should still retain sovereignty over their labor and supervision for a certain time. Would not such an orderly flowing transition be more desirable than the condition of miserable, drunken, idle, dissolute, and beggarly hordes of so-called "free blacks?".[11]

List saw the most important prerequisites for abolishing slavery and overcoming the caste system in industrialization as well as foreign trade. Without foreign trade, farm countries would be only semicivilized, "it is the epoch of slavery, aristocracy, theocracy, and despotism." At this stage, there would be freedom only for the landowners, and the richest among them would possess supreme power.

The agricultural laborer, who is bound by tyrannical laws to the soil, which is not his property, is depressed by the compulsory labor, and the labor of the enslaved agricultural laborers benefits only the landlords.

That these views also met with opposition is shown by the completely inaccurate remark of E. Leser, in the Allgemeine Deutsche Biographie, Vol. XVIII, p. 766: Some things in the essays of Friedrich List "also cast an unfavorable light on the ability of this writer to judge" practical questions, "such as the suggestion that slaves should not merely cultivate the land but also engage in manufactures." However, he said, these discussions had left no trace in American national economics, "though at the time of their publication they were very kindly received by the Pennsylvania protectionists."

List would probably have countered this criticism by arguing that the example of the American southern states taught that a country could not only produce cotton with the help of slaves and appropriate soil but also build up a cotton-processing industry. This would be doubly profitable. If Americans established cotton mills, they would compete abroad with English manufactured goods. Then, should the English make it difficult or even illegal to import American cotton, the price of cotton in their country would increase, allowing American manufacturers to sell their textiles abroad more

Fig. 10.1 The auctioning of African slaves in the United States approximately 1860

cheaply compared to English cotton goods. Either way, these measures would put England in a dilemma (Fig. 10.1).

10.3 The North American Slave Question

In the last year of his life, Friedrich List commented in an essay in the "*Zollvereinsblatt*" on the North American slavery question and its significance for the Zollverein:

> very few of our German politicians and philanthropists have any idea of the extent to which German national interests are involved in this apparently quite philanthropic question. We in our place are by no means disposed to give the word to an institution, generally considered so odious as slavery, and we would not do so even if the German national interests could be promoted thereby. However, we are convinced that the English way of abolishing this institute is a false one, in that, on the one hand, the negroes are thereby placed in a condition which brings upon them a much greater misery than slavery, but, on the other hand, the national interests of all non-English civilized peoples suffer a great disadvantage. Yes, we are even of the opinion and have already addressed it in no uncertain terms in the first volume of our "*National System*," that political rather than philanthropic purposes underlie the English motive of abolishing slavery. We set forth this conviction twenty years ago, during our sojourn in the coalfields of Pennsylvania, in a letter to Edward Livingston, who not infrequently challenged us on our views of European commercial and state relations.

The attorney, politician and diplomat Edward Livingston (1764–1836) was U.S. Secretary of State from 1831 to 1833 and subsequently envoy in Paris until 1835. Unfortunately, Livingston passed away soon afterwards, which is why List was not able to deepen his ideas with him. Regrettably this remark is obviously based on an error because Livingston was still alive and had been sent to the French capital as an American diplomat.

In this context List spoke of the "extremely important slavery question." It could not be denied that the demands for the liberation of African-American slaves were based on "much philanthropy and sense of justice" and that this zeal was a "great credit" to the advocates. Nevertheless, one should not overlook the fact that "a great deal of politics and commercial interests" also played a major role.[12]

The solution to this question must be followed with "embarrassing interest" by every philanthropist. One wonders whether this curse will be avenged or whether this problem will have a peaceful outcome. In any case, this dark chapter had become "an apple of discord", which would continue and recur as long as there were slaves on one side and blind abolitionism on the other. If this problem could not be solved peacefully, a separation of the South from the North was to be feared. Therefore, List thought of resettling the blacks residing in the North in the South in Louisiana and Texas on the one hand to abolish slavery in the North and on the other hand to grant them certain rights and securities in the South with the introduction of a mild serfdom. "Yes we fear, cannon will sooner or later solve the question which has been a Gordian knot for the legislature."[13]

This separation concern became reality just about 30 years later in the American War of Secession, the Civil War, which raged from 1861 to 1865. On one side were the Confederate southern states, and on the other side were the northern Union states. The Southern states fought to keep slavery, otherwise they would be unable to operate their labor-intensive agriculture from which the wealthy landowners made most of their money by growing and exporting cotton. The huge farms, however, could only be run lucratively with the help of cheap slave labor. There were heated debates in the U.S. Senate, including calls for the South to secede from the Union. They were opposed by the states of the Union, which relied on advancing industrialization and argued that slavery violated the civil rights and liberties guaranteed by the U.S. Constitution. The conflict was further heated up by the upcoming presidential campaign because the promising candidate Abraham Lincoln was a staunch opponent of slavery. When Lincoln was elected the 16th President of the United States in 1860, political consequences were immediately drawn in the South. Then, in April 1861, the bloodiest civilian war on American soil began, with the northern Union states ultimately victorious. In 1864, President Lincoln was reelected and then was able to bring the War of Secession to a successful end. He had saved the Union, but he could not defeat the hatred between the Northern and Southern states. On 15. April 1865, he was assassinated by the bullets of a fanatical southerner (Fig. 10.2).

Fig. 10.2 A large landowner supervising his slaves

10.4 Commercial Slavery

In addition to the enslavement of individuals, List spoke of the enslavement of economically weaker countries by leading industrial nations. His criticism in this regard was directed primarily against England. When the country preached freedom of trade, it understood this to mean selling its manufactured and colonial products all over the world and keeping out of its own markets all foreign products that might present serious competition to domestic products. List summarized, "it is to be feared, then, that the strongest nations will use the slogan of "free trade" as a means of bringing the commerce and industry of the weaker nations the more surely into a state of slavery."

Everywhere, the phrase "freedom of trade" is used to cover the many abuses and deceptions by those who use it as a nationalistic device to cover their own interests. In general, that is the mass of the people, are incapable of fathoming the questions of high politics in their full depth and are very susceptible to a confusing mixture of the differences between commercial freedom, civil freedom and political freedom. Commercial liberty, List wrote, meant only "freedom of production and means of transportation at home, while in the case of foreign trade commercial liberty may be rather equated with commercial slavery."[14]

10.5 Concluding Remarks

List's opinion on slavery and its abolition is reflected in the long bloody war of secession between the northern and southern U.S. states. It was not until 16 years after List's death that American President Abraham Lincoln declared the abolition of slavery and later paid for it with his life. Then, three years later, his successor, President Andrew Johnson, declared the Civil War officially over, and with it slavery, by signing the 13th Amendment to the Constitution.

Still, Apartheid between the black and white populations remained in effect. Even in the post World War II era blacks had to get up from a park bench if whites wanted to sit there. Blacks were forbidden to drink from public water fountains. Strict racial segregation prevailed in schools, clinics, buses and other public facilities until President Lyndon B. Johnson officially ended it with the Civil Rights Act in the 1960s. However, for all intents and purposes, segregation has not ended even today. There are still ghettos for blacks in many American cities where hardly a white person can be found and still areas where blacks are discriminated against and hardly represented. It was not until 150 years after Abraham Lincoln that a Barack Obama became the first black President of the United States. He made it clear how hard the United States still has to struggle with the inglorious legacy of slavery. He lamented, "we would be doing a disservice to those who fought against slavery if we denied that the scars of the original sins are still visible."

List's avowed desire was to help all "Negroes" to full freedom, and not only "the slaves in the plantations of the Americans," but also the "Negroes under their despots in Africa."[15] In this respect, we may regard List's opinion on slavery as another laudable facet of his ethically respectable disposition, condensed in his honorable credo, "Ét la patrie, et l'humanité."

Notes

1. List, F. and W.S. (1843); in: Das Staats-Lexikon, Vol. I, Altona, pp. 644–649.
2. Idem (1841): The national system of political economy; in: W. VI, P. 452.
3. Idem (1817): Staatskunde und Staatspraxis Württembergs im Grundriss; in: W. I/1, P. 382.
4. Ibid, p. 357.
5. Idem. and W. S. (1845): Africa; in: Das Staats-Lexikon, Vol. I, Altona, pp. 577–584.
6. Idem (1817): Emigrant survey; in: W. VIII, P. 106.
7. Idem (1827): Outlines of American Political Economy; in: W. II, P. 151.
8. Idem (1817): Critique of the Draft Constitution; in: W. I/1, pp. 205 and 210.
9. Idem (1817): Staatskunde und Staatspraxis Württembergs im Grundriss; in: W. I/1, P. 291.
10. Idem (1827): Outlines of American Political Economy; in: W. II, P. 124.
11. Idem (1841): The national system of political economy; in: W. VI, P. 413.
12. Idem (1846): The North American Slave Question and the Interests of the Zollverein; in: Das Zollvereinsblatt, No. 12, pp. 181–184.
13. Idem (1841): The national system of political economy; in. W. VI, P. 43.
14. Idem (1837): Le système naturel d'économie politique; in: W. IV, p. 176 ff.
15. Idem (1841): Das nationale System der politischen Ökonomie; W. VI, p. 411 f.

Chapter 11
The Petition to the Federal Assembly—A German "Place of Remembrance"

In the 1980s and 1990s, the French historian and publicist Pierre Nora published a seven-volume work entitled "*Les lieux de mémoire*", in which he recalled events in which French history was particularly condensed, embodied or crystallized. These can be, for example, simple memorials, monuments or graves, symbols and emblems, special buildings, selected texts by important writers or exceptional works of art. Place, however, is not regarded as a closed reality, but on the contrary always as a place in a space, be it real, social, political, cultural or imaginary. In other words we speak of a place that only acquires its meaning and significance through its context and its position in the midst of ever changing constellations.

One such Place of Remembrance is List's petition to the Federal Assembly of the German Confederation in Frankfurt am Main for the abolition of internal tariffs between the German territorial states. At this Place of Remembrance, the foundation of the "Allgemeiner Deutscher Handels- und Gewerbsverein" (General German Trade and Industrial Association) was initiated by List as the first representation of the interests of German merchants. It should also be noted that this"Place" was also the first German press organ, initiated and edited by List, that had the interests of merchants as its objective, namely the "Organ für den deutschen Handels- und Fabrikantenstand" (Press Organ for German Merchants and Manufacturers). With these activities List laid the foundation for an unstoppable discussion in the German territorial states regarding future trade policy, which finally led, after tough negotiations, to the founding of the Zollverein in 1834. This, in turn, was the precondition and the prerequisite for the technical, economic and social takeoff in Germany as well as for Bismarck's unification work in the founding of the German Empire.[1] (Fig. 11.1).

The petition to the Federal Assembly marks the beginning of a period that has entered German history as the "Vormärz". Both the beginning and the end of this epoch are closely connected with the city of Frankfurt, because the "Vormärz" found its climax and at the same time its conclusion in the revolution of 1848 and the Frankfurt Paulskirche. On 29. September 1848 in the Paulskirche, the deputy Wilhelm Zimmermann from the Schwäbisch Hall constituency called out to his colleagues in

E. Wendler, *The Political Economy of Friedrich List*, Springer Studies in the History of Economic Thought, https://doi.org/10.1007/978-3-031-24601-2_11

Fig. 11.1 The Federal Assembly in Frankfurt from 1815–1848; Collection E. Wendler

the National Assembly, "think of a highly celebrated, but long enough reviled and persecuted German compatriot, think of the great List!".[2]

The beginning of the "Vormärz" is characterized by four turning points as seen from a military, political, economic and ideological perspective:

1. The military turning point is marked by the end of the Napoleonic Wars and the Wars of Liberation. The population in the German territorial states was war-weary and longed for peace and prosperity. The aspiring bourgeoisie, expressed in the term "Biedermeier", was seen by List as the ideal to strive for, although instead of using the word "Biedermeier", he spoke of "Bürgerwürde"
2. The political turning point can be traced to the Congress of Vienna of 1815. After the Napoleonic consolidation, 38 sovereign German territorial states with autonomous governments and territorial customs sovereignty still existed. They were only connected in the form of a loose and not decision-making representation of interests, the so-called German Confederation with the Federal Assembly, also called Bundestag, which met in Frankfurt
3. The economic turning point is marked by the lifting of the Continental Blockade, which had made it virtually impossible for English goods to be exported to the European continent. After the removal of this blockade, cheap imports from England were then able to flood the markets in the German Confederation. In parallel, between 1811 and 1817, famines of almost medieval proportions

prevailed in Central Europe, which is why thousands of subjects, especially in the German southwest, were forced to emigrate to the New World

4. The ideological turning point: the Austrian Chancellor v. Metternich crowned himself Grand Seigneur of the Ancien Regime, becoming the most powerful politician in Europe, who strove to defend the prerogatives and privileges of the nobility with all his might through the so-called Restoration Policy. To this end, he had built up a networked system of informers throughout Central Europe, which served to undermine all attempts at increased freedoms. After the murder of the comedy poet August v. Kotzebue by the student Karl Sand, there was a persecution of political opponents, to which Friedrich List also fell victim

These four turning points are key in the petition to the Federal Assembly of 20. April 1819. How is Friedrich List involved in this?

During the Easter holidays of 1819, the young professor at the Faculty of Economics at the University of Tübingen undertook a journey whose destination remains obscure. We only know that he got stuck in Frankfurt and met there at the Rossmarkt with the representatives of the merchants who had gathered here for the annual Easter Fair. He struck up a conversation with the leaders and learned that the merchants were in the process of drafting a petition to the Federal Assembly to forcefully draw attention to the fact that German products were no longer competitive vs. the cheap imports from England and France and were therefore calling for the abolition of internal tariffs between the German states. List offered to interrupt his journey, to write this petition for the merchants and to present the result within two days.

The petition to the Federal Assembly was written at a time of greatest economic and social strife. Due to the involvement of the German territorial states in the battles of the Napoleonic wars, they were in a distraught situation. The years of famine were followed by the technological structural change caused by the invention of the steam engine, which brought early industrialization to England, France and Belgium, so that the ponderous, unfashionable and handcrafted German products were no longer competitive.

Two examples illustrate how depressing this hardship was on the individual states. In a short report on the Leipzig Fair in the "Allgemeine Zeitung of 15. May 1820, one reads, " our fair was excellent for the English. They sold mountains of goods at ridiculous prices. Every thinking factory owner agrees with the majority that this cannot go on. In every street one sees only headlines of Glasgow, Birmingham, Leeds, Manchester and Sheffield. This is not enough, for there are still a number of Hamburg commission agents here, who have taken possession of all the shops and overfilled them with English goods, in order to unload them at the lowest prices. On the other hand, the poor German manufacturers stand idly by their vaulted doors and have to watch with watery eyes as their customers pass by with their British purchases. In all the inns, one hears English spoken, interrupted only by German sighs. In short, everyone is astonished at the enormous quantity of English goods that have been sold at this fair. The Saxon manufacturers lay off two-thirds of their workers and face the future with fearful resignation."[3]

In view of the force with which the Chinese economy is currently pushing into world markets (keyword: New Silk Road) and the intensity with which Chinese investors are buying up key technology companies in Europe, it would not be surprising if in the foreseeable future similar trade fair reports are written in which only the word "English" is replaced by the word "Chinese".

Half a year after the cited trade fair report, Friedrich List, in the preamble to his so-called "*Reutlinger Petition*" at the turn of the year 1820/21, drastically described the untenable political, administrative and economic grievances in the Kingdom of Württemberg, as already mentioned.[4] It should not be concealed that these words put an abrupt end to his career, which had been progressing rapidly until then, as they were regarded by the King of Württemberg as an insult to his majesty, and not only cost List his seat in the Württemberg parliament but were also punished with 10 months imprisonment in a fortress and an honourable addendum.

This characterization of the political, economic and social conditions did not only apply to the Kingdom of Württemberg but basically to all German territorial states. Especially at the well known spring fairs in Frankfurt a. M. and Leipzig, the hardship of the merchants and the social misery of the population became visibly apparent. For this reason, the manufacturer Ernst Weber from Gera had already made an attempt to ban the import of English goods at the Michaelmas Fair in Leipzig in 1816, which, however, was not successful. It was not until the Easter Fair in Frankfurt in April 1819 that Friedrich List succeeded in uniting the representatives of the Rhineland, old Prussia, Bavaria, Saxony, Württemberg, the Electorate of Hessen, Darmstadt, Nassau and Baden merchants and inspiring them with the idea of a customs union. Due to the groundbreaking importance of this petition, the most important passages of the petition to the Federal Assembly are written here in full length:

> in a country where notoriously the majority of factories have either gone out of business or are dragging along a miserable life, where the fairs and markets are flooded with goods from foreign nations, where the majority of merchants have become almost inactive, is there any need for further proof that the evil has reached the highest degree? Either the cause of this dreadful decay of German trade and commerce lies with the individual or in the business order. However, who can say that Germans lack ingenuity and diligence? Has his praise not become a proverb among the peoples of Europe? Who can deny their spirit of enterprise? Did not those who now allow themselves to be abused by foreigners into smugglers and black marketeers once dominate world trade? It is only in the deficiencies of the business order in Germany that we seek and find the cause of this evil.

Reasonable freedom is the condition of all physical and spiritual developments of man. As the human spirit is held down by the bonds of thought, so is the prosperity of people bent by the process imposed upon the production and circulation of material goods. Only then will the peoples of the earth attain the highest degree of physical prosperity if they establish general, free, unrestricted commercial interaction among themselves. If, however, they wish to weaken each other, they must not only impede the import, export, and passage of foreign goods by prohibitions, restrictions, blocking of navigation, etc., but must also entirely abolish mutual communication.

Corralled in by the custom regulations of the English, French, Dutch, etc., Germany as a general state does nothing that could compel these nations to open

Fig. 11.2 Cartoon on the abolition of inner-German customs borders. The carter said, "I have nothing to declare". The front part of the wagon has already passed the Lippe border, and the rear part has not yet reached the Lippe border; collection E. Wendler

their hands to the general freedom of trade through which Europe alone can attain the highest degree of civilization. On the other hand, Germans restrict themselves all the more. Thirty-eight lines of customs and tolls in Germany paralyze internal traffic and produce about the same effect as if every member of the human body were cut off, lest the blood should overflow into another. To trade from Hamburg to Austria or from Berlin to Switzerland, one has to cut through ten states, study ten customs and toll regulations, and to pay transit duty ten times over. However, whoever has the misfortune to live on a frontier where three or four states meet lives his whole life in the midst of hostile customs officers and toll collectors. He has no fatherland.

This state of affairs is desolate for men who wish to work and act. With envious looks they look across the Rhine, where a great nation trades from the Channel to the Mediterranean Sea, from the Rhine to the Pyrenees, from the border of Holland to Italy, on free rivers and open roads, without meeting a toll collector. Customs and tolls, such as war, can only be justified as a defense. However, the smaller the state which establishes a toll, the greater the evil, the more it chokes off the vigor of the people, the greater the cost of collection, for small States are everywhere on the frontier. Therefore, these 38 toll lines are incomparably more harmful to the people of Germany than a customs line on Germany's borders, even if the tariff rates there were three times higher. In addition, thus the strength of the same Germans, who in the time of the Hanseatic League under the protection of their own warships carried on world trade, perishes through 38 toll and tariff systems (Fig. 11.2).

The petition was received with great applause by the merchants. Due to his general enthusiasm, Friedrich List, elated by his success, founded the "Allgemeiner Deutscher Handels- und Gewerbsverein" in Frankfurt. However, this initiative did not meet with unanimous approval. In the old Hanseatic cities, in the Kingdom of Hannover, in the Duchies of Schleswig and Holstein and in the Grand Duchy of

Mecklenburg, resistance to List's plans was particularly stubborn. This is why these states did not join the Zollverein of 1834 until much later.

The Free Hanseatic City of Hamburg was the last state to join the German customs territory only in 1888. Thomas Mann describes this opposition in the novel, "*The Buddenbrocks*", as, "Consul Buddenbrock was enthusiastic about the Zollverein. What a creation! At the first opportunity we should join!" His colleague, the wine merchant Köppen, on the other hand, took the opposite view, "he snorted," as Mann put it, "almost of opposition. And our independence? And our independence?", he asked, offended. "How about that? God preserve us, what shall we do with the Zollverein, I should like to know."

The analogy with Brexit is obvious. Here too, as on Easter Island, we have the famous war between the short-eared (perhaps they were short-sighted snub-nosed) and the long-sighted. These comparisons alone, with the corresponding or feared consequences, justify considering the petition to the Federal Assembly as a German memorial and revering it as exemplary and forward-looking.

When Friedrich List returned to Württemberg from his mission in Frankfurt a. M. and wanted to resume his teaching activities in Tübingen, he was sharply reprimanded by his sovereign, who was outraged by this high-handed behavior of the young professor because, as it was officially announced, he had taken on "a public task foreign to his office and this even in a foreign state" (the Free City of Frankfurt was still considered a foreign country at that time!) and forced him to give up his teaching post, meaning the loss of his civil service position. All of this for authoring the thankless and financially unsecured petition which was the impetus for the political discussion on the creation of a German economic union as a precursor to political union.

Naturally, there was a fierce headwind from the German princes initially. They feared for their sovereignty and customs revenues. List tried to convince the kings of Bavaria and Württemberg as well as the Austrian Emperor Franz I and his state chancellor Prince v. Metternich of the opposite effect. Nevertheless, the resistance was considerable. Initially, smaller customs unions were formed before the German Customs Union came into being on 01. January 1834. As mentioned, not all German territorial states joined this association at first and it took until 1888 when the Free Hanseatic City of Hamburg, some 17 years after the founding of the German Empire, was the last state to join the Zollverein.

All formulations that present the "German Customs Union" of 1834 as the solitary work of Friedrich List are inaccurate. On the other hand, he cannot be denied the merit of having put the customs question on the agenda of the German territorial states and with his efforts having contributed to initiating the political discussion. With the energetic cooperation of many politicians and statesmen of the time, this epochal unification work came about in 1834 after tough negotiations, which is still regarded today as an forerunner analogous to the founding of the European Union.

Notes

1. Wendler, E. (2019): A “memory site” of German history: Friedrich List’s petition of 20.4.1819 to the Federal Assembly in Frankfurt a. M. for the abolition of internal tariffs between the German territorial states - A plea for free trade; in: List Forum, Vol. 45, H. 1, pp. 35–48.
2. List, F. (1819): Petition to the Federal Assembly; in: W. I/2, PP. 491–496.
3. o.V. (1820): Fair report; in: Allgemeine Zeitung of 15.5.1820, No. 136, p. 544.
4. List, F. (1820/21): Die Reutlinger Petition; in W.I/2, pp. 684–688.

Chapter 12
The Labor and Exchange Value Theory as Well as the Money Theory of Friedrich List

12.1 The Importance of Labor as a Production Factor

According to List, work is "the bodily and thereby more or less mental activity of man, which is based on the intention of producing a thing useful and valuable to himself or to others, or capable of producing a force leading to this end."[1] Next to nature, labor is the main source of wealth and prosperity of an individual as well as of a nation, in that with its help man extracts from nature the means he needs for his existence and with which he can lay in raw materials and produce tools, i.e., earn the resulting capital.[2]

However, "to call the labor of man, the origin and cause of wealth alone would be to say nothing at all!" What immeasurable difference is there between the labor of a rowing servant and the labor of the engineer of a steamboat? The former, although he exerts ten times more bodily labor than the latter, does not produce even the thousandth part of the effects that the latter does. Leaving aside the power of machinery there is, for example, a vast difference between the physical labor of an Englishman and that of an Indian, between the labor of a farmer who cultivates his land in a remote region and that of a farmer who cultivates his land near a city or an industrial settlement, or between the mode of labor of a "slavish, demoralized, and superstitious people" and that of a "free, enlightened, moral, and intelligent nation."[3]

If physical labor alone is said to be the cause of the wealth of a nation, how can it be explained that the nations of modern times are incomparably richer, more populous, more powerful, and happier than the nations of antiquity? Among the ancient peoples, List said, there were incomparably more hands employed in physical labor compared with the total population, the work was much harder, and each individual possessed more land. However, the people were much worse fed and clothed than in the advanced nations of the present day.[4]

The present condition of nations is a consequence of all the discoveries, inventions, and technical improvements of the generations that have been active since ancient

E. Wendler, *The Political Economy of Friedrich List*, Springer Studies in the History of Economic Thought, https://doi.org/10.1007/978-3-031-24601-2_12

times. They constitute the intellectual capital of mankind and each nation is productive only to the extent that it can build on the achievements of earlier generations and increase them through its own efforts.

According to List, to obtain a clear idea of the productive forces and to develop and use them in a goal-oriented way, the question arises, if wealth is created through work, then through what does work come into being? What drives man, his mind, hands and feet to use them for the purpose of producing? What makes physical and mental effort effective? Everywhere it is the mind, i.e., thinking and feeling, that sets the body in motion. The hope of profit forms the powerful driving wheel of economic activity. The mere sense of duty only drives the higher man to do more than he absolutely has to do.

The more a man is convinced that it is necessary for his existence in the future and the more he is prompted by his feelings and sentiments to secure the future existence of his relatives and descendants, the greater efforts he will expend and the more he will be willing to work. The more a man is accustomed to working since his youth and the more he is motivated to set a good example for others, the more he will be ready to exert himself, to enjoy the fruits of his efforts, and the more he will detest idleness, especially as his conduct in public and in social association will earn him recognition and respect.

The less man is restrained and disturbed in his work by erroneous and superstitious opinions or by the arbitrariness of others, the more he can develop his abilities and talents and the more he can increase his mental and physical efficiency. This is why monogamy, Christianity and civil liberty are much better suited to develop the productive forces of a country than is the case in countries where polygamy, Islam, servitude and a low degree of freedom exist. Even among Christian religions, there are significant differences in the development of productive forces. Here List alluded to the different economic power between predominantly Protestant, Catholic and Orthodox regions and countries.

According to List, the productive forces, in particular man's work performance, depend to a large extent on the availability of natural forces such as water, wind, animals, steam, mineral resources and much more. However, man can only make use of these resources when enlightenment and education, science and art, manufactures and factories have reached a correspondingly high stage of development. For this reason, the output and results of the working population in civilized and highly developed nations are significantly better than those in less civilized and underdeveloped countries.

In this context, the general conditions of an economy played a particularly important role. Among other things regarding general conditions, List counted legal security and "good" laws, the greatest possible security of property, morality and the religious spirit (by which he understood above all the lack of corruption and harmful influences such as drugs as well as alcohol abuse), the quality of upbringing and education, freedom, the level of development of science and art, the protection of manufactures and factories, social justice and, last but not least, the construction of an efficient communication and transport system.

From all this, he concluded that those persons and state organs who are active in a "national society" both internally and externally also bear great responsibility, and by their powers and actions make an essential contribution to a flourishing economy, i.e., the prosperity of a nation. This being so, he necessarily concluded that the work of those engaged in developing, promoting, and protecting the productive forces of a country is no less productive than the work of those who produce effective exchange values.

Since Adam Smith regarded only the development of physical forces for the purpose of producing exchange values as the source of prosperity and wealth, he had fallen into the error of misjudging, or at least neglecting, the importance of mental forces. Had he regarded the two forces as complementary, he would not have taken the wrong path and judged international trade according to the theory of exchange values but according to the theory of productive forces.

List used the following comparisons to illustrate the errors to which Adam Smith's doctrine must lead. According to Smith's school, anyone who fattened pigs was productive, while anyone who brought up children was unproductive. Anyone who made bagpipes or Jew's harps was productive, while anyone who made music was unproductive because the sounds immediately faded away. The doctor who saves his patient's life would therefore also be unproductive, while the pharmacist who produces the pills for it would be productive. A Newton, a Watt or a Kepler would therefore not be as productive as a donkey, a horse or a plough bull.[5]

Instead, List reduced the productivity of labor to the following denominator: labor is productive either by producing exchange values or by increasing productive forces. "He who raises horses produces exchange values. He who teaches children produces productive forces."

If one were to counter that his remarks were a plea that a nation is all the more productive the more lawyers, clergymen, soldiers, teachers or scientists it counts, this could easily be refuted by a sophistical argument. The intellectual productive power of a nation is no more judged and evaluated by the quantity of achievers than is material production. This is shown, he argues, by the fact that a thousand educators or scientists who perform their duties with great zeal are capable of producing significantly more productive forces than a significantly higher number of poorly trained, underpaid, poorly equipped, and poorly motivated teachers.

In keeping with his credo "Ét la patrie, er l'humanité!", List did not ignore the social component in his reflections on labor theory. He criticized the existing exploitative practices in the factories and called for an easing of working conditions, especially in physical labor. The perfect state of the human race, he said, would be when excessively strenuous physical labor could be replaced by natural forces or machines, so that man would be left with only so much physical labor as he could do without harming his health. Every human being should be able to master his life alternating and balancing out mental and physical exertion. He hoped that in the course of time, slaves would be made of iron and bronze and driven by coal instead of by lashes. There was no mistaking, he said, that in the course of early industrialization, mankind was striving toward that goal. Already machines and inventions in civilized Europe would take over the slave labor of antiquity and the Orient of today. Already, he said, absolute idleness was rare in civilized states, intellectual labor was already being appreciated and physical labor was being rewarded with respect and prestige "Physical labor, too, is more or less spiritual in origin."[6]

To all those who fear mass unemployment in the face of the increasing digitalization of the world of work, List would have offered the argumentation that he countered the opponents of early industrialization by saying that they did not consider that the plough, the grist mill, the wheel, the axe, or even the spade were once newly invented machines and that if at all times the invention of new machines had been regarded as a misfortune, one would still have to work the earth with wooden sticks, grind the grain with one's hands and the help of two stones, and carry the flour to the city on the backs of packhorses. The whole difference between the old and the new machines, he said, was that the former were already ingrained in social and industrial conditions, while the latter, at the moment of their introduction, might render a number of people unemployed and compel them to change to another line of work or to learn the new methods of labor.

Yet, the concerns of these people are understandable because their supply situation may be disturbed. However, only short-sighted people would therefore regard the machines as an evil at all, as if the birth of a child were an evil because it is connected with pain for the mother. They do not consider that the pain passes, while the benefit remains and develops from generation to generation. The new machines will not deprive the working classes of their labor but, on the contrary, will create new labor opportunities. This is because the new machines will lower the cost of producing products and thus reduce the market price, allowing for greater demand and consumption. Although each worker would produce considerably more than with the earlier machines, considerably more could find work in a particular line of work than before.

Nevertheless, List did not fail to recognize that many workers fear losing their jobs when new technology is introduced. Indeed, this fear was often well-founded. It is true that every new machine is a benefit for the workers because it makes their physical work easier and contributes to an increase in productivity. On the other hand, it can make workers redundant, often plunging them into hunger and misery. Therefore, he said, it is natural that the individual should not be left alone in his distress, that the whole society should provide for the support of the individual. "The time will certainly come, and hopefully soon, when the whole, when society and the state will learn to understand that the momentary sacrifice of the workers in the introduction of every new machine must not fall to the individual, but to the whole, to society, since it will also receive the benefit resulting from the new machine." With these remarks List anticipates the basic idea of social insurance, especially unemployment insurance, and it is clear how differentiated and far-sighted he was in his consideration of labor as a factor of production.

12.2 The Labor Theory of Value

As labor is a principal cause of the wealth of a nation, as of that of an individual, the labor wage, along with the capital gain and the land rent, is a principal element in the cost and price, that is, the value, of a commodity. The wage is the price a worker receives for his or her physical activity. The price for a more intellectual service is called fee or remuneration. The amount of the wage, such as the price of any other service or good, is regulated by the relation of supply and demand. If the demand for workers rises, the wage rises, if the demand seeking labor rises, the wage falls. The demand for labor increases when the demand for products and services and capital increase, i.e., when agriculture, trade and commerce grows, and vice-versa.

Due to different requirements for a particular job, skilled and unskilled or common labor would have different wage levels. The higher the cost of training, the greater the effort and the more special skill and talent required to learn and perform the work, the more arduous, unpleasant, dangerous to health of the work content, and the more it is subject to change, chance and irregularity, the higher the wage.

According to List, the labor wage can vary between a high and a low point. The lowest price is given when the wage is barely sufficient to feed the worker and his family and to secure his or her future. As soon as the price falls below the lowest price in the sense of marginal revenue, the number of workers declines because the work makes people sick, the workers bring fewer children into the world, or the children suffer from malnutrition and disease. With the resulting loss of workers, the demand for workers then increases again, and consequently, the wage and the number of workers also increase again.[7]

These remarks are reminiscent of David Ricardo's theory of the natural wage, which he developed in 1817 in his major work "*Principles of Political Economy and Taxation*". As is well known, it was taken up by Ferdinand Lasalle and disseminated under the name of the "iron law of wages". However, unlike Ricardo and Lasalle, who in their social pessimism were convinced that the average labor wage would not exceed the subsistence minimum in the long run, List saw the practical way out. He made it clear that too low a wage level was highly objectionable from both a humane and a national economic point of view because it restricted and suppressed their productive power. For any country that wishes to preserve and optimize its factories, it is of great importance that the workers receive good wages and are well fed. Poor nutrition only produces a stunted and weak working class and destroys the productive power of future generations.

The highest price for labor was given when the wage enabled the worker not only to satisfy the necessities of life for himself and his family but also to accumulate savings that would make him independent, enabling him to provide for in times of sickness and the infirmities of old age. This level of wages was by no means the ideal state but should represent the normal state. Of course there were considerable differences between European countries with regard to the normal state of affairs. In countries where agriculture, trade, commerce and industry are flourishing and where a high degree of freedom is granted, the wage is disproportionately higher than in countries with little trade and commerce, especially since the demands of the workers for products and services are also greater in the more developed countries. A high labor wage, he argues, is the cause of great national prosperity insofar as it creates purchasing power and enables consumers to increase their demand and thus their consumption. It is surely not too bold to infer from this the conviction that List would be an advocate of a decent minimum wage.

These remarks on the level of wages, remarkable in themselves, are surpassed by some visionary social ideas. For List it was conceivable and desirable that international agreements be reached regarding excessive female and child labor, the upper limit of daily working hours, the care of sick workers, and the like to improve the social situation of workers and to avoid distortions of competition in foreign trade. His idea of giving the workers of large factories a share in the company as shareholders in order to secure their prosperity, to achieve a certain degree of independence and provide for old age, seems particularly bold.

12.3 The Labor Union or Confederation of Productive Forces

In the first chapter of his standard work, Adam Smith developed his famous law of the division of labor. According to List, it was above all the "discovery of this law of nature" that gave rise to the "fortune" of this work and helped its author to "authority" and "posthumous fame", although this law had already been recognized by Aristotle. However, neither Smith nor any of his successors thoroughly investigated the nature of this law and recognized its consequences. The very expression "division of labor" is misleading. It is division of labor when a savage goes hunting or fishing, cuts wood, mends his wigwam, and makes arrows, nets, and clothes on the same day. However, it is also division of labor when, as Smith indicates, ten different persons divide themselves into the various steps involved in the manufacture of a needle. The former is an objective division of labor, while the latter is subjective. The former is a hindrance to the production of goods and services while the latter is beneficial. The essential difference is that in the first case, one person divides his labor to produce different kinds of objects, while in the other case, several persons are involved in the production of a single object.

Both the objective and the subjective division of labor could also be called the "unification of labor," for the savage unites various tasks in his person, and in needle manufacturing several persons unite for joint production. The productivity of the production of services in enterprises results less from the division of labor than from the mental and physical union of different individuals for a common purpose.

This union List called the "law of the union of forces" or "the confederation of productive forces."[8] Using Smith's famous example, List remarked that in order for the needles to come into being, the one who makes the heads of the needles must

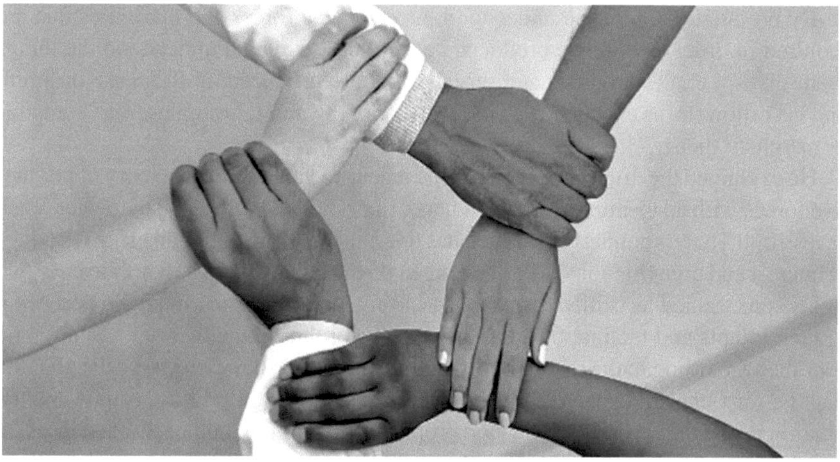

Fig. 12.1 The law of the unification of labor or the conduciveness of the productive forces

be able to rely on the one who makes the points. That is, all the operations of the workers involved in the manufacture of a product must be coordinated (Fig. 12.1).

It follows from this description that List saw an important element of the division of labor in the cooperative interaction of workers and thus propagated the idea of team work in a way that was unusual for the early phase of industrialization. Ultimately, this also hints at the idea of synergy. In this context, List already pointed out that each worker should contribute to the improvement and perfection of the respective production process. Therefore, he stated that the greater the participation of each individual in the whole process is ensured, the greater the technical improvements and production progress can be expected.

12.4 The Theory of Exchange Value

The importance of the experiences gained in American transportation for the development of List's economic theories is shown by the following confession, "formerly I had known the importance of transportation only as taught by the theory of value. I had only observed the effect of the means of transportation in detail and had only considered it with regard to the expansion of the market and the reduction of the price of material goods because of the lower cost of transportation. Only now did I begin to consider this from the point of view of the theory of productive forces in its total effect as a system of national transport. Consequently according to its influence on the whole intellectual and political life, the social interaction, the productive force and power of nations." Here, List laid down the foundation for the later known transaction cost theory.

By productive forces, he understood it to be those forces and capacities that are required in order to produce products, i.e. services, while he understood the things themselves, i.e., the products and services that are produced, in the sense of Smith and his followers, as exchange values. The theory of values, he argues, is a "comptoir or merchant theory."[9]

He explained the difference between the theory of values and the theory of productive forces with an example, "if two fathers of families who are also landowners each saves 1000 Thalers annually, and each has five sons, but one father invests his savings at interest and urges his sons to hard work, while the other uses his savings to have two of his sons trained as skilled farmers and has the other three learn a trade according to their talents and inclinations, the first acts according to the theory of values, and the other according to the theory of productive forces." When the fathers die, the first may be far richer in exchange values than the other, but in productive powers, the relation is just the reverse. The landed property of the first would be divided into five parts, and each part would be as well or as badly cultivated as formerly the whole, but each of the sons would be impoverished in the process. In the other case, the landed estate would be divided into only two parts and would be better cultivated so that greater net yields would be obtained. The remaining three sons, by virtue of their skilled education, would then be able to develop new rich sources of food. While in one family, stupidity and poverty increase with the division of their landed property, in the other, the mental powers and talents are awakened and trained, and this has a beneficial effect from generation to generation.[10]

List was firmly convinced that the theory of productive forces must stand alongside the theory of exchange value and that, for example, the theory of foreign trade should not be judged solely on the basis of the latter. He explained this with the example of the English merchants who export opium en masse to Canton, China. This is exchanged for silk and tea. This trade was extremely profitable for the merchants of both countries involved and thus, according to the theory of values, of economic benefit to both countries, or as Smith and his followers would put it, "valuable" in economic terms. In contrast, the Governor of Canton complained that the consumption of opium had a devastating effect on the morals, intelligence, domestic happiness, and public tranquility of China. The opium that the Chinese exchanged for their precious silk and tea served only to undermine the civilization and productive power of the whole people. It would be a thousand times better if the surplus production that could not be sold at home, i.e., "the price of the national poison," were poured into the deep sea instead of being exchanged for opium. "This to distinguish the theory of productive forces from the theory of values."[11]

List, on the other hand, stressed that he certainly accepted the theory of values, and least of all did he wish to diminish the merits of those who had rendered outstanding services to the development of this concept. In addition, however, the independent theory of productive forces had to be developed in order to arrive at the insight that under the existing world conditions (around 1840), the nations could be educated to industrial independence and prepared for universal confederation and general freedom of trade, for this was only possible if the most powerful and educated nations rose to the same level of civilization, independence and power. This stage, however, could only be reached by their own efforts to achieve a harmonious development of their spiritual, social and material national conditions, and this in turn presupposed the uniform development of agriculture, manufactures and trade and in the internal economy of the nation. In this way the nations would enable themselves to participate on an equal footing in world trade, navigation, and the naval power and civilization of the less developed countries. The highest degree of intellectual education and material welfare of the human race would ultimately be achieved only through global free trade.[12]

12.5 The Essence of Money

The economic activity of man ultimately consisted of the exchange of goods and services, or as List put it, "all human interaction is actually exchange".[13] Tradesmen and factory owners exchange their products for those of farmers and vice versa. The same, of course, applied to private consumption. Commerce and banks were the intermediaries between these economic entities. Domestic trade was conducted by merchants and traders, and foreign trade was conducted by export and import traders.

In the first Parisian Prize competition pamphlet of 1837, List spoke of the functions of trade. The trading companies not only saved producers the trouble of having to look after sales themselves and find consumers, but they also take over the transport of goods to places where there is a demand for them, they take over the payment of the price, they also make advances, they pile up stocks of goods that are not or not yet needed or bought at the moment, thereby facilitating the continuity of production and helping to achieve a balance between production and consumption. This short form contains practically all the basic functions of trade, namely, the market development function, the space and time bridging function, the advance financing function and the storage function, all of which have been studied and presented in detail in the functional theory of trade in the twentieth century by Oberparleiter or Seyffert, for example.

Wherever easier and more convenient transport is available for the exchange of goods, services and information, the economy will benefit from the exchange of goods and labor and contribute to the "national prosperity", as List put it, i.e., to the economic growth of a country. This effect was by no means based on "sanguine hopes", but on observations made in all countries where transport had been facilitated and where there was freedom of trade.[14]

In this context, money plays an indispensable role as a "means of facilitating exchange" or "means of circulation". Among all inanimate things there is none so restless in nature as the Thaler, "they run daily and hourly for business, and if they find none in their own country, they emigrate." Idleness was repugnant to their nature. If industry increased, the Thalers would come of their own accord. In this respect in the, "ring chain of industry," one thing always affects the other.

12.6 Coins and Banknote Money

At the time of List's work, practically the only means of payment in all countries was metal money in the form of gold and silver coins. The English financial juggler John Law (1671–1729), as director of a French bank, issued banknotes en masse in approximately 1720 but went bankrupt in the same year. This is why List also spoke of "Law's Swindles". He was also aware of the inglorious end that the assignats (money transactor) had met.[15]

Nevertheless, List advocated the issuance of paper money by the French state bank to finance the construction of railway lines and their connection to a national transport system, as List called it, a state railway network. He presented his ideas in two memoranda to the French citizen-king Louis Philippe on 5. June and 16. November 1837, the latter also in a personal audience with the monarch. In the memoranda he stated that the bad experiences made thus far with paper money should not be taken as a yardstick for its refusal. Especially for railway construction, paper money offered extraordinary advantages because its countervalue was given by the security of the railway network and its operations. The high returns that state railways promised offer an additional guarantee. It is therefore to be expected that citizens will have the same confidence in paper money as in coinage.

Neither England nor the USA had any thought of using this means of payment to finance railways. He did not disregard the fact that there was a strong aversion to paper money among the French people which stemmed from bad experiences. This reluctance could be overcome, he said, by securing paper money by special mortgages. Railways, he said, were popular, and this popularity could be transferred to the issue of bank notes. Then there would be an interaction between the progress in railway construction, the issue of paper money, the development of agriculture, industry and trade, and the need to increase the money supply.

Such an issue of paper money would not necessarily result in an increase in wages and commodity prices or in the hoarding of coinage. This would only be the case if the money supply were increased more than the increase in the needs of trade and industry. Banknotes would also have a positive effect on the lower social classes even in the least advanced provinces, especially on those who desired to make provision and accumulate savings.

Once paper money was introduced it would be as indispensable for trade as bills of exchange or coinage. However, it was necessary to limit the money supply to a certain total amount to avoid a devaluation of the currency. As a guideline, List recommended limiting the money supply of banknotes to one-third of the metal money in circulation so that there would not be, as he put it, an "anarchy of money".[16] Through the moderate use of this means of circulation, it would contribute significantly to the growth of trade and industry.

12.7 Banks and Other Credit Institutions

Just as important as the introduction of banknotes was the establishment of an efficient network of banks and other financial institutions that would provide agriculture, industry, trade and end consumers with the means of exchange necessary for purchase. What is called a lack of money, List exclaimed, is usually nothing more than a lack of sales of goods, of opportunities to obtain working capital easily, and a lack of confidence on the part of capitalists toward those in need of credit. The banks, therefore, have the obligation to create this confidence and to help traders with loans so that they can realize their business ideas. Thus, governments and wealthy individuals should take appropriate steps to build a functional banking system.

In this context, List considered the establishment of a German national bank to be an urgent task. One can imagine a financial institution spread over the whole of central Europe, including all the German and Austrian states, Piedmont, Switzerland, Belgium and Holland, set up in such a way that it would maintain branch banks at all key trading places within this wide circle and be in contact with all the main trading centers in and outside Europe. Then every businessman can, with the greatest speed, security and precision, for a small fee, draw funds from or make payments to all those countries by means of the nearest branch bank. To think what an immeasurable benefit this would be to the national as well as the international movement of goods in these countries.

List also discussed the question of whether state or private banks should be preferred. State banks, which were guaranteed by the state, might be more trustworthy than private banks in times of calm, but in times of war and general calamity, they offered the same risk as state securities in general. Private banks, if soundly financed, are generally preferable, especially if several coexist in one place, because they then compete with each other and are thus more useful to the public than large monopolizing state banks. It was necessary, however, in the interest of creditor protection, that private banks be supervised by state control, as is practiced at present by the Federal Banking Supervisory Office.

List distinguished between saving (deposit) banks, giro (checking account) banks, lending banks, bill of exchange (including currency) banks, and commercial banks, by which he meant above all the different business areas of banks, which were as a rule united in one hand. By deposit and giro banks, he understood the deposit business. In this context, he demanded strict adherence to banking secrecy, "the bank's books must remain a sacred secret." By lending, bill and note banks, he meant the payment and credit business of banks. In the process, he said, a bank also has the ability to raise capital abroad, which a private citizen is barred from doing because of the high risk involved. In the credit assessment of private banks by the government, care must be taken to ensure that there are sufficient mortgages to secure the liabilities.

In addition one must insist, that above all, the financial institutions need to ensure that capital coming from abroad is used productively and not for unproductive consumption.

This rule is violated in most countries of the world, not least in many developing countries, where foreign loans are used, for example, to finance armaments or prestige projects, such as airlines, or to accumulate the private assets of politicians, instead of being invested specifically to build up an efficient agricultural sector or infrastructure, to expand the education system or to set up and develop commercial and industrial enterprises.

According to List, when financing with bills of exchange, care should be taken to ensure that these are only issued for a relatively short period of time, with 60–90 days being the rule he had in mind. He understood slip or circulation banks to mean the issuing of cash notes or paper money, for which the following financing rules, among others, were to be observed:

- the bank had to be able to redeem paper money for metal money at any time
- the term of loans should be no more than three months
- money available on a short-term basis should not be used to finance real estate and other long-term investments.

In regards to securities trading List warned small investors in particular against an unchecked "addiction to speculation". Such "securities" often promised "an illusion with another illusion". He therefore warned small shareholders who, "cannot and should not dare anything", to be cautious because they were often promised high rates of return, but in reality they might lose all their capital. He left no doubt that paper money speculation was only in its infancy and that speculative addiction would expand and intensify considerably in the future. He warned that any stock market crisis would not be confined to a single European country but would affect other countries as well. In his bold visions List even feared that one day, "a European roulette bank in which the peoples would gamble away their fortunes and their welfare", could emerge. One might think that List was thinking of the ECB or a European "bad bank".

Gold and precious metals made up only a small part of a nation's capital, but they were a "principal intermediary" in international trade and in the circulation of capital and would form the cornerstone of the credit system and as a "world commodity". Although subject to slight fluctuations in price they would never lose their validity because their acceptance as a means of payment was guaranteed in all countries of the world and under all circumstances. In this respect, gold reserves are more important to a country than any other kind of capital. It is not without reason that the gold reserves of individual national banks in China, Russia and India, for example, are continuously increasing and that Greece, for example, has not reduced its gold reserves despite ist recent financial crisis.

List also recognized the importance of the discount rate in controlling the money and capital markets. A sharply rising interest rate was an unmistakable sign of a money squeeze, he said, already distinguishing between the money and capital markets. With regard to deposits, he welcomed the possibility of cashless payment transactions because the transfer of money would only take place through debits and credits. That is why he also spoke of "rewriting banks".

Banks and paper means of circulation adjutants complement precious metals and money and are great "fertilizers" of the credit volume, whose aid a nation can do without all the less the more its production and its domestic consumption as well as its domestic and foreign trade increase. These adjutants, it is true, are also capable of doing great mischief. However, it would be nonsensical to prohibit them and not put them into service, or not make full use of their advantages, "after all, is there hardly any good thing in the world that is used in excess or in the wrong way and would have no harmful effects."

Notes

1. Wendler, E. (2017): What can contemporary economics learn from Friedrich List (1789-1846)? Part II: Friedrich List's labor theory of value and monetary theory; in: List Forum, Vol. 43, H. 4, pp. 381–396.
2. List, F. (1845): Labor; in: Das Staats-Lexikon, 2nd ed. Erster Band, Altona, p. 606 ff.
3. Ibid. S. 606.
4. Wendler, E. (2017): Friedrich List: Die Politik der Zukunft, Wiesbaden, p. 246 f.
5. List, F. (1845): Labour-saving machines; in: Das Staats-Lexikon, 2nd ed., First volume, Altona, p. 609.
6. Idem (1840): Essence and value of a national trade productive power; in: W. V, p. 388 f.
7. Wendler, E. (1977): Das betriebswirtschaftliche Gedankengebäude von Friedrich List. Ein Beitrag zur Geschichte der Betriebswirtschaftslehre, Diss. Tübingen, pp. 169–174.
8. Notz, W. (1931): Friedrich List in America; in: W. II, P. 40.
9. List, F. (1841): The national system of political economy; in: W. VI, P. 356.
10. Idem (1837): The natural system of political economy, in W. IV, P. 192.
11. Idem (1840): The nature and value of a national commercial productive power; in: W. VII, P. 351;
12. Wendler, E. (1977): Das betriebswirtschaftliche Gedankengebäude von Friedrich List-. Ein Beitrag zur Geschichte der Betriebswirtschaftslehre, Diss. Tübingen, pp.164–169.
13. Idem (1837): Le Système Naturel d'Économie Politique; in: W. IV, P. 333.
14. Idem (1837): Le monde marche - Die Welt bewegt sich, Göttingen 1985, pp.84–99.
15. Idem, W. III/1, p. 75 and p. 150 f.
16. Wendler, E. (1996): Lists Denkschriften a den französischen König Louis Philippe, in: Idem (ed.): "Die Vereinigung des europäischen Kontinents" Friedrich List - Gesamteuropäische. The history of the impact of his economic thinking, Stuttgart, pp.190–192.

Chapter 13
Friedrich List—An Economist with Vision

13.1 Le Monde Marche—The World is Moving

The manuscript of List's second Parisian Prize competition, discovered in 1983 in the archives of the "Institut de France" by Eugen Wendler, bears the telling title "*Le monde marche*", "The world is moving". In it, the author comments on the prize question of the French Academy of Sciences, "What are the effects of steam power and the means of transport currently spreading in the old and new world´s on the economy, the civic life, the social fabric, and the power of nations?" In his analysis, List explores the many political, economic, and social impacts of steamboats, railroads, and telegraphy.

Almost 10 years later, shortly before his death, he summarized the insights he had gained in this prize submission and in the further course of development in his political legacy on the "political-national economic unity of the Germans" and reduced them to the following:

"At the present time, in all the great affairs of the world, a change is taking place which, in comparison with what has been experienced in the past three centuries, is but a small and feeble prelude. From the application of gunpowder to warfare, from the invention of the printing press, from the discovery of America, a new era began, and later, even the French Revolution was predicted to turn the world around."

Further, "there is no doubt that these causes have tremendous effects, many of which themselves resulted in revolutionary changes, whose impact far surpassed that of the original impulse. To these gigantic advances in all branches of science, the arts and institutions, to the great inventions and discoveries, and to the consequent changes in all directions in the production of human stimulants, a great increase in population and capital has been added in all advanced countries. In the following period, culture would extend to all parts of the world and to all deserts and wildernesses near and far, even to the extreme ends of the earth. From this will follow an economic upheaval which, by natural necessity, will radically change all political, economic and social conditions in all nations and countries of the advanced as well as the developing world in the course of the present and the next century."

E. Wendler, *The Political Economy of Friedrich List*, Springer Studies in the History of Economic Thought, https://doi.org/10.1007/978-3-031-24601-2_13

Today we call these observations and assumptions "paradigm shifts" and describe them with the terms globalization, digitalization, geopolitics, global warming, etc. Politicians and statesmen, List believed, are usually concerned with the demands of the present and hardly ever with those of the future. This after all, he said, is more agreeable "than indulging in notions of the possibility or probability of future uncertainties." Yet List noted that it must be remembered that the present builds on the developments of the past and at the same time builds the basis and the direction for the future. There is no doubt that the needs of the present are more urgent and that in calm times, one can be content with the problems of the present. In times of profound and rapid change, however, "looking to the future" is indispensable.[1]

In turbulent times politicians often succumb to the temptation to make their decisions only in line with the approval of their contemporaries. This behaviour, however, could lead to strong criticism from future generations. Posterity will judge such politicians all the more severely, the greater the influence of a nation on world political events could have been, or should have been, due to the respective conditions. These statesmen will be judged very critically on who is responsible for the happiness or unhappiness of all mankind. In today´s context, especially the American, Russian and Chinese political heads of state have to look far ahead to recognize the consequences of any inaction and carelessness and how that will impact the future. Only with this farsighted perspective can the responsibility for political action be derived and the obstacles, such as conflicts of interest, prejudices, corruption and inertia, which block the way to the future, be removed. List commented, "the capacity for foresight was the true profession of the politician, of the factory owners and merchants, and of the national economists."

If we think, for example, of the current challenges of global warming, environmental pollution, deforestation of the rainforests, ensuring the long term supply of water, energy and other raw materials for humanity, and above all food for the rapidly growing world population, then one realizes how visionary and relevant these topics have become.

The main points of reference for the politician, as well as for the entrepreneur who wants to give himself and others an idea of this transformation, are the increase in the population, capital and the productive forces. For this reason, looking to the future is one of their indispensable tasks.

Friedrich List was well aware that one could not predict the future, but one could try to look into the future using scientific methods. Indeed, he even had the inkling that a new science could be founded in this way, namely, the science of the future, which would be at least as useful as the science of the past, that is, of history.

To date, politics has already been oriented towards the future, but it has not been sufficiently supported either by the sciences or by statistics and the national economy. Therefore, politics has been has been limited to weak, non-quantitative diplomacy. Since the national economy has in its development not proceeded from the nature of things, namely the cosmopolitan unity of the world and free trade, so it has not been possible by scientific means to make qualified predictions regarding the future. This, one might add, is what still ails economic science today.

On the other hand, during List´s time period, as long as steam and machine power and the subsequent further developments, including mainly mass production techniques that led to rapid growth of steamboat, railroads and locomotives, etc., are not included in this future forecasting, and as long as the two great experiments of modern times, namely the development of national unity and the political and economic power of North America and the industrial and geopolitical growth of England, are not taken into consideration, a future outlook is not possible in an empirical way. If these factors are not considered, List argued, politics could hardly see ten steps forward. With the help of reformed national economics, that is, his system approach, List was convinced that it would be possible to see at least ten times further ahead in looking to the future.

At the same time, List was well aware that he could be mistaken in his visions and predictions. Acts of God, human passions, interests, appetites and aberrations may stop the natural course of events he describes for a shorter or longer time period or give them a different direction. New inventions, discoveries, and events may accelerate these developments, put a break on them, or prove his views wrong. However, some or perhaps a great deal of such visions will come to pass. One thing already seems certain, namely, that by such research into the future, as far as they are founded on scientific facts, on the correct knowledge and estimate of the present world conditions, on the correct understanding of the national character, and on factual experiences of the past, one will be able to bring to light a mass of wisdom and truth.

We are experiencing a comparable upheaval in the present because, due to digital networking in the age of globalization, the economic power coordinates are shifting from Anglo-American/continental European supremacy to East Asian-Indian dominance Fig. 13.1.

13.2 The Politics of the Future

The "*National System*" can be seen as an incomplete work of literature because only the first volume with the subtitle "*International Trade, Trade Policy and the Customs Union*" was finished by List. In reality, he intended to write a multivolume work, with Volume II being titled, "*The Politics of the Future*". With the discovery of numerous new sources from List's last creative period, we have compiled the publication entitled "*Friedrich List: the Politics of the Future,*" published by SpringerGabler. This can be seen, analogous to Friedrich Engels, who posthumously edited Volumes II and III of Karl Marx's "*Capital.*" List's visions regarding the geopolitical developments that he expected in the nineteenth and twentieth centuries are also based on these remarks.

At present, List's geopolitical visions are particularly relevant because China and, to a certain extent Russia, are preparing to adopt England's 19th-century strategy and establish "staging posts", i.e., physical bases, especially in Africa, the Middle East and Europe, to expand their spheres of influence. In our opinion, this geostrategic

Fig. 13.1 Friedrich List as a transport economist

paradigm shift is given far too little attention and is often underestimated, both in today's economics and in politics.

Friedrich Lenz and Erwin Wiskemann, the editors of Volume VII of the *Complete Edition*, drew attention to this in their commentary: it was part of the tragedy of List's life that he was prevented from comprehensively putting down on paper his ideas of the "politics of the future" because this "would have meant his very own and greatest". Even the few rudiments prove that this was an original idea with no comparable model. "The politics of the future" had remained something unique—but unfortunately incomplete.

The direction in which List was tending with his "Politics of the Future" can be guessed from the title intended for Volume III of the "*National System*", "On the Effects of Political Institutions on the Wealth and Power of Nations". With this, he evidently intended to show by practical examples how politics, including economic policy, could be used to increase the wealth and power of individual nations by appropriate governmental measures. Here, of course, he was thinking primarily of the USA, England, France and Germany.

In this connection, List also pointed out the importance of statistics: "To all nations statistics are a source for useful analysis, but most of all to industrial and commercial countries, in which it is so important that correct data on their commercial relations with all parts of the world are available, the increase or decrease of their domestic production and consumption and their causes, the effects of new inventions and events, of new institutions and measures, so that all thinking minds in the public may have an opportunity of drawing useful conclusions from them for the sake of their particular profession, or of reflecting upon them for the good of the commonwealth. Trade and commerce statistics therefore stand in all countries on an equal footing with their industry and commerce."

The first List biographer, Ludwig Häusser, reports that almost all of List's work in the last period of his life revolved around a single idea, namely, the "politics of the future", which as mentioned should have been the general theme of the subsequent volumes of the "*National System*". List had come to the conviction that "the happiness of all mankind depends on such a foresight". If one considers the reasons why the wealthy and powerful nations have attained this position, one realizes that this condition is like a plant to which the forefathers have planted the seed in the soil, but which requires perpetual care and nurturing if it is not to weaken or even die. To this end it is essential to look to the future, in which inexorable technological progress and geopolitical realities and shifts in power play a central role. This will be discussed in more detail below, insofar as it can be deduced from List's literary legacy.

13.3 Efforts for Technological Progress

Already in his earliest youth List thought about technical improvements during his apprenticeship as a white leather tanner.[2] Of course he had to learn all the standard techniques and tools of this trade, and was not spared the hard work on the scraper beam. The strenuous and foul smelling work, however, did not appeal to the young man. Instead, he thought that this work should be done by machine power which could be driven by water flowing in the canal past the workshop. Both List´s childhood friend August Merkh and the Reutlingen writer Hermann Kurz reported that such an idea was regarded as an "overbrained idea" at the time and that the young man was considered "a crazy mind" in the eyes of adults that knew him.[3]

When he then lost his mandate as a member of parliament as a result of the so-called "Reutlinger Petition" and was subsequently indicted by the criminal court in Esslingen, he occupied himself with two technological projects in which he hoped to be able to build up a decent livelihood.

The first project involved List's participation in a vitriol plant in Ödendorf, today´s Ottendorf (lying between Gaildorf and Schwäbisch Hall, east of Stuttgart). There in 1817 the mine director Ernst August Glötzge discovered sulfur gravel containing shale oil and received permission to exploit the rock deposit and build a vitriol plant. Aluminum (potassium aluminium sulfate) and vitriols (copper and iron vitriol) were extracted from the sulfurous shales of the Lettenkeuper rock. Aluminum was used as a preservative and coloring agent for hides and skins in the white tannery, for the production of dyes in cotton yarn, for sizing papers, for hardening gypsum, for cleansing water, and even as an additive for baking bread. It was used as well as in medicine as a hemostatic agent and as tooth powder. Copper and iron vitriols were needed for the production of color varnish and as sprays in fruit plantations and vineyards. In addition, vitriol containing rock was used for the production of sulfuric acid.

As Glötzge did not have the necessary equity capital, he founded a limited public company. List came into contact with the project through an acquaintance. After familiarizing himself with the technical conditions and investigating the market opportunities, he decided to take a stake in the company. It soon became apparent, however, that Glötzge was technically incompetent and of unreliable character. For these reasons List was entrusted with the management of the factory by the other shareholders in August 1821. His time in management, however, lasted only a few months. Despite intensive efforts he did not succeed in turning the company profitable, especially since Glötzge worked against him out of understandable jealousy. So after about half a year List withdrew from the company, bitterly disappointed and because of the verdict of the criminal court in Esslingen that had been issued in the meantime. Not even 10 years afterwards, in 1827, the factory was to experience its heyday, employing approximately 150 workers and thus developing into one of the most important chemical factories in Württemberg at the time.

At the same time, as List was involved in the vitriol plant in Oedendorf, he was also involved, not far away, in a suspected coal deposit near Spiegelberg in the Backnang area. In the summer of 1819 the surveyor Phillip Jakob Deininger from Stuttgart discovered a modest coal deposit embedded in the sandstone in the Dentel Valley near Spiegelberg. Since a larger deposit was suspected, a joint-stock company was also founded to establish a mine. It should be borne in mind that although people were already aware of the importance of coal for the industrialization of a country, they had no idea of the geological prerequisites where a possible deposit may be found. Due to the penetrating water, work on the test gallery in Spiegelberg became increasingly difficult. In addition it turned out that the coal was not a coal seam but merely individual coal esters of the lignite-like pitch coal. This could be used for forge fires and gas production but not for heating purposes. Nevertheless, in the spring of 1821 King William I inspected the mine and encouraged the work to continue until a reliable result was obtained. However, this only happened half-heartedly and for a short time, especially as the shareholders, especially List—were not prepared to fulfil their obligation to make additional investments.

While both investments are only marginal notes in the career of Friedrich List, they reveal his entrepreneurial initiative and his great technological interest. What he failed to achieve in both projects and the resulting high losses, he succeeded much better in the USA when he discovered an important coal deposit at the headwaters of the Little Schuylkill in the Blue Mountain area of Pennsylvania and planned one of the first railway lines in the world for its exploitation, playing a decisive role in its construction.

When he was released early while serving his prison sentence at Hohenasperg and forced by the Württemberg government to emigrate to the United States, he wrote in his diary at Le Havre, in view of the geographical proximity of the British islands, "Long live steam!". "It alone will be to the nineteenth century what all its inventions and discoveries put together have been to the fifteenth (century). It will give new impetus and direction to trade and commerce. It will bring the remotest parts of the earth closer It will give to the landlocked countries the infinite advantages of the coastlands and river districts."

In the USA, List settled in the heart of Pennsylvania in the small town of Reading on the Little Schuylkill, where he took over the editorship of a German-language weekly newspaper. There was a veritable speculative fever there at the time. Adventurers and fortune seekers were looking for further deposits in this coal-rich region. As such an active and attentive observer as List was, he could not escape this magical attraction. He also went to the coal region approximately 70 miles from Reading, followed the direction of the coal seams there, and discovered a rich coal deposit approximately 30 miles from there in the then virgin wilderness.

Considering that the world's first steam-powered railroad, the Stockton-Darlington line built by George Stephenson, did not go into operation until 27. September 1825 and that railroads were then known in North America only from reports, one realizes how progressive List's thinking was when, after the discovery of the coal deposit, he came up with the idea of building a 22 mile (35 km) railroad to the nearest navigable point where the coal could be reloaded and transported by water to Philadelphia.

After his return to Europe, he put all his energy into the construction of the first German long distance railway, the Saxon Railway from Leipzig to Dresden. Leipzig was, "the heart of German domestic traffic, the book trade and German industry". List already saw at that time this rail line as a section of a German, indeed European railway network from Cadiz to Moscow. He expected its construction to have a domino effect on the construction of other lines, which he had sketched out in his first German railway map of 1835, since he considered the Saxon railway to be one of the most profitable lines.

In this context, Jürgen Osterhammel praises, "thinking in terms of networks was not even a form of analysis until the nineteenth century." In the seventeenth century, William Harvey discovered the human body as a circulation system, in the eighteenth century, the French physician and physiocratic theorist François Quesney transferred this model to the economy and society. The next stage was a bold look into the future. Before 1850, it is impossible to speak of a "railway network" in any country on the European continent. Shrewd thinking gave planning its sound scheme, and then, when the railways had actually been built and were running, critics seized on the image and portrayed the railways as a perilous spider choking its victims Fig. 13.2.

List had similarly endeavoured to build the railway on the right bank of the Rhine from Mannheim to Basel. In 1833, he applied to the Baden State Chamber for a corresponding concession. Edwin Kelch writes, "List was then in Leipzig as U.S. consul for Saxony and from there he developed an extremely versatile and zealous plan for the construction of German railways, which owe their rapid realization and good operations to his expertise and energy. His ideas were acknowledged to be excellent, and haste was made to exploit them and reap the rewards (for the members

Fig. 13.2 The inauguration of the first German long-distance railway Leipzig-Dresden initiated by Friedrich List; collection E. Wendler

alone). It is well known how the Railway Committee that List (co-) founded, as soon as it had learned to master its purposes only to some extent, heaped upon List the crudest tricks, and finally dismissed him at the door, so that others might bask in the glory of their acquired fame."[4]

The extent to which he was interested in advancing technical progress in the German territorial states or in the beneficial application of inventions and experience from other countries is shown by his proposal to set up a technical exploratory office in the United States to deal with the practical usability of American inventions and technical processes. Significantly, this idea was directed primarily at the management of the German railroad companies. Some companies had already recognized the need to send engineers to North America to report on the latest inventions from there. However, this was difficult for the technicians selected for this purpose because they did not speak English. Under these circumstances it would be better to keep one or more resident engineers in the United States, who should immediately examine every new plant, experience, or invention, make models and drawings, and send these with a detailed report to a central office to be established in Germany. There the reports were to be duplicated and distributed to the railway companies involved. Such engineers would have to be decently remunerated. If, as could hardly be doubted, this institution proved useful, such institutions could be set up in a similar way in England, Belgium and France.

One might think that the Japanese, where even today there are some scientists who study Friedrich List, adopted this suggestion when they travelled in droves to Europe and the USA after World War II and photographed everything that came in front of their lens. It is to approach that the Land of the Rising Sun owes its industrial resurgence after World War II.

In this context, List also expected to improve the processes for the construction and expansion of streets and country roads and drew attention to the fact that in England, they had begun to pave roads with artificial granite or wooden blocks. This, he said, had already been tried in London, New York, and Philadelphia. In Philadelphia, he said, the "nasty" (i.e., unpaved) roadways between the two sidewalks had been paved. As this improvement progresses, the streets will be free of dust and debris, allowing carriages to use them without vibration or noise. At the same time, he said, a stairway or at least a step of white marble could be built to each house, and at the same time, each house could be connected to running water, which could be piped up to the roof. It would be desirable, he added, that Germany, which possessed so great an abundance of all the materials necessary for this purpose, should also undertake experiments with such paving.

During his American exile, List sent the Bavarian King Ludwig I a patent application "for railway carriages" from Philadelphia on 5. February 1829 and, after his move to Saxony, a second patent application dated 13. May 1833 for "a simple and inexpensive process for drying flour". Both patent applications are somewhat mysterious in that the files of the Bavarian State Archives contain the cover letters to His Majesty and the statements of the Ministry of the Interior and the State Ministry, but the detailed descriptions of the two "patents" have disappeared.

For Friedrich List the most important technological pioneers were James Watt, Robert Fulton and Justus Liebig. In James Watt, he admired not only his invention of the steam engine. He also praised his achievements in the improvement of windmills and other gears, as well as an improved process for the bleaching agent of hydrochloric acid invented by Berthollet, his invention of the micrometer and the polygraph, and his design of the Forth and Clyde Canal.

In Robert Fulton's case, he not only emphasized the invention of the steamboat but also pointed out that he had invented the double inclined plane, the marble sawmill and even a submersible boat. In the case of Justus Liebig, he was particularly interested in his services to agricultural chemistry. The advantages of artificial fertilization were so evident that chemistry would play a major role in agriculture in the future and help to refute Robert Malthus' population theory.

These technological pioneers were "heroes of a new age" for List. Despite his admiration for English engineers, he left no doubt that the Germans were also capable of making machines just as well as the English. Germany would soon vie with France and England in making independent technological improvements and inventions. Especially the German coal and iron mines, the mechanized factories, the glass works, the sugar and paper factories, the flax and spinning machine factories, the wool and cotton factories, etc., would in the foreseeable future be advanced to such an extent that they would not be inferior in this to any other nation on earth. In addition, this would have a positive effect on all spheres of society as, "the machine factories are the main bearers and promoters of the spiritual culture of a nation."

In the early summer of 1846, List undertook a second trip to London on his own accord to propose to the English government a German-English alliance that would enable Great Britain to secure its economic supremacy over the rapidly developing United States and help the German territorial states under the leadership of Prussia to achieve political union by peaceful means after the customs union of 1834. On this occasion, he met repeatedly with the Prussian chargé d'affaires at the English court, Christian Karl Freiherr v. Bunsen. In Bunsen he found a sincere and benevolent patron who encouraged him to send his memorandum of alliance to the Prussian king. To this request, he enclosed two memoranda on technical innovations that he had come across during his stay in London and to which he wanted to draw the king's attention.

The first concerned the possibility of creating a European market for Prussia's most important agricultural product, the potato, instead of the previous regional market. Until now, the potatoes surplus exceeding Prussia's own needs had only been processed into cattle feed and for distillery use. This was harmful to the working classes and reprehensible because of the deteriorating morals and customs. Instead, the potato should be processed into potato starch, then sold to England, where the many uses of potato starch are still largely unknown. It was suitable, for example, as an additional ingredient for wheat flour and as a syrup for sweetening wines and foodstuffs. He himself had good experiences with the use of potato starch in dishes. If the diet of the working classes were improved in this way, they would also be less tempted to take advantage of their narrow diet by drinking brandy. To date, potato starch is an indispensable raw material for many uses.

In the other memorandum, List reported on the invention of the so-called power hand loom by a Belgian. This was the invention of the power loom with high-speed shuttles. With the help of this invention, the shuttle could be moved much faster than with a simple loom. In his memorandum List reported, "we have seen it ourselves, this new product of human ingenuity, and woven with it ourselves, not only flax and hemp yarn but also wool and silk. In addition, it has cost us no more effort and skill to produce the best fabric than it costs a boy to play an aria by means of a barrel organ." Then, he listed 15 advantages of this new technical invention.

To help the poor Silesian weavers with their manual looms compete against the technically superior English competition, List suggested that the Prussian government should acquire the patent for this power hand loom and make it available to the weavers at cost.

Both memoranda got stuck in the Prussian bureaucracy and were not implemented. Had the Prussian government acted on both proposals, it would certainly have brought enormous benefits to the country and subsequently alleviated the plight of the impoverished Silesian weavers, culminating in the protests of the June Uprising of 1844.

13.4 Technological Visions—A Kind of "Science Fiction"

While the vast majority of his contemporaries were still sceptical about the railway for a long time, List had quite different technological visions that would be called science fiction today. Although the term "science fiction" was not coined until the 1930s, it can be readily applied to List's technological expectations and predictions because they sounded utopian to most contemporaries and were smiled at as fantasy at best.[5] His critics regarded such visions as the pipe dreams of a dreamer or project initiator, as the Austrian State Chancellor v. Metternich called him, or simply as crazy ideas.

In the Pfennig magazine of 1835, List not only published the first railway map in which he proposed the main lines for a German railway network but also raved about the luxury of a North American steamboat, whose cabins, in terms of spaciousness and splendor, would not have to fear comparison with the rooms and halls of princely palaces. The floor was carpeted, with mirrors and paintings everywhere. The walls, pillars and furniture were made of mahogany wood, and some of them were decorated with gilded ornaments. In the cabins of the passengers all kinds of drinks, fruits and refreshments were available, and they were equipped with elegant furniture, sofas, beds and all kinds of comforts. There was even an excellent pianoforte on the ship, and at the table, the noblest drinks were served. This description must have appeared to be an earthly paradise to the contemporaries of the time (Fig. 13.3).

List was equally taken with the idea of the telegraph. Although he may have only seen the optical telegraph in France and knew the electromagnetic telegraph at best by hearsay, he was immediately aware of the global significance of this new invention. Telegraphy, he noted, was of immeasurable benefit to science, technology, industry,

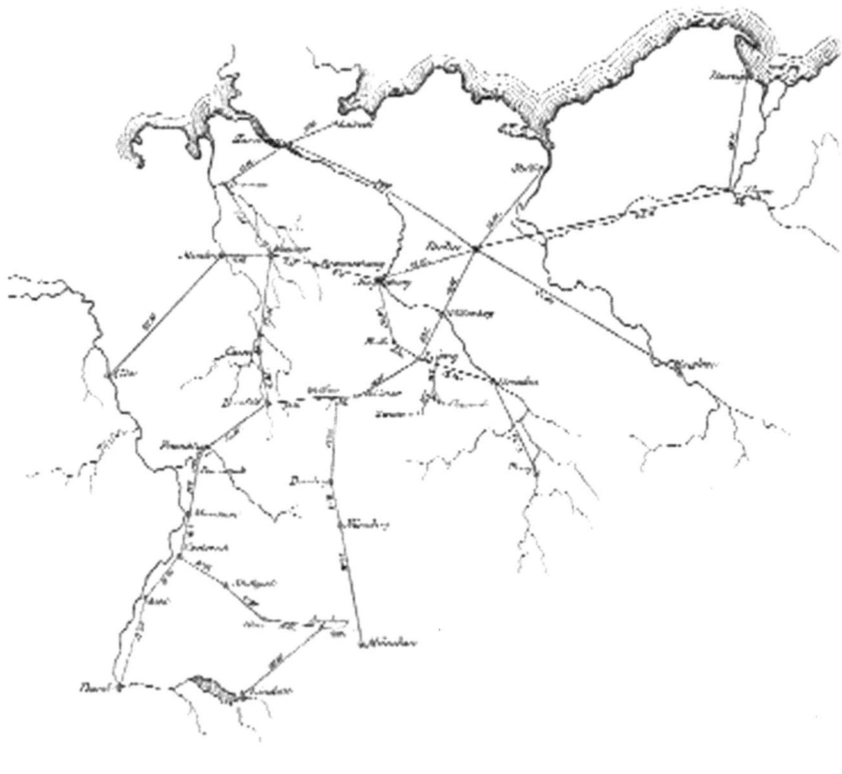

Fig. 13.3 The main lines of the German railway network according to Friedrich List's plans of 1835

and for establishing friendly relations. It was one of the most important inventions of the human mind. The telegraphic links spread across the globe allowed nations and governments to communicate and transact business as if they were only a short distance apart. Through the new means of communication, including telegraphy, man would become a more perfect being. These innovations are "gifts from the gods", which will have a beneficial effect on all human interaction, from the individual to the family, from society to whole countries, to the whole of humanity. How infinitely the culture of peoples will profit, he said, if they come to know each other en masse and share their ideas, knowledge, talents, experiences, and improvements. Full of confidence, he promised that these new techniques would help to overcome and eventually eliminate national prejudices and hatreds through the "thousand bonds of science and art, of commerce and industry, of friendship and kinship" that would now become possible.

In the truest sense of the word, List also had "lofty" expectations in regard to flying. As early as 1828, in his capacity as editor of the Reading Eagle, he commented, "a quite new invention is on the way (!), a flying machine in which one can make thirty or forty miles (48 to 64 km) in an hour. Henceforth, when Congress is in session, we shall fly away at Reading at 5 o'clock, attend the meeting in Washington, and fly home again before nightfall". Affirmatively he added, "this is indeed no joke, but utter seriousness."

Later, he remarked with some pride in the Zollvereinsblatt of 1843 that "the first idea of a flying machine was attributable to the German fatherland and emanated" from a tailor from Ulm, Germany who, after Daedalus, flew again for the first time. Then, he added that it was "irresponsible" that the people of Ulm did not give their compatriot any attention and recognition.

List was referring to the Ulm tailor Albrecht Ludwig Berblinger, who had made his famous attempt to fly from the Adlerbastei on the Danube on 30. May 1811 and had fallen into the river. His landing in the Danube was not only greeted with derision but was also associated with social relegation. He was called a liar and a swindler which meant that even the customers in his tailor's workshop stayed away. At the age of 58, he died in a hospital completely impoverished and penniless Fig. 13.4.

Daedalus was the famous Greek artist in mythical times who found refuge with King Minos in Crete but was imprisoned by him in the labyrinth together with his son Ikaros. With the help of artificial wings, both managed to escape, with Ikaros falling into the sea, as he flew too close tot he sun melting the wax of his wings, while Daedalus managed to escape to Sicily.

Under the heading "Luftschifffahrt" (Airship Travel) List reported in the Zollvereinsblatt of 1844, "attempts to solve this problem are still being made. Recently, Mr. M. Mason tried to carry out the idea of directing the balloon by means of the Archimedean screw. He made a balloon in the shape of an egg. A light wooden framework in the shape of a barge is attached underneath it, and an elongated box hangs from the center of it, to which an Archimedean screw is attached at the front. This is relatively large, but of light material, and has a rudder at the back by means of which the balloon is guided." This is the historic balloon flight of Irishman Thomas

Fig. 13.4 The tailor of Ulm during his flight attempt in 1811; Ulm City Archive

Monk Mason who, along with two other balloonists, is said to have covered a record distance of 500 miles (800 km) in 18 h in 1836.

It is only a small step from these visions to revolutionary inventions in weapons technology. The Railway Journal of 1835 contains a brief note that two six-pounder "battle rockets" were used for the first time in the siege of Oporto. "This new means of destruction and the steam destroying machines" will, List was convinced, "play a fearful part in the next wars." This communication referred to the 1832/33 siege of the Portuguese port city of Porto by the then regent Dom Miguel.

List reported on another weapon in the National Magazine of 1834, the invention of a submersible boat equipped with a special destruction assembly, the so-called torpedoes. With such a boat, one goes unnoticed under the ships that one wants to destroy and attaches the torpedo to their bottom, which only goes off after a certain time and then blows up the whole ship.

In one of his last essays in the Zollvereinsblatt of 1846, List informed his readers about the gun cotton discovered by the chemist Christian Friedrich Schönbein. This is produced by the reaction of nitric acid on cellulose. He firmly expected that this invention would be used to produce new types of shells that would change the shape of rifles and heavy guns and feared that their "pernicious" use would "encourage terrible crimes." Although gun cotton was used for explosive purposes, sea mines and torpedoes in the second half of the nineteenth century, expectations regarding its use for grenades were not fulfilled, despite attempts to do so.

List also expected quantum leaps in technological development in chemistry. He was particularly enthusiastic about "Liebig's agricultural chemistry", which would play "a major role" in farming in the future. Likewise, agricultural technology would be revolutionized by the steam ploughs invented in England. One was amazed "with what ease" the arable land could be dug up with this machine, and it was to be expected that this invention would "bring about a new era in agriculture".

In this context, he was also concerned with new methods of preserving food. For example, in a short notice in the Zollvereinsblatt of 1843, he informed his readers about Charles Payne's invention of preserving meat. He said that people knew how arduous and with what high spoilage rates it was to bring the great surplus of meat from North and South America, from southern Africa, and from Australia to the European market because the curing process was inadequate. In the process invented by Payne, the meat is placed in a cylinder which is sealed airtight. An air pump is connected to the cylinder, and brine (salt) is then pumped into the container via a pipe. This creates a vacuum, and the brine is pressed into the meat. With this method, he said, the shelf life of the meat can be significantly increased without sacrificing quality. Basically, this was the birth of vacuum packaging.

In 1834, List reported in the National Magazine that experiments had been made in the USA to cook with gas. For this purpose, the gas was fed into a tube. To concentrate the heat, a conical screen made of sheet iron was placed over the flame. The next step, he said, should be to construct a stove with which "you can fry, bake, boil, and stew at the same time."

As early as 1824, he reported in the "Europäische Blätter" published in exile in Aarau, Switzerland, on a new way of "hatching young ducklings, geese and chickens" developed in England. By this one could "give birth to a thousand chicks at once". However, he doubted whether this invention would also be used profitably in the German territorial states in the foreseeable future because it was very doubtful whether the "steam incubator would make much progress there given the aversion to all factory farming that prevailed in Germany."

At the annual meeting of German farmers and foresters in Stuttgart in September 1842, List spoke to the more than 500 participants by making some suggestions for studying agricultural systems of other nations and for irrigation of meadows. He was particularly concerned with the drainage of marshy meadows, which could significantly increase yields.

The following examples illustrate the pioneering innovations List drew attention to in the fields of construction and machine technology:

The American Charles Clinton succeeded in producing an artificial stone from burnt lime. For this purpose, lime is mixed with pearl ash and aluminum, and the mixture is finely ground. When used, the compound was then mixed with water. By adding suitable materials, he said, any color could be given to the artificial stone. Columns made from this material would have the same durability as those of marble. This technical milestone was the birth of the production of cement, to which reinforcement was later added for concrete applications.

In another press note List reported that a machine for mechanical contouring had been constructed in England. This works with a model that it traces with the utmost accuracy and does so on a scale that can be reduced or enlarged at will. Such a marvel, however, requires control technology such as that currently available.

It seemed similarly fantastic when he reported about a Russian professor who, after thorough investigations, had come to the conclusion that diamonds could be produced artificially with the help of volcanic action on pieces of coal (i.e., by high pressure), as diamonds consist mostly of carbon. As we know in the meantime this is quite feasible but because of the high cost it is technically applied only in the reworking of the ashes of the deceased into a small diamond.

All of these short reports on technical innovations represent only tiny slivers of thought in List's literary oeuvre, but in their totality and in the context of his other activities, statements and visions with a technical connection, they come together to form an impressive overall picture and show the importance he attached to technical progress. It does not seem too much of an exaggeration to conclude that Friedrich List can also be regarded and classified as an intellectual pioneer of scenario technology and trend research.

13.5 Geopolitical Visions

As part of his politics of the future, the most important geopolitical changes that List predicted for the next two centuries are summarized here[6]:

He counted England, France and the USA among the most developed nation states of his time, with certain reservations also for the politically united Germany, Russia and Spain. All other countries and nations were not only far behind in their development, they were also dependent on external circumstances and cannot solely ensure their development and existence within themselves. He considered the three most important driving forces of world political and world economic development to be population growth, the increase of capital and the promotion of productive forces.

(1) The United States of America

For the United States, List predicted strong population growth. By the middle of the twentieth century, he said, the population of the United States would be 300 million rather than 180 million. (an accurate prediction!) However, he made his estimate at a time when the U.S. consisted only of the Atlantic coastal states and had a population of 18 million. He put the absorptive capacity of North America at 400 to 500 million people. The U.S. will expand its territory to the Pacific coast and Mexico. With respect to Mexico, he expected the United States to "take vigorous hold of the poor country and probably politically develop it under something like the form of an allied confederacy." The United States, List aptly foresaw, would become "the newly emerging giant power of the West."

Andrew Jackson was the seventh president of the United States, his term of office from 1829 to 1837. Before he became a politician, he first took up the military career. He fought in various campaigns against the Native American Indians, which gave him a dubious reputation among the white settlers and the nickname "Indian hater".

Indians were increasingly pushed westward by the white immigrants. They lived constantly on their settlement frontier, the so called frontier, and were also at the center of the warlike conflicts between the colonial powers of England and France and later between the U.S. and the Indians. Thousands of Native Americans were victims of these battles. In 2005, only ca. 13,500 genetic descendants of the Leni Lenape Indians lived scattered in over seven of the Atlantic coastal states and the bordering provinces in Canada.

After the end of his military career, Andrew Jackson also entered the political arena as military governor of Florida. Due to his high profile and fame as a military commander, he ran for President in 1824. Although he was able to garner a majority of the electoral votes in the election, he fell short of the absolute majority needed to win in the Electoral College. In his place, the Senate and House of Representatives elected John Quincy Adams as the sixth President of the United States.

The majority of the settlers felt that this defeat was unjust. Because of this, a heated political argument ensued. When the next presidential election came up in 1828, Jackson received broad support. In his capacity as editor of the the Pennsylvania "Reading Eagle", Friedrich List also took part in Jackson's election campaign, as he firmly supported the election of Jackson, although he was more inclined towards John Quincy Adams in terms of his political views. However, since his principal and head at the "*Reading Eagle*", John Ritter, was a supporter of Jackson, List was also held to support Andrew Jackson. Jackson emerged from the fiercely fought election campaign as the clear winner and took office as President in March 1829.

While the founding fathers of the United States were not basically hostile to Native Americans, as President, Andrew Jackson took a combative, even downright hostile stance compared to his predecessor in office, John Quincy Adams. He denied the Native Americans respect and equal rights and forced them to leave their ancestral territories without compensation. Immediately after taking power, Jackson introduced a bill that passed the Senate on 24. April 1830, and the House of Representatives on 26. May 1830, by a vote of 102 to 97 and became known as the Indian Removal Act. It authorized the President to negotiate with Native Americans for the exchange of settlement lands in the southeastern states with their fertile forestlands for the barren, arid Northern Territories (now Oklahoma). The Act provided that the relocation would be orderly and that the Indians would be financially supported and provided with food for the first few years. This assurance, however, was criminally disregarded by Jackson. He used his authority not to negotiate fair relocation treaties with Indians but to dictate and dispossess them without compensation. When the Native American Chiefs refused to enter into such one-sided treaties, non-legitimate and heavy-handed goons were used to arrange with the Chiefs the terms of surrender and forced relocation.

These coercive measures resulted in large epidemics to which the Indians fell victim by the thousands. In addition there was a complete lack of administrative structures, mismanagement and a catastrophic supply situation. Even the promise that the allotted land would belong to the Indians in perpetuity was not honored by the United States government. The complete disenfranchisement of Native Americans and their relocation led to outright genocide. In this respect, the Indian Removal Act is one of the darkest chapters in U.S. history.

Of course, Friedrich List was also confronted with the treatment of the Native Americans. His opinion of the "Indian Removal Act", was printed in a short statement in the "*Reading Eagle*" dated 22. June 1830, about a month after the passing of this law, "A portion of today's paper is taken up by articles on the removal of the Indians. This subject is now extremely interesting, as misguided sentiments of humanity are strongly opposed to it and are used to degrade the President, who has thus recommended the measure, in the esteem of the people. All the esteem, however, that could be paid to the descendants of the natives has already been shown to the same. Indian Law clearly shows that there is not the least inequity or injustice. It is also said that most of the Indian tribes are very content to change their places of residence. Most of them are said to rather move into their new homes than live under the supremacy of the (United) States. As they are allowed perfect liberty to do the one and leave the other, any noise about removing the Indians alone seems unreasonable and unjust".[7]

In earlier research on Friedrich List we were able to show that after his return to Europe in 1832, despite his appointment as American Consul for the Kingdom of Saxony by President Andrew Jackson, was much more critical of and distanced from the latter and basically regretted that he had supported him in his election campaign,because the opponent John Quincy Adams and his economic policy concept were much more sympathetic to him than Jackson's policies. In this respect, the question arises whether he trusted the letter of the law when expressing his opinion on the "Indian Removal Act" and therefore disregarded aspects of justice and humanity, for which he otherwise stood so vehemently and was later taught otherwise. This is supported by the following evidence from 1841 where he confessed, "the North Americans are strangers to our feelings as they have a different constitution from ours, they subjugate the blacks and displace the reds, they live only for their material interests, and a wider gap exists between them and us than between England and the Continent."

In the sixth letter of his "*Outlines of American Political Economy*", under the heading "Individual Economy is not Political Economy", he mentions the Native Americans where he says, "individuals without the rules of a community are savages, and the principle of letting the individual have his way is especially true among the Indians. Again, the truth lies in the middle. It is bad policy to regulate everything from above and to promote everything when things can be better regulated and promoted by private effort. But it is none the less bad policy to let those things take their course which can only be promoted by the intervention of social power." From this, it is clear that List considered the Indians to be a prime example of individual human freedom and thus indirectly postulated their right to human dignity.

(2) The countries of South America

For the developed nations of Europe and the United States there would be no more worthwhile goal than to civilize and colonize the countries of South America, Africa,

Asia, and Australia. All could thereby increase their international trade immeasurably. One imagines that law and order, resourcefulness and knowledge will gradually spread over all of South America from Panama to Cape Horn, thereby having a stabilizing influence and a favorable impact on the creation of value in these countries. So one can understand what huge development potential the area offers, and whoever establishes firm connections here can secure them for the future. Since these countries had little power of their own to raise themselves to a higher cultural-, economic-, and political position, to introduce well-ordered governments, and to lend them stability, one should increasingly come to the conviction that help must come from outside through immigration. In this aspect the English and French were hated because of their stubborn claim to ownership of the conquered foreign lands and the mutual jealousy between these imperialist powers. The Germans, meanwhile, were very popular for the opposite reasons.

From the German point of view "a completely new and rich market for manufactured goods can be generated" in the next decades in Central and South America, including the free markets of the Caribbean. Thus, the states of the Zollverein, the German Customs Union, should pay special attention to these countries and provide them with support (i.e., development aid).[8] With the Spanish and Portuguese colonies in Central and South America having gained their independence, however, it was no longer necessary for Germany to have "colonies of their own in the hot zones". Instead, the Zollverein should endeavor to establish active trade relations with these markets and for the settlement of immigrants. Among other things List recommended the establishment of regular package shipping by steamboat between the seaports of Germany and the most important ports abroad, the promotion of private emigration, and a coordinated development of friendly cultural relations with the foreign nations. Signing trade treaties, which is not some distant and unrealistic idea as the free traders had hoped, will enable the import of raw materials and agricultural products from the hot zone directly. List advocated above all trade with Brazil but also to look at the fast growing markets Peru and Chile, especially if the planned construction of the Panama Canal came to fruition, where such opportunities as the import of valuable guano fertilizer from Peru would benefit greatly.

List criticized the fact that the Zollverein had thus far made virtually no effort in this direction. Trade agreements with these countries would be much easier to conclude if Prussia were to send a few merchant ships or warships to their ports, rather than sending only a few maps there to make the population aware of Prussia´s existence!

Realistically, however, one should not expect miracles in the medium term. Protective tariffs could not transform South American countries from poorly educated populations into well-educated, enterprising, inventive, and industrious nations in one concerted action. The precarious security of persons and property will also attract few investors to invest their capital in uncertain industrial projects. Still, if these countries were to focus primarily on exploiting mineral resources and increasing the productivity of their agricultural economies, it would be possible for them to create new needs and obtain the industrial goods they wanted from abroad. However, this would require a land reform that would turn the campesino workers into landowners.

An efficient network of German consulates and contact points should be established in the market and they should enter into correspondence with each other. Young scientists should be encouraged to travel to these countries to conduct research studies, young merchants to investigate business opportunities setting up local entities if possible, and young doctors to set up their practice there. In addition German companies wanting to settle in these countries should be supported in buying large land parcels or to acquire concessions for the extraction of mineral resources. Trading and shipping companies that have the purpose of opening up new markets for German industrial products would also have to be supported, for instance, by the establishment of regular shipping lines. The states of the Zollverein should exert efforts to gain the sympathy of the local people and governments there and should be anxious to promote public safety and order, as well as the means of communication. In sum, to provide support as far as possible, and indeed one should not be afraid, if necessary, to assist the governments of those countries by sending qualified aid personnel.

However, despite the huge potential for development, "South American nations will always remain in a certain dependence on manufacturing and trading nations." For this reason, they are "a plaything of powerful nations and will remain so," he aptly noted.

In this connection, List emphasized that he was far from wanting to assert the absolute excellence of one form of government over the others. One need only look at the southern states of America to see that democratic forms of government can be the cause of significant regress in public welfare among people who are not ready for such political structures. Let us only glance at Russia to see that people still at a low stage of development can make the greatest progress in their national prosperity under an absolute monarchy. This is by no means to say, however, that all peoples become rich under this form of government, that is, attain the highest degree of economic welfare. Rather, history teaches that a higher degree of public prosperity, namely, the flourishing of manufacturing and commerce is attained only in those countries in which the political constitution, whether it establishes a democratic or aristocratic republic or a limited monarchy, affords citizens a high degree of personal liberty, security of property, an independent judiciary, and an efficient, non-corrupt administration.

Looking at the current political situation in South America, it can be seen that in most countries there is a great dissatisfaction of the population with the respective government, so that unrest and riots are the commonplace.

(3) The African continent

Since the downfall of the Egyptian and Carthaginian civilizations, this immense continent, only one-fifth of which is as yet known, has been "a den of barbarism," which ought to engage our attention, not so much by its past and present conditions, as by the hopes that the progressive development of the social and political conditions of the world may strongly push forward their civilization. Consider the multitude of countries, with their vibrant vegetation, with their precious and varied products of the animal and plant kingdoms, with their wealth of gold and other valuable minerals. Then calculate what masses of people might live there if instead of destroying, oppressing, robbing, and making slaves of one another, they were to earn their livelihood in industry and in mutual commerce, supported by a high level of public safety and transportation facilities. Consider how these people depend on gathering their treasures from nature to exchange for European products, which neither climate, skill, nor other means enable them to produce. Consider the proximity of the African continent to Europe and Asia, the possibilities of interaction that its geographical position affords, and the extent to which recent inventions bring these countries nearer to others, and it is easy to see that the development of Africa promises inexhaustible potential and consequently prosperity to the industry and enterprise of all European nations.[9]

For sure this development path requires significant preparations. Foremost among these would be efforts to curb and prohibit the slave trade. All travelers would point to the slave trade as the main cause of aboriginal barbarism. Fathers fathered and raised children to sell as commodities. The main income of those in power resulted from the sale of subjects, so the main reason for wars and robbery was the capture of human beings. However, if people no longer had exchange value, they would have to shift to producing their own goods in exchange for industrially manufactured products from Europe. This would attract foreign merchants, and in return, the natives would have to provide them with security and transport facilities. Under the influence of foreign merchants, the tendency to warfare would diminish and contribute to the development of civilizing institutions.

However, the basic evil of slavery was far from eradicated. Portuguese, Spanish, French, and American slave traders were still able to circumvent the ship blockade of the English. Therefore, List said, every effort must be made to eradicate this disgraceful traffic in human beings at its root cause. Another evil is that about 20,000 slaves are carried off annually by caravans to Egypt and the Ottoman Empire, an evil that will only be eliminated when these countries are civilized.

For centuries the shameful activities of pirates had desolated the Mediterranean, the cradle of commerce and navigation, which, more than all seas, promoted interaction in the old world. It must be in the general interest to stamp out piracy and to establish the conviction that the welfare of each nation is inseparable from the welfare of all the others. From the growing political education of nations, the spread of the doctrines of national economy and cosmopolitan views, as well as from the spirit and progress of invention, it is to be hoped that the selfish and narrow minded jealousy of nations, especially with regard to the colonization and civilization of Africa, will give way to a reasonable interaction between the nations. This would then also include stopping piracy.

How long it will take, however, until these cosmopolitan views prevail with the European colonial powers still seems extremely uncertain. Apart from the evils caused by vicious and largely savage settlers in the African colonies, a caste of whites emerged there that strove to treat the blacks into submissiveness, immaturity and self-contempt. This was the main reason for the underdevelopment of the African continent.

The Republic of Liberia, founded in 1822 by the North American Colonization Society, occupies a special position. If the climate, which was unhealthy even for the

Fig. 13.5 Colonial imperialism in Africa in the nineteenth century

inhabitants, did not stand in the way, one could at least hope for the possibility that a system of free Negro states could emerge from it, which would help the blessings of civilization in Africa to break through. At least, List said, the principles that led to the establishment of this republic should be recognized as praiseworthy. People would be selected for settlement in Liberia who had distinguished themselves by morality, diligence, and perseverance.

The trade with western Africa was of growing importance, especially for the acquisition of natural resources for Europe. The English, French, Spaniards, Portuguese, Danes, Dutch, and also the North Americans divided the riches among themselves. For this purpose they owned buildings and factories along the west coast which, by the way, would not as a rule provide tax revenues for the local governments concerned but would more or less require financial subsidies Fig. 13.5.

On the north and west coasts, as everywhere where trade and shipping were carried out, the English played the key role. Africa was of great importance to them, not only because of its trade there but also as a trade route to the East Indies, China and Australia. On this long shipping route, List said, the possession of ports and trading points, where ships could dock, get fresh food and water, regenerate their crews, re-stock the vessels, have their sick nursed, and hire fresh sailors, was of great importance. Through these bases, England would be able to monitor and control all global traffic.

Similarly, France was striving to establish itself as a colonial power in north and west Africa and on La Réunion. After the English and the French, the Portuguese were the most important colonial power in Africa.

Spain owns the Canary Islands and certain land in Africa. In Morocco, the city of Tangier with the fort of Ceuta, as well as Melilla, within sight of Gibraltar, could one day have great importance in the event of an invasion from Africa into Europe if it should not be possible to absorb the rapid population growth through appropriate local economic development.

In general, the same characteristics apply to the colonies in Africa as to the colonies of Europeans in other parts of the world and will be discussed in greater detail later.

In most African countries, religion is a mixture of Islam and superstitious worship. The tribal rulers and kings arbitrarily controlled the freedom and lives of their subjects. They had an extremely high view of their own power and dignity, which they tried to increase through ridiculous titles. In the western parts of Africa, the plough is still unknown, the earth overturned with a wooden stake. In this way, the dense population is fed, especially on the banks of rivers.

Mobility suffers everywhere from the lack of security and paved roads but above all from a standard and convenient means of payment such as a common currency/money. In some areas small shells are used for this purpose, in others salt tablets or metal buttons are used. For the most part the economies were based on barter. From the reports of travelers it is clear that the introduction of money alone would bring about a powerful economic change.

In the north of Africa domestic trade is carried out by camel caravans. The most important trade goods for import are cotton and woolen cloths, iron and glassware, jewellery, leather goods and blankets and for export gold, ivory, skins and hides as well as ostrich feathers, palm oil and rubber, but above all, slaves.

(4) Egypt and Arabia

Egypt, once the cradle of civilization, but for millennia moved to the sidelines, seemed destined anew to play a significant role in politics and history. From the banks of the Nile the first seeds of morality, science and art had come to Greece and many centuries later, this "new world of antiquity" still stood in the same relation to Egypt as America does to Europe. Herodotus came here to study history, Thales mathematics, Solon statesmanship, Pythagoras and Plato worldly wisdom.[10]

Of all the glories for which the Greeks are still known today, for the Egyptians, however, only "a few heaps of stones remain," by which Egyptian despots and priests intended to perpetuate their memory. Science and the arts, with few exceptions that serve to satisfy the general necessities of life, had died out. Agriculture, once the pride of Egypt and brought from here to Greece, was in the hands of dirty, hungry slaves (fellahs), deprived of all possessions and pleasures and almost all human education, still using the same wretched plough from the time of the Pharaohs. The last remains of the old Egyptian culture had been trampled into the dust by the Ottomans. Since 1517, a Turkish pasha has ruled in Cairo as a viceroy. After the assumption of power by Muhammed Ali Pasha in 1806 it was believed that Egypt, due to its geographical position, was extremely important for the world traffic that was set in motion from Europe, as well as for the civilization of Asia and Africa, and that it would once again join the ranks of "orderly states". The hopes associated with this, however, had in many cases not been fulfilled. The Viceroy was not only the sole trader in products, he was also the sole manufacturer. He operated factories of all kinds, especially cotton and silk mills, as well as machine shops, which were run by skilled French and English master craftsmen.

In ancient times, as is well known, there was a channel between the Red Sea and the Mediterranean on the Isthmus of Suez, which had long since silted up. The construction of a new canal to connect the two seas has long been considered too costly and time consuming, and the result is doubtful. However, in recent times, the project of building a canal between Suez and the Nile had reappeared and was also supported by many foreign countries.

To ensure the continuity of his military government, Muhammed Ali Pasha established several military schools. The ruler sent young Egyptians to Italy, France and England for training in the administration of the country, for teaching in the schools, for the management of public buildings and factories, and for service on the general staff. All these institutions for the promotion of material wealth and intellectual culture essentially served only the power of the autocrat. This system was not capable of raising the spiritual and moral welfare of the people but had plunged them into increased backwardness.

The situation in Egypt was a good indicator of the relative position of foreign powers. England watched with the utmost jealousy every step taken by other nations that aimed at diminishing or even eliminating her influence in Egypt. Because of the tangible interests of its trade with India, it would not be indifferent to the construction of a canal between the Mediterranean and the Red Sea. If this new waterway were built, Britain would make every effort to bring Egypt into the strongest possible dependence. In this case, England would set limits on the extension of French interests. Moreover, Russia would be anxious to assert her influence more strongly on the Egyptian-Arab axis.

The seacoasts of Arabia are mostly flat and arid sandy deserts. More or less distant from the coast are mountains, whose valleys belong to the fertile regions of the country and which enclose the inner highlands, a stony, here and there fertile oases containing sandy desert, on which no European foot has ever set. On the plateau, the climate is severe, in the summer tropical heat scorches all the plants, which after the rainy season shoot up again with tremendous beauty. Coffee and medicinal plants are cultivated in fertile areas. Metals are extracted only in small quantities. From time immemorial, horse breeding has reached a high level of perfection. Nowhere are these animals so well cared for, where so much care is taken to keep the breeds pure, where a proper register is kept of their pedigree.

The main religion is Islam, including the Wahhabi sect. Trade was in the hands of the Armenians and the English. Hunting, cattle breeding and robbery were the most important sources of food for the natives. Here were the Bedouins living in tents and huts, the Fellach farming in Egypt, the craftsmen and artists, the nomads with their wandering extended families, and the Arabs ruled by the sheikhs and emirs.

The Bedouins, the largest part of the population of the Arabian Peninsula, were also the most illiterate as they did not attend schools and only memorized poems on their history. They would be subjects to sheikhs and emirs, some of whom obeyed a chief emir. Their most powerful prince is the Imam of Yemen, who holds the title of Caliph. In individual parts of the country the youth learn reading, writing, arithmetic and religion. Medicine, philosophy, astrology and astronomy are also taught in academic institutions, as well a strong focus on superstition and fables. History and poetry, however, flourished.

Since the Wahhabis played an important role in the recent history of the country, it seems appropriate to say something more about this religious sect. They inhabited the inner highlands (Rajed), believed in one God and Mohammed was a prophet to them, but they considered it blasphemy to attribute divine power to him. The Koran in its original purity was divine revelation to them, but in it, they rejected all Turkish additions. They also considered it their duty to spread the divine word by the power of the sword.

Smoking tobacco, drinking coffee, and wearing silk scarves are mortal sins for them. The rule over them exercised an emir from the family Ibn Saud.

The Wahhabis, although armed partly with firearms, partly with swords, daggers, and lances, protected all over with armor and shields, fiery, brave, and proficiently mounted, would not have withstood the much weaker but European-disciplined army of the Viceroy of Egypt. So the present cities of Mecca and Medina fell into his power in 1812. The feeble remnants of the Wahhabis are now to be ruled by the beautiful and enterprising daughter of Wahhabi, the founder of the sect. In addition it seems without a doubt that this whole country will remain for a long time, and perhaps forever, as part of the building of the state which Muhammad Ali Pasha is striving to erect on the ruins of African and Asiatic Turkey.

(5) The Asian continent

Mankind was born in Asia. Grains, grapes and many types of fruit originated in Asia. Many spices came to Europe from Asia via Greece and Italy. The first silk worms were brought to Europe by monks from China. In agriculture and some trades, the Chinese, Japanese and Indians made significant progress. However, intellectual and social development did not keep pace with industrial development because despotism and slavery often stood in the way of technical progress in Asia.[11]

While monogamy is the basis of family life in Europe, polygamy is widespread in Asia. Monogamy inevitably leads to respect for the female gender and to its equality with the male sex, and this in turn has a positive effect on the education of future generations. Property, Friedrich List said, had so little protection in some Asiatic countries, especially in Mohammedan ones, that owners had to protect themselves by concealing their wealth against predatory rulers. Indeed, people were afraid even to repair dilapidated dwellings lest they be thought of as being rich. Even the lives of subjects were regarded by the rulers as goods that they could dispose of at will.

In Asia, List commented, legislation and the administration of justice are closely intermingled with religion and the power of the ruler, medicine with the art of magic, chemistry with alchemy, astronomy with astrology, history with the world of fables. Between religion and morality, rules and law, science and learning, honor and respect, power and education, labor and prosperity, trade and security, there was often a considerable discord. A comparison between Europe and Asia must lead to the insight that the more stable the state of law, the more limited the arbitrariness of the ruler, the more enlightened and educated the people, the more respected the work and the better the remuneration, the lower the influence of the priesthood, the stronger the public control of the state officials and the freer the expression of opinion, the richer the people, the more powerful the state, the more respected and secure the ruler and the ruling dynasty.

In its main components, Asia is divided into northern, southern, eastern, western and central Asia. Northern Siberia is completely under Russian rule, with only a few hunters, fishermen and shepherds inhabiting northern Siberia. Southern Siberia, he said, possessed extraordinary wealth due to vast forests, water forces, and mineral resources. These regions, however, are inhabited by pagan and uncultivated tribes, most of whom are nomads or seminomads who only reluctantly recognize Russian supremacy.

List only counts Russia among the first class of leading industrial nations to a certain extent, "because its existence as one of the first world powers is not yet guaranteed". Its internal cohesion, its culture, and its constitutional, legal, and administrative conditions were based on a multitude of backwards nations held in check by Russian military power. He doubted that Russian policy would succeed in solving the difficult problem of nationalities. On the other hand, he saw the danger that the European continent would one day fall under the domination of Russia, assuming that this colossus continued to form a whole (political nation) and strengthened to the extent that the inexorable progress of mankind allowed it to do so. "However, this subjugation would not come about if the peoples of Central and Western Europe were to unite economically and politically." France had a key role here. As early as 1837, in his second Paris Prize competition pamphlet, List called for France to place itself at the forefront of the European unification movement on the basis of its progress as a civilization.

The most important means of consolidating Russian influence was the facilitation of transportation. If the construction of a railway from Petersburg to Moscow is now in planning, the further hope that Warsaw will one day be connected with Moscow, and that city with the southern part of the Volga, and gradually with the main points in Russian Asia, does not seem at all exaggerated. This would undoubtedly accrue great advantages to Russian Asia and give the Russian government an irresistible influence over Eastern and Central Asia. In this way, in the course of time, it should succeed in forming an Asiatic system of civilized states and in magnifying the commerce between Europe and Asia.

In the southern part of Asia, political difficulties were of a much greater dimension. The Shah of Persia, the Turkish Sultan, the Sheikhs of the non-sedentary (nomadic) and sedentary Arab tribes, could only be persuaded to cooperate through bribery and corruption. The disloyalty of the Arabs made the Euphrates the most dangerous waterway in the world. Regarding the Ottoman Empire, List was convinced that it was internally so rotten that it could not maintain itself by its own strength and was therefore heading for inevitable dissolution. The High Gate would fall, this was as certain as the leaves falling in late fall. Then the question would arise as to who would assert its power and political influence, whether the Italians, the French, or the Russians. This prognosis was also correct in principle. After the collapse of the Ottoman Empire, the Italians because of their position on the Adriatic Sea in Albania, the French because of their Romance language affinity in Romania, and the Russians because of their common Orthodox Church in Bulgaria and Serbia, were anxious to consolidate their political, economic and cultural influence and sphere of power in these countries.

When List referred to East Asia, he meant above all China, "the colossus standing on feet of clay" with an "abundance of tea, sugar, and silk to supply all of Europe, with an immense export of textiles and manufactured goods, of precious metals and gems, with the surplus of a population trained to strict obedience and production, which in a few years should be sufficient to populate the whole of Asiatic and European Russia and to enliven it with workshops and mines." However, List also criticized the political instability of the Chinese empire, whose threat and disintegration could be expected from without and from within. In this context, he spoke of a barbaric and semicivilized despotism and slavery that stood in the way of progress in all political, economic, and social spheres. As a drastic example he cited that the Emperor of China had invented a new death penalty where an eunuch sentenced to death for treason had been wrapped in yarn, wrapped in wax, and burned like a wax candle by order of the emperor.

In an essay of 1844 entitled "*The little cloud on the Chinese Horizon*", Friedrich List developed the following vision, "he would sooner believe that the throne of the Son of Heaven and with it the entire Mandarin Empire would collapse than that three hundred million people would calmly watch the English carry out the work of destroying industry". The most likely scenario, he said, "was that sooner or later the millions of workers, who had become unruly, would descend on the red-haired barbarians out of desperation and compel them to stage a new wholesale bloodbath in honor of the English petticoats (meaning the English textile industry)". On a fine day, he continued, "the Chinese free trade experiment would burst like an overheated boiler and end in horror. The red-haired barbarians would then be driven out anew and wage war, and Chinese trade would be interrupted for a long time as a result". With these words List criticized the devastating effects of English free trade which, for example, had destroyed the traditional and highly developed Chinese textile trade and produced an army of unemployed. List foresaw as already mentioned, with this assessment, the two Opium Wars and the Boxer Rebellion of 1900, and even the political and economic isolation of the People's Republic of China until Deng Xiaoping came to power.

On the other hand, List already recognized the huge development potential that lay in the most populous country on earth. Within the framework of his politics of the future, he predicted for the end of the twentieth century that alongside the giant power of the West (the USA), a second giant power would arise in the East (China). This eastern power would far exceed the population of the giant power in the West and would at least equal it in terms of prosperity. In the second half of the twentieth century there would be, as far as he could see from his limited perspective, only two giant powers and only three or four independent nations, that is a "pentarchy?!" This, too, was a brilliant prediction considering the current geopolitical power constellation that forms the most powerful economic nations on earth under the designation G7.

In terms of political and economic influence in East Asia, List expected a race between Russia and England. Russia's true interest was likely to be in making Central and Eastern Asia dependent on her. Russian expansionist ambitions in Asia, however, would put England on the spot to react. To counteract the potential of a too strong a power and market domination in Asian overseas trade, the English were about to face "the Russian battle line" with a "southern battle line". In a modern context it is important to note that this role has now been taken over by the USA.

On the English colonial empire in India, List predicted, "in the wake of commerce the European arts and sciences, European manners and customs, European schools and academic institutions, European military discipline, European norms of law and order, and European organizations and institutions of every kind are coming in. The English language, which is a general tongue of liberty and common sense, will spread among the higher classes and among the military and will gradually penetrate to the lowest classes". For further remarks on Southern Asia, especially India, East Asia (China and Japan) and Central Asia (Baluchistan and Turkmenistan), reference is made to corresponding articles in the *Staatslexikon*, which however, were not written by Friedrich List.

(6) Oceania and Polynesia

The fifth continent had only been discovered (recently) by James Cook in 1779–1780. Although nature had so lavishly endowed this part of the world with riches, it had thus far attracted little attention from the European trading nations. Only the British recognized the importance of this continent and began with its colonization.[12]

On account of the fertility of the soil in all climatic zones Australia offered them extensive possibilities in agricultural production. Cattle breeding, in particular, promised excellent results. In the long run England would benefit greatly from the exploitation of natural resources. To support the colonists, the English government had also settled criminals and released convicts in the region, who would first work as servants and if well behaved would be set free altogether. These prospects would have a beneficial influence on most of these prisoners. It is particularly gratifying, List stated, that the descendants of criminals are generally far from following in the footsteps of their parents and are rather anxious to forget the taint of birth and live a life with integrity, decent conduct, and efficiency in business.

The Australian aborigines had black skin and woolly hair like the Africans and were still on the level of barbarism in cultural terms. Between them and the settlers existed a fierce enmity, where murder from both sides was common.

New Zealand was also very suitable for the colonization and settlement of European emigrants. The aborigines were characterized by physical strength and size, while warlike still quite docile and good-natured. Their social order resembled the European feudal system with chiefs, nobility, landowners, slaves and a priestly hierarchy. Adultery and theft were punishable by death.

For the expansion of British colonization and rule in Polynesia, New Zealand seemed destined to become a major base to spur this development. For several decades there had been English settlements of missionaries and merchants. In the meantime, however, quarrels had broken out between the colonists and the natives, which had led to bloody battles. In the end it only resulted in the expansion and consolidation of British rule. The influence in Polynesia would be contested not only by England and

France but also by the United States. The USA succeeded in extending its political influence to the Sandwich Islands (Hawaii) even though it recognized their independence in 1844. In sum, there is no doubt that with the help of the English colonization and missionary system, flourishing and civilized states will emerge throughout Polynesia in the course of time, building up on what has already been achieved thus far.

Finally, Friedrich List even mentioned the island of Tasmania. Although in 1830 only about 20,000 people lived here Hobart, the capital with half of the population, already had churches and schools, an agricultural association, an insurance company, three printing presses and just as many newspapers, four large water mills, a bank and all kinds of trades and institutions.

In summary, Friedrich List was broadly correct in his assessment of the development potential of the non-European continents and clearly recognized and evaluated the significant differences. These and many other differences are still of central importance today in economic and developmental terms, despite globalization. Contrary to Adam Smith's expectations, these regions have not been reduced by free trade but have been intensified. Therefore, his economic model cannot and must not be propagated as the non plus ultra!

If we project List's geopolitical visions to the present, we find startling parallels. Just as England in the nineteenth century strove to create "stable places" for its policies and foreign trade all over the world, today the People's Republic of China is preparing to gain an analogous foothold, especially in Africa, the Middle East, and Europe. This strategy includes, for example, the purchase of land and forward-looking industrial enterprises, the securing of concessions and shares in mines, port facilities and airfields, and political influence on governments and infrastructure. Russia is pursuing a similar strategy, working massively to expand its sphere of influence, especially in the Middle East and Eastern Europe. In the second row of nations is Indonesia, which is virtually absent from current geopolitical analyses. The enormous thrust of these countries, including India, will change the current world order at least as permanently as it did in the nineteenth century.

In this context it is interesting to see how most of the member states of the European Union behave. Here, a comparison with the German territorial states of the nineteenth century is beneficial. Instead of fighting for the common goals of the Union and forging an ever stronger bond, national egoisms and centrifugal national forces are increasing. Just think of Poland and Hungary but also of the Czech Republic and Slovakia. The distribution of migrants in the Euro area is another good example, not to mention the British exit from the European Community.

List's geopolitical observations and predictions are reminiscent of the bestseller by Tim Marshall, "*The Power of Geography*" (in the original English edition: "*Prisoners of Geography*"), in which the current power poker in world politics and the tough international competition in world trade are explained in an impressive manner. In addition to the trade and war theaters focused on by List, Marshall expands his view to include the Arctic and Antarctica, as well as outer space, which already in the present, but especially in the future, will give rise to completely new and extraordinary sized distribution struggles. In addition there are the current and future core problems of the world economy which will be discussed in more detail. These pose an enormous challenge to the entire world community and give a whole new dimension to the "politics of the future". Marshall points out that the realities of the physical geography underlying national and international politics are too often ignored, even though they are fundamental to the strategic direction of policy. List certainly cannot be accused of overlooking this key attribute.

Notes

1. W. VII, p. 268 ff.
2. Wendler, E. (2018): Friedrich List—Vordenker der Sozialen Marktwirtschaft, Wiesbaden, pp. 88-102.
3. W. VIII, P. 5.
4. Wendler, E. (2017): Friedrich List—Politisches Mosaik, Wiesbaden, pp. 134–137.
5. Ders. (2014): Friedrich List im Zeitalter der Globalisierung—Eine Wiederentdeckung, Wiesbaden, pp. 79-88.
6. Ders (2016): The politics of the future, Wiesbaden.
7. Ders. W. II, p. 291 f.
8. Wendler, E.: Friedrich List und die Dritte Welt—Grundzüge der Entwicklungspolitik, Wiesbaden, p. 128 f.
9. List, F. and S. W. (1845): Africa; in: Das Staats-Lexikon, 2nd ed., Altona, Vol. I, pp. 377 ff.
10. Ders (1845): Egypt; in: Das Staats-Lexikon, 2nd ed., Altona, Vol. I, p. 370.
11. Ders. (1845): Asien; In: Das Staats-Lexikon, 2nd ed.
12. Ders (1845): Australia; in: Das Staats-Lexikon, 2nd ed., Altona, Vol. I, pp. 788 ff.

Chapter 14
Opinion About Russia, Especially About Its Ambition for Power and Its Expansionist Policy

14.1 Knowledge and Subjective Assessment

The annexation of Crimea, the warfare in Syria, the financial involvement in Cyprus, the tug-of-war over Ukraine and Belarus, and the naming of Sputnik 5 for the vaccine against the coronavirus epidemic are clear evidence of the current Russian quest for power and its expansionist policy. President Putin is currently striving to push back Western influence in Eastern Europe and return to the Soviet Union's former sphere of influence. It is therefore interesting to review Friedrich List's opinion on Russia, especially since his writings still seems as relevant today as it did 180 years ago.

Friedrich List's complete works do not contain a systematic treatise on Russia. His opinion are scattered in longer and shorter passages throughout the complete works and are summarized here for the first time into a reasonably coherent and meaningful essay.

The following should be taken into account the following points of view:

(1) List was not able to gather any direct impressions in Russia, basing his knowledge and findings on secondary sources, although he did not give any details about their origin.
(2) Most of the information is likely to have come from newspaper reports.
(3) His assessment and subjective evaluation are primarily made from the point of view of a German with the main goal of prosperity for an united Germany in peace and freedom in the first half of the 19th Century.
(4) As far as Russia's great power plans were concerned, List remarked that he naturally did not know the secrets of the Russian Cabinets, writing here merely as a theorist. He believed, however, that he could make up for the lack of knowledge by his fact based assumptions.
(5) He tried to put himself in the Russian mindset, imagining that he was charged by the Russian government with drafting the broad outlines of its policy.
(6) In this respect, it seems interesting and impressive what visions he derived from this and what development potential he predicted for Russia in the international context.

E. Wendler, *The Political Economy of Friedrich List*, Springer Studies in the History of Economic Thought, https://doi.org/10.1007/978-3-031-24601-2_14

(7) It is certainly slightly daring to deduce consequences for the 21st Century from this prognosis. On the other hand, List's deductions have been more than confirmed by the policies of Russian governments and not least by the current power politics under Vladimir Putin.
(8) List's perspective, of course, refers to Czarist Russia, i.e., an autocratically ruled country with absolutist monarchy, a form of government diametrically opposed to his Republican-Democratic conception of the state.

With a pointed pen in the "*Reading Eagle*" Friedrich List informed his American readers on the accession to power by Czar Nicholas I, who ruled the Czarist Empire from 1825 to 1855, the timeframe of his reflections on Russia. He caricatured the coronation ceremony with these words, "the coronation was carried out with all imaginable pomp. They smeared the Emperor's head with oil and put a crown on his head. That is all!" Some readers might not know what a crown is, since in the U.S. "there are no such things." Nor, he said, could he properly explain it to them! "It is a round thing to put on the head, with a brim at the bottom like a cap, but made of gold and set with precious stones, open at the top, and with all sorts of ornaments. So it protects neither from rain nor from sunshine, gives neither cold nor warm, and no one knows what it is good for. This thing was put on the emperor's head, and he himself does not know why. In addition, all the hundreds of thousands of people who watched the process with wonder and amazement do not know why either. This fun cost a round sum of 20 million Rubles. The next day, when the coronation was over, Russia is as cold as before."

> Such expensive coronation ceremonies have cost Europe, in the course of the last three or four years, more than 60 million Thalers, a sum which would be quite sufficient to finance all the vast national improvements which would give the countries an unprecedented degree of prosperity.[1]

14.2 The Sheer Size of the Russian Bear

In "*Ackerverfassung, die Zwergwirtschaft und die Auswanderung*" (the farm constitution, the dwarf economy, and emigration) of 1842 List writes, "Russia is not only already a giant, she is also growing giant, like from the inside out."[2] With a population of 60 million it possesses the natural means to increase its population three- to fourfold—indeed, should it succeed in its plans for territorial expansion, five- to sixfold. In the course of the next 40 to 50 years, the present population of 60 million will increase to 100 million, and this with its people accustomed to deprivation and hardships of all kinds since childhood, and knowing no other command than that of its military ruler. Thus, List said, the whole of Russia is a military colony, whose armed forces double every 50 years. Already in the course of half a century a military power would arise besides which the German states would appear like David versus Goliath.

This forecast roughly corresponds to the actual population development of Russia. At the turn of the 20th Century, there were ca. 125 million people, and today about 150 million. During the time of the Soviet Union, there were almost 240 million.

This did not even require any special effort on the part of the giant, for giants grow without such support. Russia had risen to "a European power of the first magnitude and now threatens Asia from one side and Europe on the other with its ceaseless striving for expansion." As such it would turn its view towards China rather than towards the East Indies, forming, as it were, the antithesis of North America. The chief difficulty of such an enterprise, he said, was to muster the power necessary for it to reach the Chinese frontier. This difficulty, however, was not insurmountable when it was considered that a government capable of raising a million soldiers and possessing an abundance of iron, timber, and labor should not find it particularly difficult to build a railway several thousand miles long. Such a route would not only be of great military utility but would also connect the several parts of this immense empire, strengthen the efficiency and administrative power of the government, prevent the dangers of famine in several provinces, and set in motion an immense commerce between Europe as well as middle and western Asia.[3]

In this respect, the serious question, not to say the fear, arises as to whether the West's sanctions against Russia are capable of shaking the giant empire to its foundations. On the one hand such sanctions are indispensable, but on the other hand they are very problematic because the West and many other countries depend, for instance, on the supply of rare raw materials, timber and grain from Russia. In this context, we refer to the problem of dependence on international supply chains, which List had already mentioned. We also do not yet have a clear idea of the social upheavals that price increases for food and energy will cause in poorer countries.

The less that distances matter because of technical progress the more Russia could draw advantages from its neighbor China and the more the latter would move into the perspective of Russian policy. However, it should not be overlooked that the higher a building is to become, the deeper its foundation is needed, and the civilization in the European part of Russia should be the basis for the Asian part and the neighboring countries. To this end, there would be no better means than the settlement of emigrants from Europe and the formation of a free citizenry and peasantry by the granting of appropriate fundamental and human rights. The most important means of giving to the Russian territory in northern Asia that degree of culture, inner strength, and vigor would seem to lie in the Russian government's founding, under its military protection, the enablement of self-governing cities and commonwealths, and in supporting the settlement of European immigrants aided by such inventions and advances like that of modern transportation.

The natural road from central and western Europe to Western Asia leads along the Danube across the Black Sea to the Caucasian coast. On this road, Regensburg is no farther from the Caucasus than Pittsburgh is from New Orleans, a distance that can now be comfortably covered in ten days by steamboat. With railways, goods and power will flow to Russia in abundance. Then, too, if the country were to encourage and develop the spirit of trade and commerce, as well as the arts and sciences by means of a mild system of custom duties and regulations, and were to establish institutions that would grant a high degree of civil liberties to the merchant, the artisan, and the peasant, the country might attain a high degree of prosperity.

Power based on the asiatic part of Russia would give the Russian government an irresistible influence over eastern and central Asia. At all times, he said, the countries of the temperate zone had exercised a strong influence on the destinies of the southern countries. However, it could not be in the interest of Russia to extend her immediate dominion, already very extensive, still more at the present time. Currently its focus, List uttered, must be to bind central and eastern Asia to itself in such a way as to make it as accessible to European enterprise and interaction as any other European country. In doing so it would endeavor to exert a strong influence on civilization and the introduction of European culture through the effects of trade and sovereignty in militarily weak countries by improving public safety and order. In the course of time it would be possible to form an Asiatic system of civilized states and to enable trade between Europe and Asia, which would far surpass the present influence of the trade of the English, Dutch, and Americans.[4]

In recent times, England insinuated to the Russian Government that the intention of gaining control over the Persian Gulf would threaten the rule of the English in India. This List said, however, was unlikely because Russia would be running an incalculable risk. The government knew too well the solid basis on which English rule over India rested. Such an attempt would involve immense expense and difficulty, especially as England was suspiciously watching over her rule in India. This does not preclude the possibility that the tide might change in "centuries".

14.3 The Political Situation in Russia

The Russian Empire consisted of a "conglomerate" of semi-developed peoples and based its size and growth on absolute power and military might.[5] Since the sole rule of the regent offered no guarantee of advanced civilization, political institutions, and a solid national character, the strength of Russia and the security of the Czar rested on the "bayonets" over which he commanded. Having become great through the bayonet and conquest, this power is able to assert itself only through the bayonet. War, the greatest hostage of civilized nations, was an important element of the dynasty, the dream of the nobility and the hope of all classes of people, because no one had anything to lose, but only to gain. The number of enlisted men increased annually by 40,000 to 50,000. It did not matter at all what the attitude of the autocrat was with regard to world peace and the welfare of mankind. Whatever the sentiments, principles and intentions of dictators, in the course of long periods of time, they would always find themselves compelled to indulge the raw passions of the national body of which they are the head.

The foundation of Russia's political strength had already been laid by Peter the Great who by facilitating transportation had made a naturally fertile country rich. This was done by promoting the building of canals and making a stretch of 4472 miles (7200 km) navigable for the transport of goods, so that Astrakhan and St. Petersburg are now connected. Since Peter the Great, Russia has been seen to advance inexorably on the course of conquest, without ever suffering a backwards step. Since a German dynasty and German intelligence guided the fortunes of that power, both had been driven by the force of circumstances. So, List analyzed, Russia had only devoured individual limbs from foreign bodies of state. Now it hopes to absorb a whole complex of underdeveloped people. Unlike small countries, Russians are self-sufficient, that is, independent of imports and able to provide subsistence resources for themselves. They produce wood, salt, iron, grain, beverages, etc., in the vastness of their national territory.[6]

Russia's national borders touch the seas, with its rivers in her control from their source to their confluence. Here, the customs system does not paralyze all the international commerce of industry as in countries of small territory. The Russian nation, he said, consists of a great majority of peasants, shepherds, hunters, and nomads, whose economic power, literary education, and civilization are but scantily developed. Civilization had stopped with the numerically small upper class and it would take a long time before it penetrated the middle and lower classes.

The impact of technological progress over the last 50 years is also hardly felt in Russia. Since its agricultural exports are not nearly keeping pace with the increase in agricultural production, this is having a very unfavorable effect on the balance of trade and the prosperity of the nation.

List did not know whether it was true that newspapers reported that the Russian government had openly protested against the completion of the German Customs Union. He did not believe this as very likely because that power was not used to positioning itself in such a clumsy manner and to raise an objection, especially as the law of nations offered it no means of doing so, and thus it could hardly be expected to succeed. List knew with certainty, however, that Russia had according to the spirit of her foreign policy every reason to enable her most secret and effective measures to prevent the Customs Union from gaining further strength. Here, a current comparison with the European Union indicates that it is basically also perceived very suspiciously by Russia and only grudgingly accepted. List summarized that since Russia's existence depends on external and internal circumstances on how its major challenges are solved, its position as a world power is currently not guaranteed.

14.4 Speculation on Russian Expansionist Policy

In a short article in the "*Reading Eagle*" of 1828, List made the following prediction on Russian expansionist policy, "Russia is a giant and has an appetite like a giant. Half a part of the world, far from satiating him, only excites his appetite for the other half. Turkey promises him special advantages and therefore (this country) will never lose sight of him. The Dardanelles in the hands of Russia would give the power of opening and closing the Black Sea at will, of organizing it like a port and trading in it, without having to build up a fleet and fear that one morning English bombs will come and set fire to the ships."[7] This, he said, England saw exactly the same way, but it was more diplomatic than any other power in the world, knowing the power and ambitions of the northern giant. So England did not object to Russia's swallowing up half-civilized countries as much as he liked, but it should not have a fleet of ships to challenge the former's superiority at sea, with the exception of smaller vessels which might easily be destroyed in case of emergency.

England would therefore try with all her power to prevent the expulsion of the (strategically important) Turks from Europe. If this is not possible Russia will seek to occupy the Dardanelles and turn it into a second Gibraltar. Currently, of course, you have to replace England with the USA and China and add modern weapons of war such as nuclear weapons, missiles and drones to the ships, in order to make a realistic assessment of military strength and strategic threat. After all, we are currently witnessing how Russia is vigorously expanding its influence and military presence in the eastern Mediterranean, especially in Syria and Cyprus, thus confirming the visions and fears of Friedrich List.

List doubted whether Russian military power would succeed in solving the difficult problem of nationalities. On the other hand, he saw the danger that the European continent would one day fall under the domination of Russia, assuming that this colossus continued to be one country and strengthened to the extent that the inexorable progress of mankind allowed it to do so. However, this subjugation would not come about if the countries of central and western Europe were to unite economically and politically. France had a key role to play here. As early as List's second Paris Prize competition pamphlet he demanded that France should place itself at the head of the European unification movement on account of its civilization, its progress, its size and state unity (Fig. 14.1).

Fig. 14.1 French cartoon of Russian expansionist policy around the middle of the 19th Century

The most important means of consolidating Russian influence was to make transport easier. In the course of time, the country would succeed in considerably expanding its sphere of influence through the construction of railways. On its southern frontier List expected greater difficulties in this respect. The Shah of Persia, the Turkish Sultan, and the sheikhs of the nomadic and settled Arab tribes could only be persuaded to cooperate through bribery and corruption.

Regarding political and economic influence in East Asia, List expected a race between England and Russia, whose true interests were to make central and east Asia as dependent on the them as possible. Russian expansionist efforts, however, would put England in a bind. To counter a too strong a power and market domination of Russia in Asian overseas trade, England was about to set up a "southern battle line" to counter "the Russian battle line". This role has now been taken over by the USA.

At the present time, we are witnessing how the Russian government, following the collapse of the Soviet Union, is trying with all its might to restore this battle line and if possible, to extend it even further. We are seeing how the USA has lost the reins of power in the Near East and central Asia, the latest since the wars in Afghanistan and Iraq, and how the Russian President Putin, Turkish Prime Minister Erdogan and the mullahs in Iran are currently calling the shots. In this respect, with his predictions about Russian expansionism, Friedrich List's motto, "Le monde mache - The world is moving", also proves true here.

14.5 Hypotheses on Russian Economic Policy

After the lifting of the Napoleonic Continental Blockade and the Congress of Vienna in 1815, Russia was initially eager to participate in the supposed benefits of free trade. In this, as List correctly notes, the German economist Heinrich von Storch (1766–1835) exerted a significant influence. The latter was a German-Russian national economist who was appointed to the military academy of St. Petersburg in 1789 and the St. Petersburg Academy of Sciences in 1804. He tutored the daughters of Czar Paul and several Russian princesses. In addition, he read to the Czarina and gave lessons to the later Czar Nicholas I. In his economic views he was an ardent follower of Adam Smith and Jean-Baptiste Say, the two fiercest opponents of Friedrich List.

According to List, the Russian Customs Tariff of 1818 took into account the principles of free trade. The consequence of this, he says, was a tremendous flooding of the Russian market with foreign products which contributed to the destruction of the domestic manufacturing power and to a considerable outflow of money abroad. "Coincident with these measures, to make the theory still more ridiculous, were the restrictions imposed by Great Britain on the importation of grain and raw materials. As a result, misery in Russia reached its peak. Nevertheless, the state held on to this system for a long time because theorists suggested to the Czar that the negative consequences of free trade were only initial difficulties and that the expected benefits would follow. In principle, they said, general freedom of trade was the best means of bringing prosperity to all nations."

However, it is equally certain, according to List, that nations depend on other nations that "follow the state-economic system of robbery."[8] It is true that robbers are not particularly blessed by their system of robbery. This may well be true, but the robbed is not less robbed because of it, nor is any good accomplished by it. Would it not be better if the deprived (robbed) person were to return an rob back, and thus make the aggressor understand that it would be better for both sides if neither robbed each other. So each, without the impairment of the world's civil rights, were to increase his fellow-man's prosperity by the exertion of his powers and by the use of the natural resources of his country. The Czar had waited for several years to understand the effects of this prophecy. Finally, the misery had become so oppressive that serious consequences were feared. Even Napoleon's Russian campaign had not weakened and ruined the country as much as the much vaunted freedom of trade. Thus, the Russian Minister of Finance, Count Nesselrode, declared on 22. March 1822, "the landowners have no market, the factories are completely ruined, the precious metals exported, and the most solid trading houses brought to ruin."

List added, "with Mr. Storch, one believed in the existence of the balance of trade. For an intelligent and enlightened man, the belief in witchcraft in the 17th Century was no less shameful and ridiculous, but now one had gained the insight that there was nevertheless such a thing as a balance of trade among independent states." The wealth of nations is no different from the wealth of private individuals as "it is only obtained by producing at least as much as one consumes and by exporting as much as one imports." Already in another publication of 1821, the most enlightened and insightful statesman of Russia, Count Nesselrode, declared, "Russia sees herself compelled by circumstances to develop her own system of trade."

Since then, Russia has changed its economic policy and oriented itself towards protectionism. As a result one has heard less about social misery, although the country is basically not yet ready for a real protective tariff system. Nevertheless, the introduction of the new system led to the attraction of foreign capital, talent and labor, especially from England and Germany, to help build up the moribund economy. With the new policy especially sheep breeding and wool manufacture flourished, and foreign trade increased greatly, especially with Persia, China and neighboring Asian countries. Trade crises have ceased altogether.

One need only read the latest reports of the Russian Ministry of Commerce to be convinced that Russia owes a great deal of prosperity to the new system and that she is making giant strides towards the increase of her national prosperity and power. It would be folly for Germany to talk down this progress. Every nation, like every individual, is closest to itself. Russia has not to provide for the welfare of Germany. Germany must look after Germany, as Russia must look after herself. Instead of complaining, instead of hoping and waiting for the Messiah of future freedom of trade, it would be better to throw the unbridled cosmopolitan system into the fire and let Russia's example teach us.

That England should regard Russian commercial policy with jealousy was quite natural. Russia had thereby emancipated herself from England and was now in a position to compete with England in Asia. Even if England manufactures her products more cheaply, this advantage in central Asia is compensated by the geographical proximity of the Russian Empire and outweighed by its political influence, List said. "If Russia is as yet a less civilized empire towards Europe, she is a civilized one towards Asia." Nevertheless, there was no mistaking the fact that the lack of civilization and political institutions greatly hindered Russia in her further industrial and commercial progress. If the Czarist government should fail to introduce productive measures that would contribute to the elevation of the people's welfare such as the abolition of serfdom, the creation of an educated middle class and free peasantry, the improvement of the means of transportation and communication, the intensification of its interaction with central Asia, the establishment of public institutions that would meet the needs of the people and of industry, the country would remain at a low stage of development. Only when basic civil rights and liberties are introduced can industrialization in Russia have its beneficial effect.[9]

In his "*Outlines of American Political Economy*" of 1827 List noted, "Russia will never succeed in becoming a manufacturing power, unless the emperors of that vast empire grant freedoms for their cities, like the emperors of Germany, whose creations grew, in a few centuries, from barbarism to a wonderful degree of wealth and civilization. (...) I have no doubt that the greatness of Russia and its trade policy, as a favorite subject of my speculations regarding political economy, has the means of making future growth possible, but I refrain from dwelling on that important subject as I do not want to infringe on the laws of propriety with these uncalled for communications".

Free trade is indeed in contradiciton to the practice and experience of nations. Russia and other countries have surrounded every article of domestic produce and manufacture, with protective and prohibitory duties. This approach, although it may have been issued from the closet of some theorists, is in direct opposition to the principles that govern the conduct of all the statesmen of Europe.[10]

However, for reforms of this kind to be possible and feasible, the Russian nobility would first have to come to the realization that in moving in this way, their own interests would be promoted the most. Instead, the nobility had only its property and agricultural interests in mind and therefore did not recognize the urgent need for a social upheaval, so that in 1917, it inevitably had to come to the revolution and the seizure of power by the Bolsheviks.

14.6 Concluding Remarks

After the collapse of the Soviet Union, the West, above all the USA, merely focused on the desolate economic and political situation of the country at that time and pursued the shortsighted goal of entering the power vacuum to vigorously expand its sphere of influence to the east, without considering that Russia will feel humiliated by this and will strive to reclaim its former geographical power. This is precisely Vladimir Putin's goal and corresponds to the self perception of the majority of the

Russian population to return Russia to its former strength. So the country sees itself once again as a world power that plays a major role in the international political arena and flexes its muscles. In this respect, Friedrich List's speculations about Russia's political and economic expansionism have lost none of their timeless validity.

Notes

1. List, F. (1826): Neuestes aus Europa; in: Readinger Adler von 1826; W. II, p. 242.
2. Idem (1842): Die Ackerverfassung, die Zwergwirtschaft und die Auswanderung; W. V, p. 501.
3. Idem (1835): Asia; in: Das Staats-Lexikon; 2nd ed., Altona 1845, p. 697.
4. Wendler, E.: (2016) Friedrich List: The Politics of the Future, Wiesbaden, p. 36 f.
5. List, F. (1841) The national system of political economy; W. VI, pp. 136-139.
6. Idem (1846): Die politisch-ökonomische Nationaleinheit der Deutschen; W. VII, p. 441 ff. and p. 482 ff.
7. Idem (1828): Jetzige Lage von Europa; in: Reading Eagle of 1828; W. II, p. 287.
8. Idem (1820): Antwort auf die Angriffe des Herrn Hartmann vom Rheine; W. I/II, p. 636.
9. Idem (1837): Das natürliche System der Politischen Ökonomie; W. IV, p. 217.
10. Idem (1827): Outlines of American Political Economy; W. II, p. 220.

Chapter 15
The Transformation of Friedrich List's Theory of State and Economy to Georgia—A Model Experiment

15.1 Geographical, Political and Economic Starting Position

Based on a recommendation from the Georgian chargé d'affaires in Berlin, I received a request in the spring of 2020 asking whether I would be willing to give a lecture at the Technical University in Tbilisi on Friedrich List's Theory of State and Economy and its transformation to Georgia. After careful consideration, due to travel restrictions during the COVID-19 pandemic and my advanced age, I declined this honorable invitation and decided instead to summarize my reflections in an essay—as a model experiment, so to speak.

I must confess that I unfortunately do not have any direct knowledge of the country, so that is why I may be accused of ignorance and naivety in some of my theses. If I had prepared this analysis 8 to 10 years ago, it would certainly have been completely different. The present contribution reflects my thoughts before the Ukraine war. In the meantime the political and economic situation changed radically for Georgia as well. On the other hand, the current political circumstances speak more in favor of my theses than against them.

In the first 20 years since independence Georgia has experienced a profound political, economic and social crisis that has affected virtually every facet of the country.

Even from the perspective of a halfway educated central European, the country lies very far away in a diffuse geographical position between Europe and Asia, "on the threshold of Europe", so to speak. The observer of a world map, on which Africa, Asia and Europe can be seen, will perceive Georgia only as a tiny dot. If the observer directs his focus on the topography, then Georgia is involuntarily reminiscent of Switzerland as they both have comparable geological features. Likewise, the territories of both countries and the population figures are somewhat comparable. While Switzerland, with an area of approximately 40,000 km^2, has barely two-thirds the area of Georgia, with just under 60,000 km^2, the reverse is true for the population. Switzerland has approximately 8.5 million inhabitants, more than twice as many as the country in the

E. Wendler, *The Political Economy of Friedrich List*, Springer Studies in the History of Economic Thought, https://doi.org/10.1007/978-3-031-24601-2_15

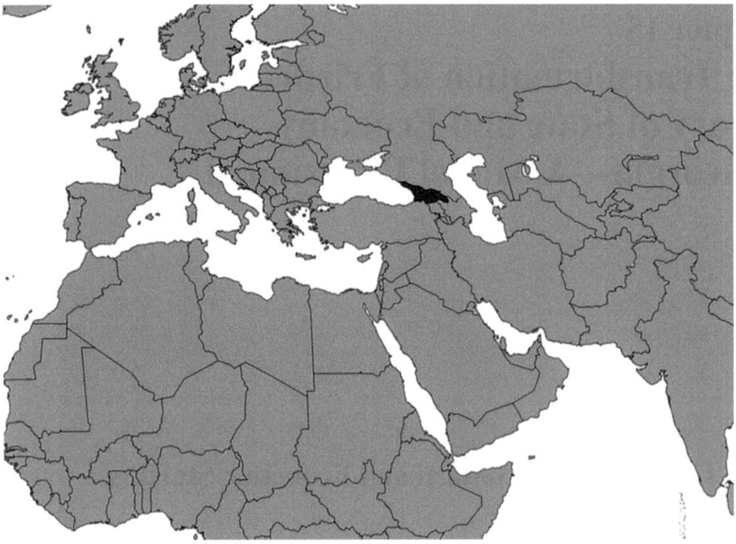

Fig. 15.1 Georgia—a small spot on the world map

South Caucasus, which has just under 4 million inhabitants. In terms of climate and vegetation, Georgia, as a Mediterranean country, can be compared to Ticino. It also has a rich, turbulent historical and cultural past [1]Figure 15.1.

Georgia lies at the interface between Asia and Europe. Geographically, the country is actually part of the Near East, but its inhabitants see it as the "Balcony of Europe". This contrasting description shows the advantages but also the whole dilemma of its geopolitical position. The inhabitants of Georgia feel a sense of belonging to Europe and the Georgian governments have been striving for close ties with the West since independence in 1991. From the perspective of central Europeans, however, Georgia is not the "Balcony of Europe", as this is an attribute he would more readily associate with the Balearic Islands, Malta and Cyprus. Rather, Georgia is but a small, out-of-the-way country. This is by no means meant in a disrespectful way but results inevitably from the perspective of the vast majority of Europeans.

The geographical outline of the country is reminiscent of the torn mouth of a crocodile, which is missing the tip of the upper snout and some teeth in the upper jaw. This is marked by a long mountainous border with Russia running across the Caucasus. In this case, the reptile with Abkhazia and South Ossetia lacks important incisors and molars. The throat is formed by the Black Sea, a relatively small fertile lowland and the mountainous hinterland with the capital Tbilisi. The lower jaw is composed of the borders of the neighboring countries of Turkey, Armenia and Azerbaijan.

These borderlines indicate that the northern border belongs to the European mainland and the southern border to the Asian mainland. The Republic of Georgia is located in no man's land, as it were. This geographical location offers advantages and disadvantages which doesn´t exactly make it easy for the country to position and assert itself as an independent state, which is clearly reflected in its checkered history.

In the recent times Georgia has undergone an impressive consolidation phase in which the respective governments have ndeavoured to initiate fundamental reforms, liberalize the political and economic framework, and create economic incentives to enable the country's take-off through structural policy investments. Commendable examples include the transformation of the autocratic presidential democracy into a parliamentary democracy, albeit an unstable and fragile one. Further progress are the tolerable respect for human rights, the fight against corruption and the debureaucratization of the economy.

Key Performance Indicators for Georgia among the world´s nations:

- 70th in the 2016 Human Development Index
- 46th in Tranparency International's Corruption Index
- 61st in Reporters Without Borders Press freedom Ranking
- 97th in Freedom House's Level of Democracy
- 6th in the To-Do Index for Business Activities

In respect to this Business Activities KPI, Georgia is considered a model student in the Caucasus region. On the other hand, after the parliamentary elections of 2016, a strong concentration of power of the ruling party was noted, so that in international commentaries doubts were expressed as to whether there is a de facto separation of powers in Georgia. "Rugged mountains, hip clubs, chic cafes, plus historic backdrops and laid-back people. This is the image that has been conveyed of Georgia for some years now. In the capital Tbilisi, a layer of mostly young people with free-spirited values has emerged. They are mobile, multilingual, and cosmopolitan. However, they are part of a society in which the Orthodox Church, which also has great political influence, is very popular with its restorative appeals."[2]

What applied 5 or 10 years ago may already be outdated. In some areas one will notice an analogous implementation of List's ideas from the first half of the nineteenth century. As if it were in time-lapse, one can demonstrate their realization, which is remarkable. In contrast, this progress level has not been achieved to the same extent in many African countries, which have more or less been treading water, over much longer timeframes.

On the other hand, many aspects that play a central role in List's thinking, such as the harmonious development of economic sectors, the fight against poverty, the consideration of social standards, the long time demand for ecological standards, or the resolution of the border issues with Russia, have thus far been neglected. Moreover, political processes are never complete. Therefore, it seems useful to point out List's thought patterns and warnings so that they might be heeded and applied to Georgian conditions in the future.

It is not easy for an external observer to obtain a reasonably coherent picture of the situation because the available data sources are partly contradictory, as the following example shows. According to official statistics the unemployment rate is approximately 13%. According to unofficial estimates, however, it varies between

35 and 40%. Youth unemployment is estimated at 32%, and according to surveys, 70% of the population describe themselves as underemployed. Taking these figures as a yardstick, Georgia's current economic situation appears nowhere near as rosy as it is portrayed in official and semiofficial reports for foreign investors.[3] For all the progress made in the past decade, it should not be overlooked that Georgia is still a poor developing country.

15.2 Historical Review

By "politics", List understood "the statesmanship of leading a people standing on a low stage of development towards its maturity, of gradually curing the infirmities of the state without shock and violent measures, of improving its organism, and of helping the principle of law to recognition."

Georgia's historical development in the nineteenth and twentieth centuries was marked above all by constant efforts to achieve national independence, i.e., territorial detachment from Russia. Throughout both centuries, Czarist Russia and the Soviet Union were eager, as List predicted, to bring the Caucasus region under its or their control. It took Russia the entire first half of the nineteenth century to achieve this goal. In the process, Georgia became increasingly interlocked with the Czarist Empire through intensive Russification.

At the same time, Russian rule opened the Caucasus region to Western influences. Tbilisi became the Paris of the East. On the other hand, national consciousness and the desire for independence developed into a national liberation movement. In 1905, a large scale peasant uprising broke out, which was followed by political reforms and somewhat dampened tensions with Russia.

After the October Revolution, the independent Republic of Georgia was proclaimed on 26. May 1918. A quarter of a year later the Soviet Union renounced the annexation of Georgia in an additional agreement to the Peace of Brest-Litovsk, but two years later, the 11th Russian Army marched into Georgia. After brief resistance the country capitulated and was incorporated into the USSR as the Georgian Soviet Socialist Republic. Shortly thereafter, land ownership was expropriated and nationalized. From 1921 to 1936, Georgia was part of the Transcaucasian SFSR and after its dissolution until the collapse of the Soviet Union in 1991, the Georgian SSR. In association with the USSR, Georgia experienced the beginning of industrialization. Agriculture was oriented towards the cultivation and sale of tropical fruits, and the republic was developed into an important tourist and holiday region for Russian tourists.

In 1924 there was an uprising against Soviet occupation which Stalin put down and executed their leaders. More than 30,000 Georgians, mainly members of the political and social elite, were killed at that time or disappeared in Soviet prison camps. Between 1935 and 1950, approximately 60,000 Georgians fell victim to the Stalinist and post-Stalinist regimes.

During the late 1980s, a strong independence movement again emerged in Georgia. On 9. April 1991, before the collapse of the USSR, the country rose up against Soviet subjugation and declared its independence once again. Georgia's first president after gaining independence was Zviad Gamsakhurdia. He was succeeded by the former Georgian party leader and Soviet Foreign Minister Eduard Shevadnadze, who is held in high esteem in the Federal Republic of Germany because of his services to German reunification together with Michael Gorbachev. Shevadnadze introduced democratic reforms. However, the economy stagnated at an extremely low level, there was widespread corruption and several electoral frauds.

After peaceful mass demonstrations, the so-called Rose Revolution, Shevadnadze was forced to abdicate in November 2003 and was succeeded by Mikheil Saakasvili. During his term in office, which lasted until 2012, the so-called Caucasian War of 2008 took place. In spring 2008, tensions with Russia over Abkhazia and South Ossetia increased almost daily. Troop movements, skirmishes, and propaganda campaigns, especially by Russia, brought the situation to a head, there were several border violations and deaths. In early August 2008, the confrontation escalated into open warfare. Georgian formations advanced on the capital of South Ossetia with ca. 8000 troops, resulting in a Russian counteroffensive. Russian troops pushed back the Georgian army and advanced to the Georgian heartland. The ceasefire lasted for 5 days. By the time of the ceasefire on 12. August, a total of approximately 850 people had been killed and between 2500 and 3000 wounded. Under the mediation of the EU, in particular French President Nicolas Sarkozy, a ceasefire was reached on 15. and 16. August 2008, and Russian troops withdrew from the Georgian heartland.

A scandal over torture and rape in Georgian prisons brought down the Saakashvili government in October 2012, and Prime Minister Bidzina Ivanishvili took power as the winner of the election. He was succeeded by Giorgi Gacharia, who served as Prime Minister from 8. September 2019, to 18. January 2021. Due to a dispute over the planned arrest of an opposition leader, Gacharia was forced to resign, leaving his post at the disposal of current Prime Minister Irakli Garibashvili. This rapid change of office is a visible sign of the country's domestic crisis and instability, which has been exacerbated by the COVID-19 pandemic.

Giga Zedania, Rector of Ilia University in Tbilisi, summed up the period of government over the past 25 years as follows, „regardless of the fact that groups with completely different social and cultural backgrounds have been in power, one thing has not changed: The ruling party always did everything in its power to make it impossible for the opposition to get into government one day. To do so, it used legal and illegal, formal and informal means, from suppressing freedom of the press to creating alleged opposition parties to oust the real opposition, to attacking NGOs. Similarly, the ruling party has always rallied around a charismatic leader endowed with great power and is thus more reminiscent of an entourage than a modern organization."[4]

All parties, ruling and opposition alike, regard politics as a zero-sum game. Every change in power leads to the ousted rulers being legally prosecuted. Every election is therefore tantamount to a revolution, a radical new beginning. There is no clear separation of private and public, and the role of the charismatic leader renders formalized channels of communication and decision-making meaningless because behind this façade, real politics take place, with informal networks operating according to informal rules.

The conclusions for practical politics that can be drawn from Georgia's history, using Friedrich List's theory of the state as a basis, can be summarized in several "construction sites". In this context there is at least one delicate Achilles heel which Georgian politics currently seems to be avoiding and that is the relationship with Russia. Russia is the natural export and import market for the Georgian economy and remains closely intertwined with the country in cultural terms. All attempts to circumvent Russia are therefore doomed to failure. This is made abundantly clear by the current state of war between Russia and Ukraine. Georgia cannot escape its geographical position and must, for better or worst, strive for a good neighborly relationship with Russia.

The key terms for understanding List's conception of the state are freedom and national unity. That is why he was fundamentally opposed to national fragmentation. He compared a fragmented nation to the splitters of a broken jug. For this reason, he also spoke of the "broken piece nation". This phrase can also be applied to Georgia with the breakaway provinces of Abkhazia and South Ossetia. Figure 15.2.

List always advocated peaceful reforms, which is why he strictly rejected civil wars. This can also be seen in connection with Abkhazia and South Ossetia, which are formally independent but in reality Russian vassals.

After the collapse of the Soviet Union, Georgia put out its feelers to the West and has since been striving for full membership in the EU and NATO. This was especially pushed during the presidency of Mikheil Saakashvili. It seems naïve and unrealistic to believe that the EU member states could be motivated to permit Georgian EU Membership with the thesis that Georgians are the descendants of the "oldest Europeans"[5].[6] These EU and NATO goals meet with iron-fisted resistance in Russia and were perceived as a provocation and hostile attack. The parallels to the current developments in Ukraine, with Russia´s occupation of the Donbass region and annexation of the Crimea in violation of international law should be a lesson not to be overlooked.

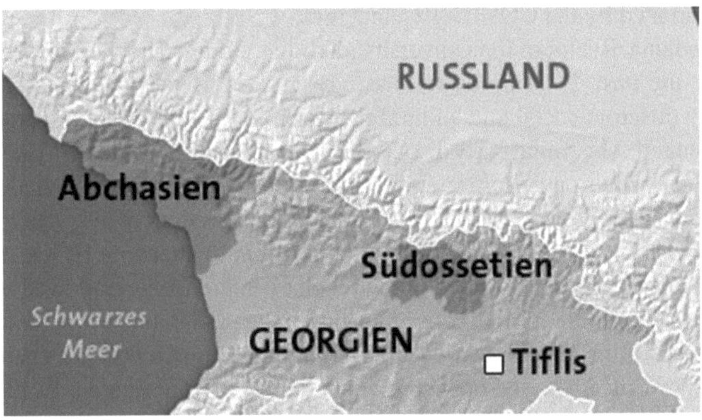

Fig. 15.2 The political situation in Georgia

Neither Russia nor the EU and the US are currently prepared to grant Georgia full membership to the EU and NATO because the military but also the political and economic risks are simply too great, and nothing will change in the long term.

15.3 Political Starting Points

How could Georgia escape this dilemma? In the spirit of Friedrich List, it would make sense not to court the favor of the EU and NATO and to agitate Russia but rather to develop a reasonable degree of sovereignty and national pride, daring to come to a common understanding with Russia. In relation to the EU, Georgia has already achieved the maximum possible status at present with the signing of an Association Agreement, which entered into force on 1. July 2016. On this basis, the country should consistently continue to intensify its political and economic relations with the European Union.

At the same time, Georgia should reconsider its relationship with Russia and strive for normalization. The establishment of diplomatic relations as a first step towards confidence building measures would be advisable. There is no sensible reason why this should not be done. This would also be a necessary precondition for finding a viable way forward in the Abkhazia and South Ossetia conflict. Following the establishment of diplomatic relations, a direct air link between Russia and Georgia should be reintroduced as well as a transit arrangement with Abkhazia implemented. Both measures would be of great benefit to foreign trade and tourism. Since a military reconquest of Abkhazia and South Ossetia, even as a tactical measure, seems unthinkable, with the Russian bear not moving on its own accord and neither the USA nor the EU showing any serious efforts in this direction, it is up to the Georgian government to restart the dialog with Moscow going and to reach an understanding through confidence building measures.

Georgia has thus far been too one-sidedly committed to a east–west course, neglecting its north–south orientation. The Corona Virus crisis in particular suggests rethinking the focus. It is not yet clear how this crisis will affect international trade and tourism, which play a crucial role in Georgia's economy, in the mid- to long-term. In this respect, it may be necessary to develop or revitalize previously neglected markets. To this end, the repositioning of the country can be helpful.

The two geographical regions of Abkhazia and South Ossetia have been struggling for independence for over 100 years. Abkhazia lies south of the Caucasus on the northern coast of the Black Sea. It considers itself an independent state under the name "Republic of Abkhazia" but is not recognized under international law and by the international community, with the exception of Russia and three other countries, as it is regarded as part of Georgia. Abkhazia has had its own constitution and state structures since 1993. Georgia currently does not exercise any sovereignty over this territory, which is populated by approximately 250,000 people and in which both Georgians and Russians form a minority. Russian colonization began in 1880, and by the end of the nineteenth century, Abkhazia had already become a popular tourist attraction for Russian aristocrats. After the October Revolution the region was constituted as a short-lived North Caucasian Republic, which was formally recognized by the young state of Georgia but soon after was forcibly incorporated into the Georgian territory. In 1921, the Red Army occupied all of Georgia, and thus Abkhazia also became part of the USSR. Abkhazia became one of the most popular tourist destinations and was nicknamed the "Red Riviera". In 1931, there was a popular uprising, but it was bloodily put down. Abkhazia was reunited with Georgia, deprived of its national identity and cultural autonomy and and all attempts at freedom were punished as counterrevolutionary.

South Ossetia is a mountainous region south of the main ridge of the Great Caucasus. The area is sparsely populated, with population figures varying between 30 and 80,000 people. The majority of the inhabitants are of Russian origin and not Georgian. The region declared its independence during the last stages of Soviet rule. In a 1991 referendum, 90% voted in favor of statehood, but this was not recognized by Georgia or the international community. In 1996 both sides sought a peaceful settlement of the conflict, and in 2004 Georgian President Mikheil Saakashvili presented a three-step plan to the UN General Assembly to reintegrate Abkhazia and South Ossetia into Georgia, but it was rejected by the other parties. After Georgia failed to achieve its goal, the so-called Caucasian War broke out in 2008.

The conclusions that can be drawn ist hat the Georgian Government alone has the power to act. Every effort should be made to agree on a modus vivendi with Russia to resolve this problem amicably. As further international diplomatic recognition of the two republics is not to be expected, the current political state of affairs is unsatisfactory for both sides. Both parties could only gain from a peace treaty agreement. A long-standing conflict would be eliminated, which would certainly motivate foreign investors to become much more involved in the Caucasus region. Such a paradigm shift seems essential if the status quo is to be changed for the better. Of course, Russia would demand a high price for this and a very high degree of autonomy for both regions. This would still be better than the current state of affairs. If Russia were to insist on a military presence in Abkhazia and South Ossetia, Georgia would probably have to "swallow this pill" as well Fig. 15.3.

We are not in the position to point the finger at Georgia as to whether and to what extent human rights are respected by the state authority. In this context, of course, police and judicial power play a central role. If one takes an article by Barbara Christophe from 2004 as a yardstick, then there are considerable doubts about respect for fundamental and human rights in Georgia. Her essay is entitled "*Culture of corruption? Notes on the political order in Georgia*". In it the author states, among other things, "the main perpetrators are officials at the lower and middle levels of leadership, who repeatedly succeed in paralyzing state monitoring and control mechanisms and using their office for personal enrichment purposes against the will of an ultimately helpless political leadership." [7] Almost all influential businessmen in Georgia aspire to political office, which they use for circumventing the law, to extract preferential conditions for their companies. The transformation of the state into a self-service institution for the members of the ruling apparatus has serious consequences for the development of the productive forces and for social stability and justice in Georgia.

Fig. 15.3 Cartoon on Russian greed for Georgia

In parallel the trust in the political caste is understandably very low. Georgia has ratified the Convention on Human Rights. Nevertheless, there is often arbitrariness on the part of the authorities. Members of the opposition and journalists are often subjected to severe harassment and violence. The right to express one's opinion is repeatedly severely restricted. Journalists who report on opposition demonstrations are subjected to reprisals.

The Amnesty International Report of 2017 points to irregularities in the Georgian judicial system, according to which judicial decisions often have a biased character.

In the 2019 reporting period Amnesty International observed an increasing deterioration in human rights compliance for Eastern Europe and Central Asia. For Georgia, there are complaints of systematic repression of freedom of expression, association and assembly. In addition, certain population groups, such as ethnic minorities, lesbians and gays, and religious minorities are discriminated against. Violence against women and children is also widespread. In addition, landowners are often brutally expropriated in government and private construction projects without being adequately compensated with land or money. All of these points can also be traced to the thinking of Friedrich List.

Barbara Christophe introduced her essay with, "the Rose Revolution of Mikheil Saakashvili has once again brought to light with unmistakable clarity what has actually been clear to everyone for a long time. Corruption has become a pervasive phenomenon in Georgia!" In the meantime, corruption in Georgia has been fought and pushed back. According to the Corruption Perception Index for the public sector, measured at 82 points in 2003 it was almost twice as high as it is in 2019, with 44 points. This puts Georgia in 46th place in the world rankings. Since 2018, corruption has risen slightly again but has fallen considerably compared to 2003.

In her 2018 book "*Georgia, Rewritten*", Professor Luka Nakhutsrishvili of Ilia University in Tbilisi takes rather sober stock of the achievements of "a neoliberal experiment" since independence. From 2004 to 2011, under President Saakashvili, the country's Gross National Product rose from 4 to 13 billion US dollars. However, poverty indicators increased at a considerably higher rate during the same period. The state became richer, while the citizens became poorer and poorer. The average monthly income was USD 526 in 2014 fell back to USD 417 in 2019 (EUR 377 in 2018). Excluding high earners, including senior management in public institutions and companies, the real average income in the capital region was only between EUR 250 and EUR 280, in the rest of Georgia in the range of EUR 150 and EUR 200. Only one-fifth of dependent employees earned a monthly salary of more than EUR 300. A similar negative trend can also be observed recently for foreign direct investment, the equity ratio of companies, tourism, money supply, household incomes, the current account deficit and the projected current account balance, as well as for the Consumer Price Index, the growth of retail sales and the growth of real Gross Domestic Product (GDP).[8]

Distributive justice, the socially just allocation of resources, and the idea of the welfare state are branded with the spectre of the Soviet Union. As soon as one mentions the role of the state in controlling and organizing the economy or, even more modestly, refers to its social functions, one is involuntarily reminded of the Soviet experience. In this case, the Soviet Union is equated with the term "welfare state", and that is the end of the discussion. In view of such a mindset, it is not surprising that iron-fisted capitalism exists in Georgia.

In the long run, however, according to Friedrich List's ideas, a state can only exist if social peace is ensured. This presupposes that the principle of the welfare state is not only enshrined in the constitution but is also reflected, for example, in tax law, social law and labor protection regulations and can be enforced accordingly. If this principle is criminally neglected, sooner or later, there are likely to be demonstrations and in the worst case, revolts and the overthrow of the government. If Georgia wants to be a modern European state, then human dignity demands that the welfare state principle not only be one of the constitutional prerequisites but also be implemented politically.

15.4 Economic Starting Points

List saw one of the main evils in the small division of land ownership, that the farm workers turn into "walking skeletons". While the grandfather was still working with four beautiful horses and had enough cattle and food to feed his large family, the grandson was gnawing at the hunger cloth year in and year out. "If his children now follow in their father's footsteps and participate in the poor land ownership," List asked himself, "where will the people for industrial production come from? "

It is certainly not foolhardy to recall the French Revolution in this context. We are also now witnessing, again and in general, that there is considerable social tension between the first and the third generations, which thus far can only be felt in mass emigration. This also applies to Georgia, whose population has fallen since independence from just under 5 million (also due to the departure of Abkhazia and South Ossetia from the state federation) to just under 4 million by 2019 because many citizens have emigrated.

The majority cannot participate in the economic development of the country as 45% of the population is employed in agriculture and produces mainly for their own consumption. The development of the agricultural economy is hampered by unproductive land use, inadequate infrastructure and low processing quality of the products as well as inadequate working conditions.

In her collection of stories, "*If only there were love before Dark*", the Tbilisi-born writer Iunona Guruli paints a bleak picture of the social situation in Georgia.[9] According to her, the consumption of hard drugs is astronomically high. The situation of women is particularly bad. The public is not only conservative, and the majority is strictly religious but also strongly dominated by men. Many of them believe that they can dispose of women as they please and inflict violence on them.

Referring to the social ills of the poor and in the less developed countries, List said that the well-to-do and decently dressed city dweller considers, "the bad clothes of the country people, their narrow and dirty dwelling, and the eternal dish of potatoes without salt and meager milk quite adequate," although these people do the hardest work. The well-to-do deluded themselves that poor people are not used to anything else and do not consider that they, too, would be very receptive to decent clothing, proper housing, and better food. Similarly, List thought of children, the sick, and the aged, "of those huddled, gaunt, and lean figures, with rattling legs, the sad and dull appearance, their sluggish gait, and the awkwardness of all their movements."

Countries such as Georgia, expect prestigious but costly events to bring them international awareness and recognition and as a result the attention of foreign investors. In recent years, Tbilisi has hosted numerous major events, including the UEFA Super Cup and the 2015 Rugby World Cup, as well as many business and political forums. The Georgian government had also bid to host the Winter Olympics as well as the 2020 UEFA European Football Championship together with Azerbaijan. The investment cost calculator should not be left out of this process. The question should always be examined whether such a small and economically weak country can afford such events or whether only foreign investors will profit from them and whether, after the end of the major event, considerable follow-up costs, such as empty stadiums or hotels and destroyed nature, are to be feared.

A cautionary example is the special economic zone granted by the Georgian state to the Chinese Hualing Group. The main business of this group is the construction, leasing and management of shopping malls and hypermarkets, as well as the construction of hotel chains and other development projects. In 2012 the contract was signed for the acquisition of 420 hectares of prime land located on the Tbilisi Sea, for the construction of the Olympic Village and related infrastructure. The buyer committed to investing US$150 million on the purchased land within 10 years. For the investor the price of the land was significantly lower than the market price and he was exempted from paying VAT on imported building materials and technical equipment, as well as from future taxes on profits.

In reality, this created a Chinese enclave in which the Georgian state has practically no sovereign rights. The real beneficiary is the investor, not the Georgian state. Such a danger also exists in other efforts of the Chinese government to integrate the Caucasus into the Silk Road project. To this end, generous loans are being granted and construction work is being carried out with Chinese workers so that hardly any consideration is given to local labor. With such "development projects" one should be aware that it is a matter of hard-nosed business and that in many cases the foreign investor gets far more out of it than he invests.

In a dissertation at the University of Bamberg, Giorgi Doinjashvili examined "*The Effectiveness of EU Development Policy in Georgia and Armenia*"[10]. In several case studies concrete development projects were tested according to four criteria/dimensions:

- political-institutional
- economic
- sociocultural
- ecological

In the process, shortcomings and grievances were ruthlessly uncovered, systemic recommendations for action were developed, and future perspectives were identified.

Systemic shortcomings of development aid were identified as insufficient funding, poor sustainability and a lack of multidimensional perspectives. Overall, the author draws a sobering balance when he states that, despite some successes, the EU's development policy, "has not been effective" and requires significant improvement.

15.5 Starting Points for the Development of the Secondary and Tertiary Sectors

Because farms are so small it is not worthwhile for many farmers to purchase modern machinery. As a result while almost 50% of the population works in agriculture, this sector generates barely 10% of GDP. As agriculture offers no prospects for many Georgians, they leave the farms and head for the capital Tbilisi to try their luck. The processing industry is also underdeveloped with products are often marketed on the farm. The poor infrastructure drives up prices even in the high season, making it difficult for most farmers to even place their own produce in Georgian supermarkets, let alone export it to other countries. As a result, cheaper competing products, especially from Turkey, crowd out local fruit and vegetables. Experts are therefore calling for, in the spirit of Friedrich List, the abandonment of smallest-scale farming and land reform so that larger plots of land can be created and leased or sold to investors, who would drive forward mechanisation in the agricultural economy and considerably increase its productivity.

Since independence the production of citrus fruits, especially mandarins, has fallen by two-thirds, of wine by 50% and of tea by as much as 95%. In many cases the harvest spoils in the fields because there is a lack of transport and marketing opportunities and the real cost is higher than the market price of cheap imports. Although Friedrich List did not advocate protective tariffs for agricultural products because this would not slow down the shift from the primary to the secondary and tertiary sectors, in the case of Georgia the question arises as to whether temporary subsidies or protective tariffs would be appropriate for certain agricultural products.

To date, the secondary sector is clearly underrepresented and underdeveloped. Only 11% of the labor force is employed in industry, while agriculture and the service sector are almost on par with 44%. According to research by the World Bank, industry accounts for only a quarter of GDP value added, while the shares of agriculture are 9% and services, with a focus on tourism at 66%. Especially in view of the COVID-19 crisis, it becomes clear how dangerous such low diversification is because the dependence of the national economy on tourism is far too great, and therefore, strengthening of the secondary sector is urgently needed.

Here, too, it is worthwhile to refer to some of Friedrich List's basic theses. For him, manufacting and factories were "the mothers and children of bourgeois freedom, of the Enlightenment, of the arts and sciences, of internal and external trade, of navigation and transport improvements, of civilization and political power." They were, he said, "the chief means of freeing agriculture from its chains. A state is as independent and powerful in proportion to the development level of its industry and productive forces." An agrarian state, as Georgia still is, will never attain such a powerful intellectual and material potential as an industrial state.

List was aware that the industrialization of a country was a lengthy and costly process. He considered the development and expansion of the necessary infrastructure and education to be the basic prerequisites for building up a national manufacturing power. Even when these conditions are fulfilled, a considerable period of time is required to train the necessary number of skilled workers and, above all, to transform the population used to agricultural work into qualified factory workers. Foreign investors who would be willing to invest in Georgia under certain circumstances often criticize the fact that there is a great shortage of local skilled workers. Therefore, the Georgian government would have to put a clear emphasis on vocational training.

List used the image of nurturing and protecting a young plant to explain why state aid is needed to build up an internationally competitive industry and how problematic the free trade agreement between Georgia and the People's Republic of China appears in this context. This is based on an essay by Franziska Smolnik, a political scientist at the Stiftung Wissenschaft und Politik in Berlin.[11] Among other points, the author states, "economic cooperation between Georgia and China has developed rapidly in recent years. In the 1990s, trade was marginal. According to the Georgian statistics authority, until 2000 Georgia imported goods from China worth less than US$ 3 million (!) annually and exported goods worth less than US$ 1 million to China. This has changed dramatically. The volume of trade grew more than a 100-fold. Chinese exports, in particular, have increased sharply. For 2017 imports from China were over US$730 million while exports to China amounted to approximately US$200 million. From the numbers it is clear that from Georgia's perspective there is a drastic trade deficit in its foreign trade with China. While a negative balance is a general characteristic of Georgia's foreign trade, it is particularly pronounced in relation to China. "There is also an imbalance in the range of goods traded. While China supplies diverse goods to Georgia, Georgian exports to China are not very diversified. In 2016 exports to China were dominated by ores and metal waste. They accounted for nearly 90%, while beverages, mainly wine, accounted for only 9%."

> Not least against this background, Georgia's leadership considers the free trade agreement with China, which entered into force on 1. January 2018, a particular success. The agreement is considered groundbreaking for the further development of international economic relations and for Georgia's future as a hub between East and West. On both sides import duties were abolished for over 90% of product categories. Products for which Georgia maintains import duties, albeit comparatively low, are mainly food and luxury goods such as poultry products, nuts, milk, honey, certain fruits and vegetables, fruit juices, wine and tobacco.

The Georgian government assumes that its own country in particular will benefit from the agreement as most imports from China were already exempt from customs duties, an expression of Georgian economic liberalism. A feasibility study prepared in advance came to similar conclusions. With the free trade agreemen Georgia expects above all the duty-free export of Georgian wine to the People's Republic.

Franziska Smolnik points out that the free trade agreement with China was negotiated "in just seven months" (!). This, however, should make one wary and cautious. If one remembers how long China hesitated to join the WTO and if one knows that the Chinese government is more inclined towards protectionism than free trade, or in other words, preaches free trade and practices protectionism. It is therefore safe to say that China expects to gain considerably more from this agreement for itself than Georgia will gain.

We agree with the criticism that fears asymmetry/one-sidedness in this treaty because it leaves the Georgian economy, especially the secondary sector, defenceless against Chinese competition. This also in light of the fact that the Georgian Government has concluded similar free trade agreements with Ukraine, Belarus, Moldova, Kazakhstan, Kyrgyzstan, Uzbekistan, Turkmenistan, the neighboring countries Armenia, Azerbaijan and Turkey, the EFTA countries Switzerland, Iceland, Liechtenstein and Norway, as well as with the EU Member States. In its relations with the USA, Canada and Japan, Georgia has negotiated Most-Favored-Nation (MFN) agreements and has thus also agreed to virtually free market access. This apparent liberality is extremely problematic because it practically and realistically eliminates the development of its own secondary sector.

Already during the time of the Belle Epoque (at the turn of the nineteenth and twentieth century) the Caucasus region, especially Georgia, was a tourist magnet for Russian aristocrats who wanted to escape the cold city life of St. Petersburg in winter. During the time of Soviet rule the Black Sea coast, the so-called Russian Riviera, was the most popular tourist destination. After the collapse of the USSR, the country attracted few tourists in the first years thereafter. Since then many efforts have been made to shed the musty, post-Soviet image and build mass tourism. At the turn of the millennium the number of tourists was still 300,000 per year. Today, with a population of 3.8 million, there are approximately 7 million tourists per year and this number is estimated to rise to 11 million by the end of this decade, which seems rather uncertain in view of the coronavirus-related travel restrictions. On the other hand, the country is already suffering from the tourist boom. The population reacts very reservedly to the monumental hotel buildings, which generally do not fit into the landscape at all. Georgia is in the process of losing much of its unspoiled charm. Although Tbilisi is called the "Paris of the East", you can only get an impression of the former flair along Rustaveli Boulevard and a few other streets. Otherwise, one can observe many excesses of the unbridled building mania in the old town. Many skyscrapers that were built in recent times often look like ruins. Although they are inhabited they are left in an unfinished state due to cost reasons. They often do not have a well maintained and paved entrance and lack the work of a caretaker and the regular maintenance of the elevators. There is also an unimaginable shortage of parking spaces. There is undescribable chaos on the public roads, especially since the traffic rules are practically not adhered to by the car and truck drivers.

The government should try to transfer typical historical building elements to the present in close cooperation with the country's best architects, aiming to give the its new buildings a certain independent and unique charm and character. A mix of Mediterranean, Oriental, especially Turkish and Persian style elements with modern Western architecture seems desirable.

The country is still an insider tip for individual tourists, but this is changing rapidly. Hotels and restaurants are trying hard to adjust to the European level. Nevertheless, the quality of service is still lacking. On the other hand, the tourist development of the country hardly takes nature into consideration. That is why worried voices can be heard who wants to put the brakes on mass tourism and warn of a tourist collapse, at least in some mountain regions. Georgia, like many other tourist hotspots, seems to be aiming for mass over class, which can only be warned against. Georgia should not position itself as a cheap country with unbridled mass tourism but rather, as Friedrich List would recommend with regard to the country's national independence, protect its cultural identity and its nature and rather be content with fewer but more affluent tourists. There would certainly be a great demand for this among the Russian upper class, which is why the establishment of diplomatic relations and a modus vivendi with Russia would be beneficial in this regard as well.

15.6 Starting Points for Infrastructure Development

Although the term "infrastructure" did not exist in Friedrich List's time, he recognized its fundamental importance for upgrading a developing country. The Georgian government is endeavoring to further expand the country's infrastructure in terms of road construction as well as rail and maritime transport. This should make the South Caucasus a much more attractive business location and as a transit route between

China and Europe. At present, however, the southern route is still deeply overshadowed by the northern routes, which cross Russian territory, because these are favored by China. Two projects in particular are intended to change this:

- the new or modernized Baku-Tbilisii-Kars (BTK) rail link, which connects Azerbaijan, Georgia and Turkey. The BTK was completed at the end of October 2017 after approximately ten years of construction. However, its long-term significance is highly controversial. For one thing, part of the line is not electrified, the signalling technology is outdated, and there are weight restrictions on individual sections, making the line unsuitable for large container wagons.[12]
- the mega-project Anaklia, a deep-sea port on the Georgian Black Sea coast, which is estimated to cost USD 2.5 billion.

The current shipping traffic is handled via the two Georgian Black Sea ports of Poti and Batumi, which, however, do not have the necessary water depth for container ships of the Panama class. Therefore, the cargo destined to and from Georgia has to be reloaded in Istanbul or Constanza, which means additional costs and a loss of time. This is why the deepsea port of Anaklia provides a remedy. This project is considered to be the project of the century. To everyone's surprise it was not a Georgian-Chinese consortium that won the contract but a Georgian-American consortium. The decisive reason is said to have been that the latter plans greater participation of local labor. "This is an indication that there is greater scepticism about Chinese involvement because in other infrastructure projects with Chinese participation, not only many specialists but also many workers were brought into the country from China, and Georgian workers hardly benefited."

On rail network development, according to forecasts for 2027, only 3% of Eurasian train traffic will be completed via the southern route. That is the majority of traffic will use the Central Asia route, bypassing Georgia. A study commissioned by the European Parliament supports this assessment, according to which the northern routes in particular will benefit from the further growth of rail transport between Asia and Europe. This is also seen by the current cooperation efforts between Russia and China.

Here the question arises once again as to whether Georgian policy-makers should not rethink their previous foreign trade strategy and decide on a paradigm shift. We believe that it would be much more obvious to build a railway connection with Russia and in the direction of Ukraine and to handle Georgian foreign trade via these routes as opposed to a very costly transit connection bypassing Russia. In this respect, we agree with those critics who argue that Georgia should position itself primarily as a hub for regional trade between the South Caucasian and Central Asian states and focus less on transit trade between Europe and China.

In sum it would be timely for Georgia to bid farewell to certain dreams and come to a realistic, self-confident and identity-affirming assessment of its position because it represents only a small but a spot with certain potential on the world map.

15.7 Concluding Remarks

From the intensive reseach of Georgia, which I inevitably had to undergo in the preparation of this study, I have learned that the country in the South Caucasus impresses with its “downright raw beauty” and is a real insider’s tip for tourists. In addition to the unique scenic beauty and cultural sights the country is said to impress with its proverbial hospitality, the joie de vivre and its culinary delights. The capital Tbilisi is characterized by European, Oriental and Asian influences, which combine to form a charming synthesis.

The Georgians joie de vivre is also said to have been the reason why the Lord God allotted them this blessed land. Actually, according to an old legend, God wanted to reserve the land for himself. However, the Georgians failed to ask the Lord God for a piece of land as well because they were partying hard all the time and in their celebrating mood, forgot to ask for land of their own. When all the lands were finally distributed they realized that they might go away empty-handed. However, the Lord was so pleased with the Georgians joie de vivre that he decided to forego a land of his own and give the Georgians the land he had reserved for them.

In the further development of the political, economic, social and cultural dimensions of the country, one would hope that all inhabitants are aware of this divine grace and do not sacrifice this precious patch of earth to mammon and the greed for profit and do not turn it into a desert in ecological terms. In the sense of Friedrich List, one would like to wish Georgia that it will find its happiness neither in monocultures nor in mass tourism, neither in soulless concrete blocks and residential barracks, nor in the uncritical adoption of “Western culture”, neither in senseless prestige projects and large-scale events, nor in congested roads and traffic gridlock, neither in the thoughtless devastation of the environment such as the deforestation of the native forests, nor in the unrestrained exploitation of mineral resources, but strives to cultivate its unique Garden of Eden, developing the productive forces of the country and its people in harmony with nature.

Notes

1. Ammon, P. (2020): Georgia between statehood and Russian occupation, Frankfurt a. M.
2. Demography and social issues in Georgia; in: Eastern Europe, 68th ed, h. 7, 2018, p. 103.
3. Dreamland Georgia; in: Eastern Europe, 68th ed, h. 7, 2018, p. 3. Gazer, H. (2005): The Georgian Orthodox Church; in: Schröder, B. (ed.): Georgia - Society and Religion on the Threshold of Europe, St, Ingbert, pp. 55-70.
4. Zedina, G. (2018): Simultaneity of the nonsimultaneous - paradoxes of politics in Georgia; in: Eastern Europe, 68th ed. 7, pp. 106-116, p. 11.
5. Maisuadze, G. (2018): “The oldest Europeans”; in: Nakhutsrisvili, L: Georgia, respelling, Bielefeld.
6. Saldastanishvili, K. (2004): Georgia on its way to the European Union; in: Schröder, B. (ed.): Georgia - Society and Religion on the Threshold of Europe, St. Ingbert, 2005,
7. Christophe, B. (2004): Culture of corruption? Notes on the political order in Georgia; in: Schröder, B. (ed.) Georgia - Society and Religion on the Edge of Europe, St. Ingert, pp. 33-46.

8. Nakhutsrishvili, L. (2018): Georgia, spelled anew; edited by the Heinrich Böll Foundation.
9. Guruli, I (2018): If only there were love before dark; o. O.
10. Doinjashvili, G. (2017): The effectiveness of EU development policy in Georgia and Armenia; Diss. Bamberg.
11. Smolnik, F. (2018): Ambitions, conditions, restrictions - Georgia on the New Silk Road; in: Eastern Europe, 68 Jg, H. 7, pp. 131 ff.
12. Diakonidze, A. (2018): It is all about work; in: Nakhutsrishvili, L.: Georgia, spelled anew, Bielefeld, pp. 153- 162.

Chapter 16
Friedrich List and European Integration

16.1 The Idea of Integration

In the liberal-democratic atmosphere of Switzerland, Friedrich List could dream during his exile in Aarau, "he who stands on the highest level of education will be a citizen of the world and will desire a cooperation of all presently independent states in a confederation." Only by means of treaty agreements, he said, could one attain "freedom of world trade," by which alone the highest level of prosperity could be attained. One could think that List had already thought of the League of Nations or the United Nations with this statement and perhaps also of the World Trade Conference in Bali, which ended on 6. December 2013 with a joint commitment by all states to liberalize world trade.

List was enough of a realist to know that this wishful image was an unattainable ideal in his time. Moreover, he did not believe in the utopia of eternal peace. In the union of states into a nation under a uniform legal system, he saw the greatest possible union of individuals at that time. In this context, his political goal was, of course, primarily directed towards the economic and political unification of the German territorial states.

The consistent application of reason, he said, demands close cooperation with other peoples not only in business life but also in the entire economic, political and social spheres. The confederation of productive forces urges cooperation and integration with resulting irresistible power. In the process, he said, resistance and friction are inevitable. However, just as friction ignites a fire, the friction of the spirit is indispensable for human progress. That is why in the future we can expect increasing business, scientific, private and political communication on a national and international level and a growing exchange of goods and ideas.

At the same time, List was already thinking about the necessity of a union of independent European states to strive for what one used to call the "European system of states" or the "European equilibrium". In the introduction to a three-part article on the subject, "*Idées sur les réformes économiques, commerciales et financières, applicables à la France*", which he published in the "*Revue Encyclopédique*" during

E. Wendler, *The Political Economy of Friedrich List*, Springer Studies in the History of Economic Thought, https://doi.org/10.1007/978-3-031-24601-2_16

his stay of several months in Europe in 1831, he pleaded for "le modèle d'une bonne administration et préparer l'équlibre future de l'Europe, fondé sur la sainte alliance des peuples."[1]

Already in his memorandum on 14. April 1819 to the Federal Assembly on the abolition of internal tariffs, he expressed the conviction that only through general freedom of trade could Europe "attain the highest degree of civilization. Only a strong and rich Germany will be able to maintain the equilibrium on the continent; a poor and exhausted one will succumb to every attack, whether it comes from the east or west."[2]

In another memorandum, in his mission as delegate of the Handels- und Gewerbsverein (trade and industry association), which List presented to the Austrian Emperor Franz I on 2. March 1820, he writes, "the theorists will have to admit to us, after all, that it would be very conducive to German national prosperity if all European states were open to German products and that corresponding trade treaties would be very desirable."

After his conviction by the criminal court in Esslingen for the "*Reutlinger Petition*", List initially fled to Strasbourg. There he wrote a series of articles to which he gave the name "Themis" after a Greek legendary figure. The first volume was dedicated to none other than Marquis de Lafayette, who as a young nobleman played a prominent role in the American struggle for independence and later in the French Revolution. Friedrich List was privileged to accompany Lafayette for two and a half months in 1825 on the latters triumphal tour of the Atlantic coastal states in the USA.[3]

In the corresponding preface of the article List writes, among other remarks, "no false national pride in our days keeps peoples from letting foreign experience serve as a lesson and from establishing institutions in their own country that have been tried and tested abroad," for so he added, "my eyes are fixed on Europe!".

16.2 The Journalistic Implementation of the European Idea

After the scathing verdict of the criminal court in Esslingen, List fled to Alsace (in today´s France across the Rhine River) and then to Switzerland, where he obtained a residence permit in Aarau and met other German emigrants there. To build up a material existence the emigrants founded their own newspaper in Aarau, which they sensibly gave the title "*Europäische Blätter*" (European Papers). The driving force behind this project was undoubtedly Friedrich List. Since the editors had to strictly refrain from political topics, they concentrated their efforts on informing their readers about the most important German, French, English and sometimes Italian and American developments in the fields of trade, industry and technical inventions. For this reason, the contributions to the "Europäische Blätter" written by List do not contain any commentaries on political issues of the day or even visions of European politics.[4]

Later, he wanted to take up a similar project again when he suggested to the publisher Georg v. Cotta in 1837, "could not one revive the European Annals with commercial, national economic, financial, constitutional and historical tendencies?"[5] Cotta, however, did not comment on this suggestion. A book project that List proposed to Cotta a year later also remained unrealized. In a letter dated 6. September 1838, he asked the publisher whether he would print a book with the title "*Über die Freiheit der Nationen, des Weltverkehrs und die Vereinigung der Nationen unter einem Rechtsgesetz*" (On the freedom of nations, world traffic and the unification of nations under one law). Unfortunately, Cotta did not respond to this idea either, although this title would be particularly interesting from today's perspective.

In a short series of lectures on the "*Encyclopaedia of Political Science*" that he gave at the Lehrverein (Teaching Association) in Aarau, List had the vision that one day there would be a European Tagsatzung, at which interstate trade relations could be regulated, disputes between states could be settled, and joint agreements could be made to absorb the surplus population (!). The term "Tagsatzung" was used in Switzerland to refer to the federal parliament, i.e., the government organization. From this statement one can probably deduce that List might already have had the idea of the Council of Europe in mind at that time. This visionary flight of fancy, however, was immediately followed by a sudden awakening that caused him to descend from this "almost poetic height" and return to harsh reality.[6]

Among the scientific disciplines of political science, he included the so-called philosophical international law or world law, as well as practical international and state law. The philosophical law of nations addresses the necessity that all nations in the distant future recognize the general law among each other and realize that animosities in military and mercantilistic matters mutually weakens their moral and material forces. A struggle between one hundred thousand people will in the future be fifty thousand times more repugnant than a struggle between two.

In the case of practical international and state law, the question is "to what extent the law has in reality come into effect among the various peoples and states." This question included international treaties as well as the so-called "law of war". It was futile to distinguish between lawful and unlawful wars, as was done in theory. The practice is rather to wage wars and to hurt others if one expects advantages from it. For incomprehensible reasons, List said, the conquest of peoples has been brought into a system as if people could be conquered in any other way than through civilization and by establishing their inherent rights. In reality, he says, "the violence of arms also sanctifies unlawful conquest."[7]

Often peace and friendship between peoples are concluded for eternity, and no thought is given to the possibility of this bond being limited in time. Therefore, such insights should lead to emphasizing the need for state unification and striving for a European system of states.

16.3 Economic and Political Integration

List saw the main obstacle to a closer "unification of the European continent" in the desolate situation of economically and politically fragmented Germany.[8] "Instead of being a mediator between the east and west of the European continent in all questions of territorial division, of constitutional principle, of national independence and power due to its geographical position, by a federal constitution which excludes all fear of conquest among neighboring nations...by its religious tolerance and cosmopolitan tendencies, and finally by its elements of culture and power...this center is the bone of contention over which the east and the west quarrel......because they both hope to draw to their side this middle power, weakened by lack of national unity and always wavering uncertainly to and fro. If Germany, on the other hand, were to constitute herself as a powerful commercial and political unit, with the seaboards belonging to her with Holland, Belgium, and Switzerland, and if this powerful national body, with its existing monarchical, dynastic, and aristocratic interests, were to fuse together the institutions of the representative system, thus far as they can be reconciled with each other, Germany could guarantee peace to the European continent for a long time to come and at the same time form the center of a permanent continental alliance."[9]

In such a united and liberalized European economic union, Germany would form the great commercial thoroughfare between eastern and western as well as between northern and southern Europe and would build up its prosperity under the umbrella of external and internal peace. When this is realized, the customs frontiers and the general German trade and industrial association and the name of its intellectual originator Friedrich List, will have long been forgotten.

Through the new means of communication the market reach of every producer and every trader could expand, according to Thünen's Circles (model of spatial circles in connection with business location and expansion) ist agricultural production, and production and consumption could increase in accordance with the proportional expansion of the market so that international trade would eventually spread across the entire globe. Here, globalization is already anticipated from the outset.

The railway would act as an iron band for the European continent, bringing about the definitive union of economic areas and cultural zones, such as the three linguistic areas of Switzerland. The European continent and its rail network, which would extend from Cadix and Lisbon to St. Petersburg and Moscow, from Naples to Le Havre, via Paris (the railway junction and where the center of these two giant lines would be situated), and from Paris across Germany, Austria-Hungary to the Black Sea, would expand its trade on an immense scale, without depending on any maritime great power. This closing phrase, maritime great power, of course alludes to England.

In one of his most important essays in the *Staats-Lexikon* on "*Railways and Canals*", List made clear at the same time how much Germany in particular would benefit from such a rail network. In his writings he dared to make the following prediction, "the travel traffic of foreigners from all European countries, in which Germany also attracts more foreign travellers because of its spas, the diversity of its institutes (such as) fairs, schools, universities, art exhibitions, etc., will be of great benefit to the country. Germany will attract more foreign travelers than any other country. If one considers the character of the people and the country, the prevailing order and the cosmopolitanism of the nation, one would like to hope that Germany, would become the point of unification of the entire European continent in terms of trade and industry, as well as in terms of science and the arts." Finally, the time would come when Europe, fragmented into numerous small states, would also have to strive for political unification. There was a danger that the Russian colossus would continue to expand its giant empire to the west, as far as western civilization would allow. This would give rise to the danger that Russia would attempt to bring the states of central and western Europe under its control. However, this subjugation would not occur if these countries were to unite economically and politically.

List saw another threat to Europe, that being the population pressure from Africa. If one did not succeed in absorbing the population growth of this continent through a corresponding economic development, then this could become dangerous for Europe at some point. Thus, he writes in an article of the *Staats-Lexikon* of 1834, „if one does not succeed in eliminating the main reasons for the backwardness of the African continent, one day the Spanish enclaves Tangier with the Forts of Ceuta and Melilla could become important (for Europe) in case of an invasion from Morocco. "Of course, at that time he hadn't yet thought of Lampedusa, Libya, Syria and the Balkan routes of today´s refugees.

List, in his time, probably only had in mind a political integration of the states that we now call "core Europe": Germany, Belgium, Holland, France, Switzerland and Denmark. He certainly did not have eastern and southern enlargement in mind, especially since the Ottoman Empire still reached as far as the border of the Habsburg Monarchy and Italy, for example, was not yet united (Fig. 16.1).

With regard to the eastward and southward enlargement of the European Union, it should be noted that List demanded two preconditions for economic and political unification. First, it had to be voluntary, and second, only those states that were at roughly the same stage of development should join together. In certain recent times for Greece and other critical Euro countries, the first condition is undoubtedly fulfilled. However, whether the second condition was met, in the sense of political positioning, for joining the monetary union may be more than doubted.

Because of its high level of civilization and resources, List believed that France should be at the forefront of European unification efforts because it was the most advanced country on the European continent politically, legally, economically, and culturally. As the center of European trade, the French capital Paris would become the geographical crossroads of Orient and Occident, as well as of Northern and Southern Europe.[10]

That the Belgian capital Brussels would be an important center for such European bridge building was hinted at by List as early as 1831 in a letter to the US Secretary of State Martin Van Buren, in which he requested from the American government a diplomatic function in Belgium, pointing out that Brussels was a central point between Germany and France.

With regard to Switzerland's position on European integration, List also made a pertinent announcement. From an economic point of view, he said, it was hard to

Fig. 16.1 The EU—a peaceful island in a stormy world sea

see why "Switzerland, with the small size of its territory and its present constitution wanted to hold onto its own trading system. A customs union with the Zollverein, Austria or France would certainly bring it great advantages. "In whichever of these three bodies of commerce Switzerland entered, it would everywhere rise to the industrial level of that body. Nevertheless, for higher political reasons, Switzerland might have misgivings about accepting an offer of this kind, from whatever side it might be made. Material wealth is desirable only if it can be acquired without prejudice to more valuable goods. "[11]

16.4 List's Efforts for an Anglo-German Alliance

From the rapidly growing spread of the new means of communication that he expected, List also reached the conclusion that England would derive great benefit mainly from the consolidation and expansion of her colonial empire. The more its colonies and possessions in Asia, Africa, and Australia grew in population, civilization, and prosperity, the greater its sales of manufactured goods, the more significant its population, its wealth, its financial power, its shipping, and consequently its naval and land power. England could be expected to pave a "world lane" as far as China and to annex the "houses" to the right and left of her dominion.

One only has to think of Gibraltar, Malta, Cyprus, Aden, India, Ceylon, Singapore and Hong Kong when making this prediction. No one could predict when this time would be reached. However, it may be boldly stated that the child of the man is already born who will see all this accomplished. England will create outposts for her trade all over the world. Moreover, it will try to impose its culture and its language on the people of these countries, who are accustomed to servility and work.

To maintain its position of world power, List concluded, England must be very interested in entering into an alliance with Germany, but not with the Germany as it is at present (i.e., approximately 1850), but as it should be and become with England's help. Namely, with the help of a close political and economic alliance. There was every reason to intensify Anglo-German cooperation and to strive for a political-economic alliance as that could only be to the advantage of both sides. In this way England would assert its economic supremacy. In return, it should support Prussia in integrating the German territorial states that did not yet belong to the Zollverein, i.e., the economic union, including Austria, in terms of trade policy.

Furthermore England was to help Germany build up its productive forces and facilitate the achievement of political unity. As an effective means of this support, List demanded that the English government tolerate a temporary protective tariff system.

> "Certainly, England does not know the future significance of Germany. Proud of her present supremacy, she has not yet taken the trouble to form a clear conception of what fate this nation is destined to meet with if her present fragmentation continues, and what influence this nation, hitherto so little respected by her, is destined to exert upon her own history."

To propose this alliance to English politicians, he traveled to London for the second time in the spring of 1846 on his own initiative. He submitted his alliance memorandum to the English government, i.e., to Prime Minister Robert Peel, the leader of the opposition, Lord Palmerston, and Queen Victoria's husband, Prince Albert of Saxe-Coburg-Gotha.

The ultimate rejection of the Alliance memorandum in no way diminishes the mature political insight with which Friedrich List anticipated Bismarck's alliance policy from the outset. It puts the final gloss on the "herald of German unity", as he was called in a popular biography by Uller.

It seems remarkable that Friedrich List, although he could only appear as a private citizen, was received with respect and courtesy by both Prince Albert and Viscount Palmerston and that his Alliance memorandum was carefully reviewed. The Prussian ambassador at the English court at the time, Christian Karl Freiherr v. Bunsen, wrote to the Prime Minister a few days after Peel's refusal, "List is a sincere patriot. Although the measures he proposes for the good of his country cannot be realized, they are nevertheless fundamentally correct."

The editors of Volume VII of the *Complete Edition*, Friedrich Lenz and Erwin Wiskemann, commented on this in 1931, "if they (the English politicians) objected to List and especially to his Alliance Memorandum relating to the idea of a political alliance between the strong England and the weak German Confederation, in that it was in itself illusory, there is little to be said against this historically." On the other hand, both recalled, "the anxious visions of the old Bismarck, who, nearly half a century later, for the sake of preserving a united and strengthened Germany, sought to include England in his system of alliances for European peace." However, it was precisely in this that "the greatness of List's forebodings would become quite clear, notwithstanding the lack of real preconditions for a German-English alliance in his day." After all, the chemist Justus v. Liebig also attested to him that no one "knows the English conditions, which I (Liebig) know fairly well through my travels there, better than Herr List (describes), but what a gulf between his views and the accepted views of our statesmen."[12]

On the other hand, Lenz and Wiskemann also point out that List, "misjudged the deep and tenacious roots between utilitarianism and idealism in the British character". Notwithstanding this psychological error, however, List recognized better than England of the nineteenth and twentieth centuries that the British, in the long run, could not avoid a close alliance with a strong Germany.

After the disappointing outcome of his second trip to London, List was left only with the hope of a continental alliance with close cooperation between France and the politically united Germany and the countries forming the core of Europe. Perhaps in the future one will have to get used to the term "continental alliance". A quotation handed down in a paper by A. Wetzel from 1898 also fits into this scenario. In it, the author quotes, albeit without precise reference to the source, the famous American national economist Henry Charles Carey (1793–1879) with the words, "around List is a silence that points to something better. The true monument of List will be German Europe!"[13] The only thing displeasing about this quote is the word "German", because in this context, it sounds hegemonic, which is not at all what List meant. He saw Germany's future role as an integrative, albeit very important, piece in the puzzle of the European community of states.

Notes

1. Ders (1831): Idées sur les réformes économiques, commerciales et financières, applicalble à la France; in: W. V, pp. 59-91.
2. Ders, W. V, p. 226.
3. List, F. (1823): Themis I - Geschichte des Jury - aus dem Französischen des Herrn Aignan, Heidelberg, Announcement and Preface.
4. Ders (1984): Leben und Wirken von Friedrich List in der Schweiz und sein Meinungsbild über die Eidgenossenschaft, Diss. Konstanz, pp. 130–148.
5. List, F. Letter to G. v. Cotta, dated 30.10.1837; in: W. VIII, p. 49.
6. Wendler, E.: Leben und Wirken von Friedrich List in der Schweiz, Diss. Konstanz, p. 116.
7. Ibid. S. 115–117.
8. Ders. (1989): Friedrich List - Politische Wirkungsgeschichte des Vordenkers der europäischen Integration, op.cit., p. 188 f.
9. List, F. (1837): The Natural System of Political Economy; W. IV, p. 40.
10. Ders (1843): Letter to A. Duckwitz, 7.5.1843; in: W. VIII, p. 670.

11. Wendler, E. (1984): Leben und Wirken von Friedrich List in der Schweiz, op.cit., p. 259.
12. W. VII. S, 623.
13. Boianovsky, M. (2013): Friedrich List and the Economic Fate of Tropical Countries. In: History of Political Economy, Vol. 45, No. 4, pp. 647–693.

Chapter 17
How Would Friedrich List Comment on Brexit?

17.1 The Die Is Cast

At literally the last minute the British government and the European Union had agreed on a comprehensive free trade agreement to prevent a disorderly Brexit. After years of tough negotiations, the jubilation is restrained, but there is relief on both sides of the Channel because a modus vivendi has been found on which future relations can be built and continued. Only time will tell whether the British dreams of a prosperous Brexit will be fulfilled. In any case, the mood is now one of disillusionment, not to say hangover.

The strategy and tactics of the English governments on Brexit and in the withdrawal negotiations are reflected in the experiences that Friedrich List had to make exactly 175 years ago in his efforts to establish an Anglo-German alliance. Due to the insular and trade supremacy strictly followed by England even then, he had to admit that England was stubbornly defending this position and therefore frustrated and disillusioned, abandoned his plans for promoting an alliance. He then pinned his hopes on a continental alliance of European nations, as it has now emerged following Britain's withdrawal from the European Union. Perhaps we will now have to get used to the term "continental alliance" and in the process be reminded of List's foresight.

On the other hand, the motto of List's second Paris Prize competition pamphlet, "*Le monde marche–The world is moving*", also applies to English politics, albeit with a completely different situation than 175 years ago. The world trade axis has shifted from the western to the eastern hemisphere, the British Empire is history, the rate of global change has accelerated dramatically, and despite its lingua franca, England, especially from an Asian perspective, appears only as a small speck on the world map. If the Scottish government were to follow through with its intentions and achieve independence from the United Kingdom and even if Northern Ireland united with the Republic of Ireland, Brexit would prove to be a disastrous boomerang.

So now the die is cast! The protracted and sometimes undignified tug of war between the British governments over Brexit has come to an end. However, the tablecloth was not torn because a hard Brexit was still avoided at the last minute.

E. Wendler, *The Political Economy of Friedrich List*, Springer Studies in the History of Economic Thought, https://doi.org/10.1007/978-3-031-24601-2_17

A new era of British-European cooperation is now beginning. From a European perspective, Brexit may be regretted, from an English perspective, it seems consistent.

Here, one reminds us that in 1846, the last year of his life, Friedrich List set out on his own initiative to propose a German-English alliance to the English government and the opposition and how disappointed he was when he had to admit the failure of his mission. This begs the question of how List would comment on Brexit today.

17.2 The Failed Attempt at an Anglo-German Alliance

After List had already set foot on English soil for the first time in 1824, he planned, as already mentioned, a second trip to the English capital in the spring of 1846 to win over the English government with the incumbent Prime Minister Robert Peel and the parliamentary opposition under Lord Palmerston for the plan of a German-English alliance.[1] Commenting on this mission, Gustav Kolb, then editor of the *Allgemeine Zeitung,* friend and confidant of List, "before List went to England, I had had some very serious conversations with him, in which I explained to him how he could not possibly achieve his purpose in England. He insisted that this was the most glorious mission of his life and that the purpose was so great that he felt rewarded for having striven for it."[2]

List could not be dissuaded from his plan, although common sense must have told him that it was doomed to failure from the outset. At least he found a financial supporter of this journey in Anton Bachmaier, the co-owner of the trading house F. J. Bachmaier in Vilshofen. On 16. March 1846 Bachmaier wrote to List, "I repeat to you that I fully support your project and find no greater reward than the awareness that through my help I can also contribute a stone to the great work that you have been building for years with noble sacrifice and true patriotism".[3]

Anton Bachmaier even launched an appeal to form a committee of the most important industrialists, merchants and large landowners with the aim of raising funds to finance List's trip to England. This appeal was quite successful, as the significant sum of 6,000 Florins was raised. Kolb reports that List did not touch these funds and deposited them with a banker. Only after his death did Kolb hand over the sum to his widow.[4]

On 19. June 1846, List arrived in London. He stayed for two months at the Hotel Royal in Bridgestreet, Blackfriars. The hotel was built before 1845 as a luxury hotel and existed until the First World War. It mainly accommodated visitors from other European countries.[5]

It goes without saying that this mission was bound to end in failure from the outset. List had neither a political mandate nor could he hope for broad support among the German people.

Kolb commented, "Peel received the memorandum coolly, remarking in a polite letter to List, he may have been guided by good intentions, but the happiness of the peoples would not be promoted by such prohibitive and blocking measures. England, therefore, could not lend a hand to List's intentions. Nor does he seem to have found a lot attention from Lord Clarendon." Georges William Frederick Villiers, 4th Earl of Clarendon, his full name, was then President of the Board of Trade, that is, English Minister of Commerce. After all, the Alliance memorandum appealed to him enough to invite List to a personal debate.

In a lengthy statement, opposition leader Lord Palmerston made further arguments in favor of the English free trade doctrine. Like Robert Peel, Palmerston certified that List's political views were well founded but that his conclusions on economic policy were wrong. If List held that England should enter into a permanent alliance with Germany for the benefit of both nations, he argued, this was beyond dispute. However, if, at the same time, he demanded that Germany, to achieve her political unity, should for the time be renouncing free trade and instead pursuing a policy of protective tariffs, this was a misguided course. Free trade, like charity, began in one's own house, and if List rightly praised the advantages of the Zollverein for Germany's economic development, it was precisely this success that was based on the principles of free trade. The best examples, he said, were Bavaria and Württemberg, which had achieved a great economic upswing as a result of the Zollverein. Protective tariffs were equally detrimental to production and to increasing the prosperity of a nation. Thus, protectionist measures could make a country neither prosperous nor strong.

In this respect, this mission was a total failure. Resignedly, List noted that the English government neither knew the general mood of the Germans nor had it "duly considered" the long-term consequences of its negative attitude for its own country.[6] He returned to Germany, as Gustav Kolb reports, "disheartened, almost he would like to say, humiliated." List never recovered from this blow and put an end to his life a quarter of a year later. Despite his criticism of this mission, Kolb commented on the memorandum with the words, "it is the calmest, most consistent, wittiest account that has ever come from List's pen, and yet it was written at the very time when we observed those precarious spiritual phenomena in him."[7]

17.3 English Insular and Commercial Supremacy

Friedrich List introduced an essay from 1843 with the words, "the English are a great and respectable nation, which the German holds in the highest esteem of all nations, with which he sympathizes the most and by which he himself is best understood, most justly and correctly judged. The English as individuals are upright, lawful, lovers of truth and justice, magnanimous, understanding, capable in everything. However, as a nation they are this only up to the point where their monopoly of trade comes into discussion. From then on they are, as all their predecessors were in regard to commercial dominion, and as no doubt all their successors will be, unjust, deceitful, insolent (i.e., impudent and presumptuous), insatiable in possessiveness, a Harpax among nations (a Roman weapon that can be used from land like a harpoon fired to board enemy ships)."[8]

List described Great Britain as an insular nation with commercial supremacy, due to its economic strength and trading power, and as such is unique versus all other countries. With regard to agriculture and industry, to fleet and colonies, to internal wealth and the importance of foreign trade, as well as to the level of technical development of machinery and means of transport, the country stood far above any other nation. The factories of this commercial and industrial supremacy have a thousand advantages, including skilled and trained laborers in the greatest numbers and at the lowest wages, the best technicians, the most accomplished and cheapest machinery, building infrastructure, the greatest advantages in buying and selling, especially the cheapest means of transportation for obtaining raw materials and shipping finished products, great credit ratings with the banks at low interest, business connections, etc., such as can only be gathered and established in the course of human generations. In addition, an immense domestic market and an equally immense colonial market.[9]

Civil liberty had developed earlier in England than in other countries. The interests of monarchy, aristocracy, and democracy were united and combined there earlier than elsewhere, with the general aim of increasing the productive powers of the nation within and trade with the inhabitants in all directions. Agricultural, manufacturing, and commercial forces were at the highest level of perfection and most beautiful equilibrium. There, the practical application of the custom laws was powerfully supported by the insular situation. There, it is seen how for centuries, with the exception of a brief interlude, the development and progress of the productive forces have steadily taken their course. The perpetual peace in the domestic industry and the vast superiority of naval power is the basis for extending foreign trade still further Fig. 17.1.

Considering the available capital List called "the English nation the bankkeeper of all the nations of the globe." However, a nation that manufactures more than all others will always exalt itself by its narcissism and national egoism and tend to arrogance. Although reason dictates that one should renounce ever increasing jealousy and ill-will, although this realization tells one that war between nations is as foolish as it is cruel, and although the awareness that eternal peace and freedom of trade are capable of raising all nations to the highest level of wealth and power, the readiness for peaceful cooperation and international division of labor is still extremely underdeveloped. The best means of improving and deepening international economic relations, he said, were trade congresses, to which the most competent national economists of their respective countries be sent to deliberate on what common interests and objectives should be pursued as a matter of priority. In saying this he by no means meant to assert that there should be no supremacy, and the supremacy of England was desirable more than that of any other. It seems to be in the order of nature that the plants of politics are as different as the plants of nature, and his desire does not go thus far as to say that all the trees of the earth should be oaks. List only demanded that "the other nations of Europe should not be so overtopped and prevented by England and her daughter nations from revolving on their own axis and pursuing their own course, in summary that they should not be degraded to mere satellites of England." Nevertheless, he said, "England is tempted by her avarice to stop and disturb the progress of nations which are harmoniously forming their national forces, not of course, by the use of brute force but, what is more dangerous, by the use of a false

Fig. 17.1 Caricature of the Supremacy of Britannia in the mid-nineteenth century

doctrine, tactical persuasion and diplomatic shrewdness. It is only in these respects that he is a serious opponent of England."[10]

The famous chemist Justus Freiherr v. Liebig (1803–1875) was not unaware of List's work. He wrote to a friend, "no one judges the English conditions, which I know fairly well through my travels there, better than Herr List, but what a gulf between his views and the accepted views of our statesmen."[11] Liebig may have been referring here to List's *Zollvereinblatt (customs trade journal)*, which reported in numerous articles on the political and economic situation on the island.

17.4 Brexit and the Continental Alliance

After the unsuccessful efforts to form an Anglo-German alliance, List had to come to the realization that England could not be counted on for European integration. He had already hinted at and expressed this in corresponding formulations. Some evidence is cited here, "Love for Britannia is like love for Jupiter: whoever wants to embrace her will be consumed by her fire like Semele."[12] In Greek and Roman mythology, Semele is the daughter of the goddess of Concord, namely Harmonia. Jupiter, the father of the gods, appeared to Semele as a mere mortal and fell in love with her. His wife Hera therefore became jealous when she learned of this love affair and sowed discord, which is why Semele came to have doubts about her love. To dispel these doubts Semele wished that Jupiter might show himself in his divine splendor. When this wish was fulfilled, Semele, like a body that comes too close to the sun, was struck by lightning and scorched by heat.

In the 9th Chapter of his *Outlines of American Political Economy*, List writes, "the more English policy at the present time seems to contradict itself and shrouds its decisions in ominous mystical darkness, the more difficult it is to understand its attitude. If one asks about the intention of the English government, it becomes apparent that this consists of strengthening its own economic power in such a way that no other country can compete with England. To achieve this end, the government supports liberal principles at home, while in Asia, it plays the conqueror and supports the despotic governments there, and in the West Indies and Canada, it is content with a paternal government. Always, she has adapted her conduct to the circumstances, applying liberal principles at one time and place, and then again employing power and money either to promote liberty or to suppress it, as suited her ends." List contented himself with this realization because he did not intend to discuss European politics here. He merely intended to show that English policy always pursued the aim of working against the European continental powers.[13] At the same time, he remarked, "The (source of the) strength of Germany is the strength of England."[14] However, "Germany is shown the dangers threatening her on the right and on the left, she is made to feel how desirable and necessary England's friendship and help are to her, and as a reward for such service she (Germany) is demanded to sacrifice her striving for trade and industrial independence to trade supremacy (of England)."[15]

If one considers the immeasurable interests that continental nations of Europe possess, one must recognize that a "refined continental system" 20 is now necessary. Such a "continental alliance" can only succeed if France does not make the mistakes of Napoleon and we add, Germany does not make the mistakes of the Wilhelmine era and National Socialism. List states, "an effective continental system can arise only from a free union of the continental powers, and can succeed only if it has as its objective the equal distribution of the advantages which flow from it." One can clearly see how a collective continental system is in the making, where once again England will then use all means, permitted as well as unpermitted, to assert her old supremacy[16]–Fig. 17.2.

Fig. 17.2 After Brexit, the EU shrinks to a "continental alliance" (Friedrich List)

However, the British, who are all too thirsty for superiority, would be hard hit when they then find that the Continental Alliance is gaining more economic power and political influence than they possess. The same causes that lifted Britain to its then lofty level would be likely, over the next century, to lift the United States and China to a level that will far surpass Britain. Thus, in the not too distant future, the necessity that dictated to the French and the Germans the foundation of a continental alliance would at some point also suggest to the British to place themselves (again) under the protection, security and prestige of the European continental nations. So it would be beneficial, List recommended, if England would secure the friendship of the European continental powers at some point and get used to the idea of being "the first among equals!."[17]

What would List advise the Germans in view of the UK's exit from the EU and the Brexit Agreement? He would perhaps say to them, "let us tell the English, you need a capable ally on the continent. We sympathize with you in every way and to a greater degree than with any other non-EU nation. However, we would like to be sincere and capable allies. Therefore, you must cease to intrigue against our advances in trade, commerce, and navigation."[18]

17.5 Concluding Remarks

In view of List's trip to London in the spring of 1846 and his efforts to forge a German-English alliance, most will wonder how this complete hubris and loss of reality can be explained. There is no conclusive answer to this question. Certainly, political decision-making processes in the first half of the nineteenth century were less complicated and quicker to carry out than they are today. However, this is not sufficient to explain List's motivation.

We start from the following conjecture: after List succeeded in 1819 in providing the first impetus for the economic unification of the German territorial states with his petition to the Federal Assembly and the founding of the Handels- und Gewerbsverein, he now wanted to provide the first impetus for political unification as well with his idea of a German-English alliance. In doing so, he certainly did not expect immediate success. He probably only had the expectation that the English government and the opposition would receive his idea positively and consider it seriously. This would already have been a great success for him. Then he could have addressed the Prussian government with the same request, and from this, an important signal would have gone out for German unity. Moreover, for List it would have been a considerable image booster. Since none of this occurred, his disappointment must have been boundless and robbed him of his last ounce of energy.

Notes

1. Wendler, E. (2013): Friedrich List (1789-1846 >)—. An Economist with Vision and Social Responsibility, Wiesbaden, pp. 289–300.
2. Kolb, G. (1849): Letter to L. Häusser; in: W. VIII, p. 854.
3. Ibid.
4. Bachmaier, A. (1846): Letter to F. List; in: W. VIII, pp. 799 and 802.
5. Wendler, E. (1989): Friedrich List—Politische Wirkungsgeschichte des Vordenkers der European Integration, Munich, pp. 206–221.
6. List, F. (1846): The true fundamental conditions of an Anglo-German alliance; in: W. VII, pp. 263–296.
7. Kolb, G.: (1849): Letter to L. Häusser; in: W. VIII; p. 854.
8. List, F: (1843): The English alliance and German industry; in: W. VII, p. 250 f.
9. Idem (1841): The national system of political economy; in: W. VI, pp. 315 f, 349 and 369.
10. Idem (1837): The natural system of political economy; in: W. IV, pp. 220–225.
11. Idem (1839): Announcement and plan of a state library; in: W. IX, p. 99.
12. Idem (1827): Outlines of American Political Economy, ed. by Michael Liebig, Wiesbaden, pp. 120–122.
13. Idem (1845): Die wahren Grundbedingungen einer deutsch-englischen Allianz; In: W. VII, P. 263.
14. Idem (1843): The English alliance and German industry; in: W. VII, p. 252.
15. Idem (1840): Essence and value of a national trade productive power; in: W. V, p. 380.
16. Idem (1839): Announcement and plan of the State Library; in: W. IX, p. 99.
17. Idem (1841): The national system of political economy; in: W. VI, pp. 415–7.
18. Idem (1843): The political national unity of the Germans; in: W. VII, p. 254.

Chapter 18
For the Emancipation of Jews and Against Anti-semitism

The hatred and persecution of the Jews has been one of the darkest chapters in German history since the early Middle Ages. The atrocities of the Holocaust by the National Socialists in the Third Reich are beyond any reason, based on the erroneous belief in the master and superior race. However, both before and after, discrimination against Jews has a long history. Individual shocking crimes and incidents in the present prove that there are still those on the right-wing fringe of our society who are filled with dislike or hatred and express this more or less bluntly. That is why it is always necessary to draw attention to this intolerance and to fight against it with historical memories and rational arguments so that the misery of the Nazi era is never repeated.

"Jewish emancipation" is the term used to describe the development of the Jews and their integration into the Christian society of the Occident in the first half of the nineteenth century. After centuries of being ostracized in Europe and relegated to a marginal position in society, Jews were granted citizen status by the French National Assembly as a result of the French Revolution following the constitution of 1791. Nevertheless, they continued to have few opportunities to take up middle class professions and still had to be content with banking and money transactions and with the role of petty traders.

On 30. May 1806, Napoleon again permitted Jews to practice their religion. In the Jewish Edict of 1812, Prussia also granted the Jews the right of citizenship, the Grand Duchy of Baden had already gone ahead with this in 1809, and Bavaria followed in 1813. In 1866, the Jews were granted freedom to settle in Switzerland, and in 1874 they were also granted the right to practice their religion freely. Thus, as of 1874, all Jews in western and central Europe were formally equal citizens of their respective states. Despite this legal equality, however, social discrimination remained. From 1830 onwards, many liberal democrats called for "civic improvement" with regard to the acceptance of Jews. Many intellectuals and already assimilated Jews were baptized. Heinrich Heine also saw this as a ticket to European culture. With the Reich Constitution of 1871, all remaining restrictions on civic rights were lifted. In particular, the right to vote and to stand for election, i.e., the ability to participate in

E. Wendler, *The Political Economy of Friedrich List*, Springer Studies in the History of Economic Thought, https://doi.org/10.1007/978-3-031-24601-2_18

municipal and state representation and to hold public office, were now independent of religious confession.

Friedrich List commented on the "Jewish Question" in only two places in his literary works. In his "*National System*", he very briefly discusses the consequences of the Inquisition in his economic history of Spain where he writes, "Spain was in possession of all elements of greatness and prosperity when fanaticism, in alliance with despotism, set to work and suffocated the high spirit of the nation. This work of darkness was opened with the expulsion of the Jews and ended with the expulsion of the Moors, by which two million of the most commercially industrious and prosperous inhabitants were driven out of Spain along with their financial capital."[1]/[2] Elsewhere, he notes, "I do not want the oppression of the Jews, but neither do I want the rule of the Jews." By the latter, he understood the "disgraceful Jewish exchange"; i.e., the fact that Jews often did not engage in respectable money transactions and thereby brought misfortune to many. On the other hand, privately he was friends, or at least well acquainted with several Jews, among them Ludwig Börne, Heinrich Heine, and Felix Mendelssohn-Bartholdy.

If one may rely on the triangle symbol that identifies List as the author, he commented on Jewish reform in an article in the "*Allgemeine Zeitung*",[3] "the other day, for people who do not look at the matter in depth, very strange views were put forward about a partial emancipation of the Jews. It is worth the trouble to consider this slightly more closely. It was feared that such an emancipation would bring the greatest disadvantage to the existing Judaism, indeed that it would thereby lead to its complete dissolution.

This assertion ties the salvation of the Jews to the strict maintenance of Talmudic-Rabbinic Judaism. What does it want by this? It wants to bind a religious community to human statutes, for the Talmud consists of rules of Jewish scribes, which in many cases determine in the highest degree sophistical explanations and applications of Old Testament passages for the worship and life of the Jews and, with the exception of a collection of excellent sayings of ancient Jewish sages, contain such an abundance of verbosity, pedantic sophistry, and adherence to the letter that one does not consider such aberrations possible until one has convinced oneself of them by one's own insight.

To the human authority of the authors of individual parts of the Talmud, to the tradition of the rabbis then, the Jews in our day are pointed, and every effort to free themselves from this burden and to purify the simple beauty of the Old Testament from the defaced glaring human ingredients is declared to be a step toward self-destruction. As if the divine text did not precede all human explanations, as if Moses and the prophets and the other books of the Old Testament were not continually read in the synagogues, as if the distribution of this people over the whole earth, which is a miracle of history, still preserved its character after eighteen centuries so faithfully as to be recognizable at a glance. As if the distribution of this people prevented it from imbuing itself with the moral law of the divine document, with the consolation and enlightenment of the Psalms, with the sublimity of the prophets, with the wisdom of life of the writings of the Old Testament. As if the cessation of the theocracy had blocked up the eternal springs from which doctrine, consolation and higher instruction continually flowed to them. One must have seen the pressure exerted by the old Talmudic rabbis upon the believing Jews to understand the longing for deliverance from this pressure."

A small number of writers allowed themselves to be infected by a false objective of the time, namely to fight straightforwardly not only against the interests of Judaism but also against the well understood interests of Christianity. What the abrupt segregation of the Jews from other peoples, what the pressure of the rabbis and the pressure of the Christians has made of the Talmudic-Rabbinic Jews, is obvious. That in this way no thought was given to the human education of this minor group and that its moral elevation was not accomplished must be obvious even to the most ignorant. This naturally perceptive people must be freed from prejudice. It was the duty of Christians to promote this goal through humane and brotherly counsel, and certainly not the duty of Christians to point them from the holy source to the deceit of demagogues.

Friedrich List was very much aware of the situation of the majority of the Jews and he certainly could not gloss over it. As he considered the situation untenable, he tried to propose a solution. In this connection, he was well aware that the relationship of the peasants to a part of the Jews in Germany was disturbed, as he had seen live and up close. However, he was convinced that for the moral and intellectual advancement of the Jews, a few more generations were necessary and that this could not be achieved with serious and degrading pressure. He was well aware that when considering a small part of that people engaged in commerce and usury (outrageously high money lending interest paysments), one should not take the whole into account, but only the relevant part. Nevertheless, it is certain that the Jews must become different and that becoming different can only take place on the path of free education on the basis of the divine word. If one leaves the overgrown tree as it is, it will bear bitter fruit year in and year out. If on the other hand, one takes pains to graft a noble rice on it, all its juices will push towards the rice and on a bright morning one will pluck sweet and mild fruits from the formerly despised tree.

Notes

1. List, F. (1841): The national system of political economy; in: W. VI, pp. 110–12.
2. Idem (1846): Letter to the learned gentlemen; in: W. VIII, p. 788.
3. o. V. (probably F. List): Die Judenreform; in: Allgemeine Zeitung No. 147 of 27.5.1846, p. 1172 f.

Chapter 19
Broad Development Policy Guidelines

19.1 The Division of the World Into Temperate and Hot Zone Countries

In 2013, Mauro Boianovsky, Professor of Political Economy at the Faculty of Economics of the Universidade de Brasilia, published a major paper on "*Friedrich List and the Economic Fate of Tropical Countries*".[1] In the Introduction, the author argues that List's views at the time on the development policies of backwards countries are still relevant for the developing and emerging countries of the 20th century and beyond. What we call "developing countries" today, he argues, is roughly equivalent to what List called the countries of the tropical or hot zone. Boianovsky points out, however, that the term "tropical zone" is inaccurate with respect to South America because List included under it Chile, Uruguay, and Argentina, which are not in fact tropical countries. List's division of the world into a temperate and a tropical zone should better be distinguished into the industrialized northern hemisphere and the predominantly commodity exporting southern hemisphere.

Boianovsky refers to several authors who have put forward the thesis that List based his development policy only on the countries of the temperate zone and did not trust the countries of the tropical zone with an industrialization process. This interpretation is certainly not entirely wrong. If one takes into account the desolate political, economic and social situation in many developing countries, especially in those of black Africa, one cannot but agree with List's pessimistic assessment and perspective. On the other hand, it would be fatal and irresponsible to shrug one's shoulders and accept this state of affairs. The continuing wave of migration is a cry to all politicians and economists to do their utmost to reduce this evil. However, the corresponding efforts are a drop in the bucket as long as the political instability, lack of understanding of democracy, limited freedom of action, legal arbitrariness, corruption, tribal feuds, exploitation by large landowners, domination of the military and the aristocracy of officials, nonsensical prestige projects, the irresponsible deforestation of tropical forests, the overexploitation of agribusiness and mining by foreign investors, and the neglect of education, health and infrastructure, to name only

E. Wendler, *The Political Economy of Friedrich List*, Springer Studies in the History of Economic Thought, https://doi.org/10.1007/978-3-031-24601-2_19

the most important, persist and are not broken. As long as there is no real political will to reform, developing countries will remain what they are, namely developing countries. As such mass migration will remain an outlet to release excess pressure from "social steam boilers". In these countries, science, development policy and aid come up against narrow limits.

Examples such as the Asian tiger economies, Vietnam, Malaysia and Rwanda in Africa, but above all the People's Republic of China, prove that the transformation process can indeed succeed if the political will is there and the necessary framework conditions exist. In the final sentence of the "*National System*", Friedrich List summed up the basic prerequisite for a successful development policy, "everything that will be required on the part of governments to achieve this can be summed up in a single word, it is called, energy!" Contrarily, one cannot simply dismiss List's thesis that the countries of the temperate zone, simply because of their climatic, geographical and topographical conditions, have better conditions for industrial transformation and technical progress.

19.2 The "Free" and "Unfree" Countries of the Hot Zone

List understood the "unfree" countries of the hot zone to be the colonies that the English, French, Dutch, Spanish, and Portuguese seized in Africa, Latin America, and Asia. When he refers to the indigenous population as "barbarian" or "semibarbarian", this is due to the use of the word "civilization" at the time, by which one meant the way of life of the upper middle classes in the first half of the 19th century in central and western Europe, the Biedermeier period, which cannot be compared with the culture and way of life of the inhabitants in the colonies.

List associated the countries of the hot zone, also called tropical countries, with the idea that they were hardly capable of their own industry and should therefore concentrate primarily on the agricultural sector and the extraction of mineral resources because they possessed a natural monopoly here. The exchange of industrial products from the temperate zone for agricultural products (colonial goods) from the hot zone would lead to a cosmopolitan division of labor and a confederation of forces, i.e., "to great international trade."[2] He was of the opinion that it would be a disadvantageous undertaking for the tropical countries to build up their own industrial potential. In this there is, however, the danger that the free, as well as the unfree, countries of the hot zone will become totally dependent on the industrial nations. This danger could only be countered by the emergence in the temperate zone of several nations or power blocs possessing roughly the same economic and political power. Only then would it be guaranteed that no nation or confederation could abuse its superior power over the less powerful states of the hot zone.

World trade would only be dangerous if it were monopolized by a single nation. This is not the case at present, but in fact, the industrial nations dominate the WTO and have thus condemned the developing countries to free trade. According to List, it was clear that a monopoly of world trade, such as existed at that time through the free competition of English manufactured goods on the European and American continents, was in no way more beneficial to the welfare of mankind than a protective system that sought to develop the manufacturing power of the temperate zone in favor of the agriculture of the hot zone.

List also pinned his hopes on the fact that in all civilized nations "the better heads" would come to the conviction that mutual hostility through wars and trade barriers in colonial policy only do harm and that the insight would prevail that countries torn apart by anarchy or run down by bad governments should be helped to stable governments. These would guarantee security of person and property, legal security and the right of every inhabitant to act freely, thus enabling them to acquire the industrial products they need as cheaply as possible and to exchange them advantageously for their agricultural products.

Of course, international trade only developed on account of the colonization of the Europeans in Africa, the East and West Indies as well as in North and South America. It should not be concealed that the transfer of the Negro slaves to America and the West Indies contributed significantly here.

Regarding the treatment of the Europeans with their colonies, List drew a differentiated picture. He criticized the English the least because they respected the existing customs, laws, religion, and cultural institutions of the indigenous population. The English were more lenient against traditional customs and superstition than the other colonial powers. Above all, they sought to win the trust of the natives and lead them to the better by example, self-interest and instruction. Under their rule, farming and the economic situation improved significantly.[3]

Contrarily, the Spaniards and Portuguese supported their monks and nuns in all lands, imposing their intolerance on the natives. Agriculture, trade and commerce would thrive there only meagerly under the rule of priests and despots. Elsewhere, List criticized that the Spaniards and Portuguese had extorted their then and former colonies in South America.

The French would have the will but not the patience and not the tact and perseverance, to civilize the native peoples. Their eagerness to bring home the riches they had acquired as quickly as possible rarely led them to take a lasting interest in settling in the colony. Only with the help of slaves did they succeed in cultivating new tracts of land. Under their rule the institutions of liberty, public improvements, and education made little progress.

The Dutch were monopolists. They lacked education, cosmopolitanism, liveliness and mobility. None of their colonies would last, perhaps not so "negative" as it was to be expected that the African colonies, like the United States would throw off the colonial yoke and gain their independence one day.

At present we are witnessing a new form of colonialism on the African continent, practiced by both the European Union and China. Due to the heavily subsidized agriculture sector in the EU, African products are hardly competitive, apart from tropical fruits. Foreign trade with Africa is mainly concentrated on arms supplies in exchange for raw materials. Of some 35,000 German companies only about 1,000 are currently involved in Africa. When considering investments many German companies complain about the lax handling of property rights, widespread corruption, rampant bureaucracy and inadequate security for people and property.

The People's Republic of China, on the other hand, is pursuing an aggressive strategy. It recognized Africa's importance for its resources and agricultural potential years ago and positioned itself very skillfully on the continent as a major power without a colonial past. China has clear priorities, especially that of ensuring the future food supply of its population, and to this end it is building the continent's infrastructure. Only recently has it become known that the Chinese are building a megacity of millions between Cairo and the Suez Canal, which does not even have a name yet. China wants to create a bridgehead to the African continent through this artificial metropolis. In addition, the Chinese government has announced that it will invest the gigantic sum of USD 60 billion in the infrastructure of East Africa.

Since the Chinese usually bring their own workers the Africans hardly profit from this local construction boom. Through so-called "land grabbing" large areas of agricultural land and virgin forests with clearing concessions as well as mining rights for mineral resources are often sold to international corporations under often dubious circumstances, from which the domestic economy hardly benefits. Russia is currently also making intensive efforts to secure further sources of raw materials in Africa.

19.3 The Diversity of Developing Countries

The term "Third World" was coined in 1952 by the French demographer Alfred Sauvy. Although he distanced himself from this phrase in 1989, it has nevertheless come to be used as a synonym for "developing countries". Originally, "Third World" was intended for the nonaligned states to differentiate themselves, as they did not belong to either of the two military power blocs of NATO or the Warsaw Pact. These countries wanted, as the economic theorist of the Prague Spring of 1968 Ota Sik expressed it in his book, "*The Third Way–Marxist-Leninist Theory and Modern Industrial Society*", to follow an independent path.

At the conference in Bandung, Indonesia, in 1955, 29 countries initially united together under the Third World term, all of them poor developing countries that were able to free themselves from the colonial yoke but suffered from extreme poverty and discrimination. In the mid-1960s, the number of countries that counted themselves as part of the Third World increased to 77, and today 130 countries feel that they belong to this grouping. It includes almost all the countries of the Southern Hemisphere, Latin America, Africa and Asia, with the exception of Japan and the southeastern + "Tiger States", as well as Australia and New Zealand.

Although all of these Third World countries have some kind of development deficits, they are characterized as heterogeneous and diverse due to their different geographical, climatic, political, cultural, ethnic, economic and social conditions. Since there are considerable differences in levels of development, growth potential, poverty and population size, to name but a few parameters, the term Third World is also used as an umbrella term for the emerging economies and the countries of the Fourth World.

Newly industrialized countries are those developing markets that have relatively high growth rates due to their level of industrialization and industrial capacity, wielding considerable global economic power and possessing vast territory, such as Brazil, China, India and Indonesia.

The number of emerging markets fluctuates between 10 and 55 because there are no universally valid and measurable criteria. One can only conclude that compared to developing countries, these countries have above average growth rates and much higher labor productivity with comparatively low wage levels. On the other side, these countries still have more or less major deficits compared with industrialized nations in terms of political stability, security, respect for civil rights and democracy, protection of property, legal certainty, corruption and quality of life.

In comparison, the countries of the Fourth World, the so-called Least Developed Countries (LDCs) and Less Developed Countries, are experiencing only low, often stagnant or even declining growth. Their social structure is characterized by mass poverty. These countries include above all the African countries in the Sahel zone. Although these countries are dominated by agriculture they are hardly able to provide sufficient food for their own population. The necessary food imports then lead to an increase in national debt. Since there are hardly any jobs in industry these developing countries have particularly high unemployment rates. Due to the lack of capital and the low export opportunities, these countries are more or less dependent on development aid. Additionally, there is high population growth, frequent civil wars, large-scale corruption and political repression. Other characteristic features are a low standard of living, poor hygiene and health care, high infant mortality, low life expectancy, a high illiteracy rate, low per capita income, extremely unequal income and wealth distribution, a low propensity to save and invest, unfavorable trade terms and trade balance, strong social disparities between urban and rural areas, inadequate infrastructure, severe environmental degradation and much more. All this is the breeding ground for the current wave of migration from Africa to Europe.

In view of the great and diverse differences that exist between and within the countries of the Third World, there can be neither a uniform development theory nor a uniform recipe for development policy. Friedrich List´s thesis is still valid today in that, contrary to the teachings of the economic classics, it is necessary and indispensable for each state to follow its own path in its development policy on the basis of its individual circumstances, possibilities and requirements. This is the strategic imperative of every responsible government.

The division of the world into countries according to different levels of development was already demonstrated by Friederich List, where he classified the nations of the earth into "5 Worlds"[4]:

1. Supremacy Nations: countries with the highest level of development, which secure their domestic and export markets with high quality and low priced products due to technological progress
2. Second-Tier Manufacturing Nations: countries that lag behind in industrialization but are strong enough to keep up with the Supremacy nations
3. Independent States: countries that restrict their foreign trade to raw materials and agricultural products
4. Colonies
5. Agrarian States: countries that are too weak to build up their own industry and therefore need protective tariffs and free market access to the Supremacy Nations.

19.4 Stage Theory

To explain the different stages of development of the various economies and to draw appropriate conclusions, Friedrich List used the term "economic stages" and divided countries into the following five states of development[5]:

1. The Hunter State (also referred to as the Wild State) which is characterized by hunter-gatherers living in caves or simple dwellings and roaming in tribes or extended families in forests and steppe similar landscapes, preying and feeding on game and berries
2. The Pastoral State where the inhabitants of a region move across the country as sedentary herdsmen or nonsedentary nomads with their herds or caravans
3. The Agrarian State where farmers are sedentary and manage their land holdings in village settlements/communities
4. The Agrarian-Manufacturing State in which the agricultural and forestry economy of the peasants is supplemented by craft and industrial production in commercial and manufacturing enterprises, whose workers are recruited from agriculture
5. The Agriculture-Manufacturing-Trading State, the highest level of development, in which the three economic sectors of agriculture, industry and commerce are harmoniously developed and, as we have learned from Fourastié, there is a shift in the structure of employment from the primary to the secondary and finally the tertiary sector.

The speed with which the individual countries pass through these stages varies greatly. Taking China as an example, we can see the rapid and breathtaking development that this country has undergone in the past 40 years from an Agrarian State to an Agriculture-Manufacturing-Trading state, while the countries of the Sahel have remained Agrarian States.

The Manufacturing State is quite different from the Agrarian State. Manufacturers, List explained, were the mothers and children of civil liberty, enlightenment, art and science, internal and external trade, navigation and transportation improvements, civilization and political power. They were the most important levers for freeing the Agrarian State from its shackles and transforming it into an advanced industrial state.

Even if this classification no longer corresponds to the current conditions in the age of globalization and at least the Quaternary sector is missing, Friedrich List's Stage Theory still seems very descriptive and useful for explaining the development gap between the northern and southern hemispheres. Basically, List complained that the free trade theorists had not recognized that economic policy must necessarily differ with regard to the respective economic stages and individual characteristics of the national economies. Thus, there were still considerably greater differences between the Agrarian State and the Agrarian-Manufacturing state than between the Pastoral State and the Agrarian State. In the pure Agrarian State there is arbitrariness and servitude, superstition and ignorance, lack of culture, means of traffic and transport, poverty and political impotence. In these states, only the smallest part of the mental and physical powers of the people slumbering in the nation and only the smallest part of the existing mineral resources and natural forces are used, and only little capital is formed.

List spoke of a crippled state of agriculture when the peasants share their land until the property of each family has become so small that it is sufficient only for the barest necessities of subsistence, and practically no surpluses are generated with which to purchase any agricultural tools and machinery, and virtually no other consumer or durable goods, whether manufactured at home or abroad. In such countries, the villagers would often sit idly around the town´s well or lime tree to keep "mother wit and inventiveness as well as lungs and tongue in exercise by all kinds of gossip", to counter boredom, as well as to debate about the village finances and the local administration. Occasionally, the existing differences of opinion may be out carried out with strong emotions and fisticuffs. If everyone had sufficient landed property at his disposal, there would be no reason for wasting money and time, no idleness and no reason for gossip, bickering and quarrelling, and, we add, no reason for migration.

19.5 Thoughts on Development Aid

With regard to the social grievances in the "dwarf economy"[6] List said that the wealthy and decently dressed city dweller considered "the poor clothing of the country people, their narrow and dirty dwelling and the eternal dish of potatoes without salt and meager milk to be quite adequate," although these people do the hardest work. The well-to-do console themselves with the fact that these people are not used to anything else and do not consider that these poor, too, would be very receptive to decent clothing, a decent home and better food. Similarly, he thought of children, the sick, and the aged, "of those huddled, gaunt, and lean figures, with rattling legs, sad and dull appearance, their sluggish gait, and the awkwardness of all their movements." However, so he added,

> do not pervert the meaning of our words. We are far from thinking that it is possible to bring about a state of things in which all those people who are now comprehended under the word peasants can eat and drink, dwell and clothe themselves, think and behave, as well as the well-to-do and educated in the country. Always and everywhere there is and will be a numerous class of people who will have to be content with basic food and scanty clothing. He who believes that this can be done differently is now a fool, and he who believes that it can still become different in the course of many centuries is a dreamer. The sensible politician confines his views to what is attainable now in the country and in the next century, and this he has in view and nothing else.

He believed that by means of agrarian reform the numerous, respectable and useful peasantry could and should be assimilated to the middle bourgeoisie in their pleasures as well as in their outward appearance, in their manners and in their intellectual education. He further believed that both the educated bourgeoisie, i.e. the nobility, and the ruling upper class would profit immeasurably from it, and that the reforms would not only take place at the expense of the social lower class, i.e., the peasants and workers, but would be of immense advantage to them.

Finally, List appealed to the conscience of the educated and wealthy classes. It would be irresponsible, after all, to delude oneself out of lazy habit, that such untenable social conditions are getting worse and worse, and therefore lapsing into inactivity and waiting to see how the problems develop. Such passivity would also not be compatible with List's motto, which he prefixed to his published works, "*National System*" and "*Natural System*", "Ét la patrie, et l'humanité!"

List considered it untenable for the upper and lower classes of a country to live side by side like two foreign nations or to be sharply divided, as the Brahmins and the Parians are in India. Sometimes it happens that clergymen but also merchants, civil servants and doctors marry a wealthy farmer's daughter and exchange the farmer's way of life for the city's. This seldom goes well, because the husband's relationship is acknowledged with nose-rubbing when such an educated man marries an ill-fitting farmer's daughter and is therefore looked at skeptically by his colleagues. The woman is then often treated like a leper even by her own caste and cut out by the educated class because of her lacking nobility status.

Very rarely would sons from the educated middle class work in the peasantry. Even in the case of mentally weak and indolent subjects, everything possible was done to place them in the civil service, however makeshift, or to try to employ them in retail trade or or similar. If a young man from the upper class nevertheless wanted to work in agriculture, he would at least have to study at university to escape the ignominy of being excluded from the caste. With biting irony, Friedrich List added that even those who planted cabbages, shook the plums from the tree, guided the hoe, or mucked out the stable would then have to have completed a course of study to be armed against disgrace and exclusion.

On the basis of the conditions in the German territorial states at the time, List also addressed the grievances and infirmities in agriculture and made appropriate proposals for improvement.

A generally valid conclusion for the countries of the Third World can be stated in List's own words, "should we not now, as an American cattle breeder says rather generally, but nevertheless very enrichingly, take the bull by the horns? Should we not tackle the evil that reaches its extreme with dwarfism, namely emigration, according to the principle: simili similibus curentur, in order to cure the disease from the bottom up while it is still curable, or at least to put a stop to its further prevalence?" This should be understood not only as a reminder but also as an indispensable challenge for those in power in developing countries and highly developed industrial nations. In view of the fact that we now live in the age of globalization, the wealthy upper class that List is addressing here is not only focused on the national sphere of power but also globally to understand that the rich countries must assist the poor, for example, in climate protection, in improving infrastructure or in health care.

Of course we do not find any concrete statements on development aid in List´s time, but we can take the following principles of development aid from his treatise on "*Die Ackerverfassung, die Zwergwirtschaft unf die Auswanderung*" (the farm constitution, the dwarf economy and emigration):

1. it is only successful if it is not siphoned off by those in power or fails because of bureaucracy
2. it only makes sense if it is understood and provided as support for self-help
3. it should focus exclusively on concrete development projects and be coordinated and monitored by investors (The Peoples Republic of China's "development aid" in Africa offers numerous examples of this)
4. it should always be holistic, combined and integrated with school education and technical training
5. it should set clear priorities as to which projects are to be implemented based on their urgency.

If the German government calls for an internationally financed Marshall Plan for Africa, it is to be feared that this will fail due to the national egoism of the individual donor countries. Perhaps it would make sense to select individual countries to work out and implement a country-specific Plan on their own and in close cooperation with the respective government. This could perhaps create a domino effect and spur other industrialized nations to make similar efforts.

According to OECD guidelines, the target for development aid by industrialized nations should be 0.7% of the Gross National Product, which has been the accepted number since 1970. To be sure, the 29 donor countries raised a record of approximately USD 143 billion in development aid in 2016. The USA ranked first, followed by Germany, the UK, Japan and France. However, it should be noted that most of the so-called ODA (Official Development Assistance) funds go to housing and caring for migrants in the donor countries. This is referred to as "phantom aid" or "inflated aid". If one considers that China has now announced development aid of USD 60 billion for Africa, a sum that exceeds those of every other donor country put together, then one understands what development offensive China is pursuing.

19.6 The Infant Industry Argument

(1) *Friedrich List, protectionism and Donald Trump–an untenable linkage*

During his election campaign and after taking office as President of the United States, Donald Trump used his slogan "America First" to scare and frighten European and Asian countries by professing protectionism and declaring it the central principle of his economic policy. He threatened to impose punitive tariffs on some 20,000 imported goods. This program was attributed to Trump's then-advisor Stephen Bannon, who was described as "Trump's dark whisperer" in the book by Tilman Jens. After Bannon was dismissed, Trump continued his protectionist course undeterred.

Whenever the word "protectionism" is tossed around in the discussion of economic policy, Friedrich List has to serve as the chief witness. Indeed, he is elevated to the status of the "father of protectionism". In surveys of economic experts, the word protectionism crops up repeatedly like an old castle ghost, and people associate it with the greatest danger for the global economy. For example, Thomas Fuster made the adventurous claim that Friedrich List was the chosen patron saint of the American president in a column in the NZZ of 2. February 2017 with the headline "*Trump's Patron Saint*". This fits with a remark by P. Sai-Wing Ho in an essay from 2005, in which he complains that there are still too few empirical studies on the overall problem of protectionism. Mainstream economists have taken few constructive steps in this direction. Instead, List and others more recently have been misused as straw men in regard to branding protectionism and attaching the label "protectionist" to List. Then, the same argument was always set in motion to criticize and denigrate it. In this respect, this debate would have to be refined considerably but unfortunately, this refinement was not expected to take place in the foreseeable future.[7]

As already quoted, List, in his memorandum to the Federal Assembly, expressed the opinion, "only then will the peoples of the earth attain the highest degree of physical prosperity if they establish general, free, unrestricted commercial integration among themselves." By this, he quite obviously meant not only the German territorial states but also all world trade. This did not, however, exclude the possibility that protective measures in the sense of the infant-industry argument might be advisable and necessary for the industrialization of backwards countries.

(2) *Some scientific findings*

In the academic discussion it is undisputed that the infant-industry argument goes back to the first American Secretary of the Treasury, Alexander Hamilton (1755–1805), as well as to Friedrich List. However, there is confusion and disagreement about its useful application and practical significance. Frank Weiler, who dealt with it in his 1996 dissertation, "*The 'Infant-Industry' Argument for Protectionist Measures–Theoretical Classification and Economic Policy Relevance*", concludes that "in addition to a large number of ambiguous cases, there are also a large number of cases in which infant-industry protection measures must be assessed as failures but also some cases in which they must be regarded as successes". The author does not base his summary on a "multitude" of cases, but limited to 10 international studies, so in this

Fig. 19.1 Protectionism versus free trade; i.e., poor versus rich

respect, it is doubtful whether his results are valid. At the end of his paper, Weiler irritates the reader with the remark that, "the infant-industry argument should thus by no means be understood as an argument for temporary protective tariffs." Makes one want to ask: For what else? Then, the author concludes, "against the background of this work, it appears rather as a plea for a change of perspective, through which social learning processes are moved into the center of economic theory and economic policy considerations". Here, too, one would ask, why "societal learning processes" and not "technical" and "economic" learning processes, as already implemented by List?[8]—Fig. 19.1.

Since this work unfortunately did not take us one step further, we refer to further studies on this topic, and first to an essay from 2005 by Mehdi Shafaeddin titled, "*Friedrich List and the Infant-Industry-Argument*". Shafaeddin is a graduate of Oxford University and was a lecturer at the University of Neuchâtel until 2011. In his paper he rightly points out that List is largely ignored in the professional community and, when mentioned, is often misunderstood and misinterpreted. He once again summarized the following points on which List's argumentation is based:

1. Customs policy is only an economic instrument for industrial take-off
2. Safeguard duties are an integral part of a dynamic economic policy with a singular application
3. The application of safeguard duties is considered to be a selective measure aimed at promoting certain industries
4. The infant-industry argument implies a dynamic and flexible perspective
5. Safeguard duties must not be too high to stifle foreign competition completely and not too low to avoid killing off domestic competition

6. Producers should be aware in advance of the dismantling of safeguard duties so that they can prepare for it in advance
7. Tariff rates cannot be determined theoretically, they depend on the specific circumstances and factors affecting them
8. Imported raw materials and semifinished products as well as agricultural products should be exempt from protective tariffs, as should luxury goods which can, however, be taxed at above average rates by means of appropriate financial tariffs
9. Safeguard duties should not favor monopolies as they should facilitate the establishment and promotion of domestic industries and support government export incentives, as has been done in India, for example, with 100% export-oriented companies
10. Protectionist measures that demand higher prices from consumers at the beginning are compensated by later economies of scale. These so-called learning costs are the price that has to be paid for the industrialization process.

For List, protective measures were not a panacea, as Dieter Senghaas rightly notes, "he considered particularly harmful the protectionist measures that owed their existence only to assertive lobbyist interests, but did not follow a coherent development strategy. In the critical early phase of catch-up (take-off) development, it was necessary to find the industry- and sector-specific dosage of openness to the outside world and (the accompanying) protective measures. List was thus an advocate for a qualified mixed strategy of selective world market integration and selective decoupling, with a view to avoiding overtaxation as well as undertaxation, and he saw the mixing ratio as dependent on the self-assertion and competitiveness of the productive forces already mobilized in each case. Finding the right path was the task of higher-level state policy. The decisive development policy concept consisted of neither overtaxing nor undertaxing one's own economy."[9]

> Of course, it is easier to formulate such a motto than to put it into practice. The aim of the promotion and accompanying protection measures was the formation of a broadly effective, well-proportioned structure of agriculture, industry and services,[10]

As commented in the bestseller book published in 2003 by Ha-Joon Chang, "*Kicking away the Ladder–Development Strategy in Historian Perspective*". Since 1990, Chang has been Professor of Political Economy at Cambridge University. His numerous works have been translated into 12 languages. He has made a name for himself as an advisor to governments, NGOs, international organizations and corporations. Chang was awarded the Myrdal Prize in 2003 and, together with Richard Nelson, the Leontief Prize in 2005.

Already in the title of his book, the author uses a vivid image to infer that in general it is shrewd, regardless of whether from a personal or organizational perspective, that when someone has reached the summit of his development, he no longer needs the ladder on which he has worked his way up and can thus tip the ladder away. Therein lay the secret of the cosmopolitan doctrine of Adam Smith and that of his greatest contemporary, William Pitt, and of all his successors in the British government. Any nation that had reached the pinnacle as an industrial and maritime power by means of protectionist measures could do nothing more clever than kick the ladder away and preach free trade. Here the ladder symbolism is based on a translation inaccuracy as the original uses the symbol of crutches. From my perspective the difference is not trivial in that crutches are more appropriate here because it is more accurate in describing the situation in developing countries than the concept of the ladder.

Some authors argue that the World Trade Organization (WTO) does not allow trade policy in the sense of the infant-industry argument. Shaffaedin contradicted this with the remark that under the rules of the WTO, a selective application of this principle is very much permissible and would contribute to a fairer trading system. Even in the U.S., he said, this is often done. In 1997 for instance, 58,000 companies alone received subsidies from the government. Nobel Laureate Joseph Stiglitz commented, "do as we say, not as we do!" Sai-Wing Ho, Professor of Economics at the University of Denver, in "*Distortions in the Trade Policy for Development Debate: A Reexamination of Friedrich List*", remarked between 1950 and 1970, "it took a lot of time and huge efforts by developed countries to win developing countries over to free trade". However, this has been cleverly circumvented by East Asian developing countries to climb higher on the development ladder. Against this background, one should not overlook the national interests that lie behind the current liberalization pressure.

In the cited essay by Sai-Wing Ho, the author attests that List's visions are much broader than the orthodox reduction which "protectionists" express.

In 1992, Jürgen Backhaus, then a full professor at Maastricht University, published the article, "*Friedrich List and the Political Economy of Protective Tariffs*". In contrast to the two aforementioned authors, Backhaus states that there are only a few economists who have received as much attention in the secondary literature as List, his name appearing regularly in textbooks.

Unfortunately, this observation must be contradicted. Regardless of whether one picks up the specialist literature, whether in German or English, on economic and development policy, on economic theory and globalization, on economics and political economy, on the social market economy and economic ethics, or even on the economic history, one will generally search in vain for Friedrich List's name, and if he is mentioned, then at most as a marginal note or in a footnote.

However, Shafaeddin and Ho must agree that List's views, if they are mentioned at all, are usually presented in an abbreviated, one-sided, and erroneous manner. Even Backhaus is not exempt from this when he claims that List's contribution is not a theory in the classical sense. Anyone who reads List's work with a critical eye would be irritated, since in contrast to List's work, the real innovative content of countless other works on economic theory often seems very thin.

Among the few German scholars who have dealt with Friedrich List is Dieter Senghaas, who has repeatedly referred to him in his work. In a recent contribution he dealt with "*Weltordnungspolitik und Weltrecht in einer zerklüfteten Welt*" (Global political order and legal constitution in a complex world), stating, "the macrostructure of the world is characterized by an extreme hierarchization. There is a gap between a center of gravity, characterized by dense symmetrical interconnectedness and the rest of the world. This center of gravity, the OECD world, which accounts for 15%

of the world's population and 75% of the world's Gross National Product, now sets the tone in every respect. On the other hand, the orientation of the rest of the world, and thus of the majority of the world's population, towards this center of gravity is characterized by asymmetrical interdependence with the consequence of structural dependence."

Friedrich List already had a premonition that such centers of gravity would emerge. As already mentioned in the context of his "*Politics of the Future*", he predicted that in the second half of the 20th century, as far as he could see with his feeble eyes, there would be only two giant powers and three or four independent countries–in other words, a "pentarchy" If we add the EU, Russia, Japan and India to the USA and China, we find that this vision has been fully confirmed.

In another essay, Dieter Senghaas points out, "the development successes of the emerging economies of East Asia were not based on free trade pure and simple, but on a development scenario à la Friedrich List: selective integration in the world economy. Selective decoupling for a time in order to develop one's domestic market broadly, and in the long run, a free-trade order."

In his book, "*Geo-Imperialism–The Destruction of the World*", Wolfgang Effenberger mentions the transatlantic free trade agreement TTIP, which, as is well known, was called off by Donald Trump. On this Effenberger says that the Europeans concerns at the time, "about the lack of transparency and undemocratic arbitration procedures seem to have been well-founded. However, the insight of economic theorist Friedrich List may weigh even more heavily. As early as the 19th century, he proved that free trade between different economies at different levels of development does not lead to possible convergence. In contrast, it further consolidates the different levels, leading to increased dependency and a drain of resources in favor of richer nations. That is where the USA's dogged fight over TTIP makes sense! "[11]

19.7 The Improvement of Infrastructure–A Key Role of Development Policy

(1) *The blessing of the new means of transport and communication*

Although the term "infrastructure" did not even exist in Friedrich List's time, he recognized its fundamental importance for the advancement of a developing country. In a seminal contribution to the "*Staatslexikon*" of 1837 on "Railways and Canals, Steam Boats and Steam Car Transport", he set out his basic ideas regarding transport infrastructure. He prefaced the essay with the following timelessly valid insight, "the efficient, rapid, safe, and regular transportation of persons and goods is one of the most powerful levers of national prosperity and civilization in all of its ramifications."[12] Shortly thereafter, he summed up this insight in the second Paris Prize competition pamphlet, "Le monde marche–the world is moving."

The necessity of building railroads, steamboats, canals, and the consequent blessing to nations by the increase of intellectual and material powers, was so obvious that even those who were skeptical of technical progress should be enthusiastic here.

Steam navigation has already produced immeasurable benefits. Journeys from one European country to another have ceased to be risky and costly, the movement of people, letters and goods is much faster and safer. Hundreds of thousands of Englishmen travel annually to the continent to make friends with the French and Germans, Europeans flock to the island to marvel at the wonders of industrialization, and whole caravans of Scandinavians visit the German territorial states. In other words, the people get to know each other and are spurred on by the frequent visits. With the aid of steam navigation, trade with East Asia and North Africa becomes possible with regular business connections. Without this, France could never have thought of founding a colony in Algeria. Regardless of the fate of this enterprise, it is certain that through steam locomotion, even though it is still in its infancy, all countries with ocean access will experience a tremendous upswing.

New inventions were made daily by which the output of machinery would be increased, the cost of fuel would be decreased, the safety of travelers would be increased, and the use of steam power to overseas destinations would be made possible. In this, as in other fields, the Americans were leading by shining example, and especially if the latest news were to be true, in which "an invention concerning the application of electromagnetic force" is reported, that is, a foreshadowing of the development of the electric motor.

What steam power was to sea and river navigation, the railway meant to land transport, a "Hercules in the cradle", which would deliver the nations from the plague of war (!), of dearness and famine, of national hatred (!) and unemployment, of ignorance (!), and the slovenliness that will fertilize their farmlands, enliven their workshops and mines. It would give strength even to the poorest in society to educate themselves by visiting foreign lands, to allow all to seek work in distant places and to restore their health at distant natural springs and seashores. For, List stated, it was far too narrow a view to expect railroads merely to reduce the cost of transportation for the manufacture and distribution of goods. In reality he said, the railroads will bestow many more human than material blessings, that is, it will be of more use by men than by things, for the formation of productive forces than for the trade in goods (i.e., the creation of value), and, last but not least, will be of more use for the education, welfare, and satisfaction of desires of the working classes than just for mere consumption Fig. 19.2.

Imagine that all the countries and cities of Europe were connected by steamship and/or railroad, which immeasurable advantages would result. The doctor, the lawyer, the scholar, and the artist could now extend his sphere of activity to distant cities and countries. A great actor would be able to perform today in one city, tomorrow in another, and the day after tomorrow somewhere else. An entrepreneur who learns of an invention that interests him will be able to travel there to obtain more detailed information. The merchant and manufacturer would expand his business circle and clientele, enrich his knowledge, establish joint enterprises, cooperate with people in distant places, settle differences of opinion and find employees.

Fig. 19.2 Old school wall map illustrating the possibilities of travelling by rail; collection E. Wendler

The railway was even more important for the education of all classes. Even the less well-off student would be able to visit famous universities at home and abroad and to become acquainted with foreign countries directly. There would be a large number of annual congresses for lawyers, historians, national economists, theologians and linguists, educators, fine artists and musicians, technicians and engineers, chemists and physicists, miners and ironworkers, farmers and foresters, sheep and silkworm breeders, etc. Viewed from this angle, he said, the railways were the greatest invention in the old and new ages, "they are real machines of popular welfare and education."

Nothing is more detrimental to the development of man than clinging to the soil and simple agriculture, where neither the spirit nor the productivity of physical work is improved and determines to a large extent the low education level of the population. From the example of the Asiatic and African peoples, he said, one can see where it leads to when people work for centuries in the same activity, methods of work and tools, the same prejudices and limited views, the same carelessness and unmotivated way of doing business. Most owners give the laborers little pay, so that this is only sufficient for a meager diet, and frequent unemployment is the result. This, List concluded was undoubtedly due to a great variety of causes, but did not go into these further as this would lead too far away from his subject. In summary, he simply stated that the decisive impetus for the development of these peoples could only be promoted by exemplary examples and their imitation, especially by better working techniques and tools.

However, he did not limit the infrastructure topic to its theoretical implications, as during his stay in the USA and after his return to Germany, he himself became a railway pioneer.

(2) *The construction of the Little Schuylkill railroad in Pennsylvania*

In an anthology by Lance E. Metz from 1990 entitled "*Canal history and technology proceedings*", an essay by Spiro G. Patton on the subject "*Frederick List's Contribution of the Anthracite Railroad Connection in the United States*"[13] is included. At the time Patton was a professor at Widener University, a private university in Chester, Pennsylvania. In the article, the author recalls that Friedrich List's ideas were highly respected in the industrial circles of the United States in the first half of the 19th century and that his services for the transportation of anthracite coal were particularly appreciated.

In the USA, coal became known as an energy source approximately 1750, when bitumen, so-called soft coal, was discovered and mined in Virginia. In the last decade of the 18th century, hard coal or anthracite was discovered in Wyoming, Schuylkill and in the Lehigh Valleys in northeastern Pennsylvania. These deposits could not be mined, however, because they were too distant from usable waterways. During the British blockade of 1812, when the sea route for transporting Virginia coal to major North American ports on the Atlantic was cut off, in parallel American manufacturers were experimenting with coal as a source of energy, resulting in a growing interest in anthracite coal.

By 1820, three companies were engaged in coal mining in the northeastern Pennsylvania valleys, the Lehigh Coal and Navigation, the Delaware and Hudson, and the Little-Schuylkill Navigation Company. While the first two focused only on the exploitation of deposits, the third also aimed to transport coal by canal. A canal was to be built between Port Richmond in Philadelphia County and Port Carbon in Schuylkill County. The small town of Reading, Pennsylvania was intended as the central location. When Friedrich List moved to Reading in 1827, the canal had just been completed.

With the opening of the canal, the search for other mining deposits of anthracite coal in the mountains and valleys of southern Schuylkill County began to intensify. After arriving in Reading, List observed the coal fever with great interest and noticed that the seams extended in a northwesterly direction parallel to the course of the mountains. Therefore, he decided to turn his focus to the valley of the Little Schuylkill. In the immediate vicinity of the Indian settlement Tamaqua, he found what he was seeking. He recorded the discovery in his diary, "I got off my horse to look more closely. Suddenly I caught sight of shimmering black rock. I examined it and realized it was coal, wonderful anthracite coal. I dug deeper and more and more coal appeared. Then, I covered the dug-up place and rode toward the hill that lay before me. I dug again. Again new coal showed itself. I was sure that I had discovered a coal deposit. Carefully I covered all traces of my search!"

With the cooperation of Dr. Isac Hiester, the nephew of the Governor of Pennsylvania, who also lived in Reading, List was able to acquire large tracts of land in the immediate vicinity of the discovery site. After a canal construction initially planned by the Little Schuylkill Navigation Company fell through, List sensed his chance to transport the coal with the help of a railroad. After approval by the Pennsylvania Legislature, the Little Schuylkill Navigation, Railroad and Coal Company was incorporated on 23. April 1829. Because of the special location, Hiester and List planned to establish a settlement at Tamaqua to provide housing for railroad workers. After lengthy efforts, they were able to procure the necessary capital from the Thomas Biddle bank in Philadelphia.[14]

After the financing was finally secured, List and Hiester found a capable engineer in Moncure Robinson, who was only 27 years old. The groundbreaking was on 1. June 1830 and construction of the railroad line was done very quickly. The 22-mile (35 km) long railroad line was completed on 18. November 1831, which is an incredible feat considering that the raging Little Schuylkill riverbed had to be crossed 17 times. Initially, the coal cars, commissioned from Richard Imlay in Baltimore, Maryland, were pulled by mules and horses. At Port Clinton, the coal was then transferred to boats and transported to Philadelphia.

According to S. G. Patton, it was only the third most fully completed and operational railroad in the United States. List's efforts would have inspired many other companies in the Schuylkill region to build railroads. Then, beginning in 1850, anthracite coal became a major export of the United States.

To significantly increase transport capacity, the "Comet" and "Catawissa" locomotives were ordered by List from Edward Bury in Liverpool. They had the type designation 0 -1- 0, weighed just under 8 tons, and cost $5000 each. These arrived in Philadelphia early in 1833. They were then disassembled into parts and towed by sled on the frozen Schuylkill Canal to the operational site at Port Clinton; Fig. 19.3.

Fig. 19.3 The "Catawissa" of 1832–the first locomotive ordered by Friedrich List in England for the Little Schuylkill Railway; Smithonian Museum Collection

The test run of the "Catawissa" took place on 27. February 1833, and was the first steam-powered locomotive operating in Pennsylvania. During the second test run on 8. March 1833, an accident occurred because the locomotive derailed and the 13 coal cars were more or less damaged. With the help of horses, it was possible to salvage the locomotive. It was transported to Tamaqua with the demolished cars and repaired there.

The "Comet" was inaugurated with a trial run beginning on 11. March 1833. From mid-April 1833, both trains ran regularly between Tamaqua and Port Clinton. The 16 coal cars were loaded with approximately 3 tons of anthracite coal each and ran twice a day between the two end points so that in total about 200 tons of coal could be shipped daily.

Since the rails initially consisted of wooden ties (sleepers) shod with sheet iron, which was of course completely inadequate, they soon had to be replaced by iron rails. Two years after its commissioning, another accident occurred, this time with the "Comet" because it derailed again and fell into the river. Whether it was then still usable seems uncertain.

The "Catawissa", on the other hand, served well for many years. When the Little Schuylkill Railroad was taken over by the Pennsylvania Railroad Company in 1863, the locomotive was still part of the inventory; it was not taken out of service until 1870, when it was sold for the scrap value of $4,000.

Spiro G. Patton acknowledged List's contributions to the construction of the Little-Schuylkill Railroad by noting that List recognized coal as a source of energy and railroads as a means of transportation and linked the two for the development of a national economy. In concluding his essay, Patton lamented that the younger generation of American national economists were unfamiliar with List's "*National System*", and Patton hoped his essay would go some way toward changing that.

(3) *The importance of telegraphy*

In the transmission of messages by means of telegraphy, a distinction is made between optical, cable and wireless telegraphy. The age of optical telegraphy extended from the 17th to the middle of the 19th century. The signal telegraph developed by the French inventor Claude Chappes was very successful, and there were over 500 stations of this technology in France. This enabled short messages to be transmitted via visual contact. It is possible that Friedrich List had only seen such signal telegraphs and had only heard about wired telegraphy from hearsay, but this was enough for him to recognize the outstanding importance of this new means of communication.

Wired telegraphy, also known as electrical telegraphy, was developed experimentally by various pioneers in the course of the 19th century. The first to be mentioned here was the Barcelona-born physician, meteorologist and physicist Francesco Salvá i Campillo, who believed as early as 1795 that it would one day be possible to transmit messages wirelessly using electric telegraphs.

In the case of the wired apparatus, the anatomist Samuel Thomas v. Soemmering should also be mentioned, as he constructed the first electric telegraph in Munich in 1809. In 1832/3, Wilhelm Weber and Carl Friedrich Gauss carried out the first experiments with an electromagnetic telegraph. At the same time, Paul Schilling v. Canstadt developed a needle telegraph in St. Petersburg, which the Englishman William Fothergill Cooke saw in Heidelberg in 1836. Cooke subsequently constructed the first operationally reliable telegraph cable for a railway line in England in 1837. From then on railway companies were the technical pioneers of telegraphy. Carl August v. Steinheil constructed the first printing telegraph in 1836 and built a 5 km long working cable connection in Munich in 1837.

The real breakthrough of telegraphy came in 1837 when Samuel Morse constructed the first, and in 1844 the improved writing telegraph, which was used to build the continental telegraph network beginning in 1850. The laying of the first overseas cable began in 1850, but it was not until 1866, after several costly failures, that the first permanent telegraph link between Ireland and the United States was put into operation.

Well before, List had already commented on telegraphy in his second Paris Prize competition pamphlet of 1837,[15] "Telegraphy, which today already performs great services in the administration of the State (meaning France), could be of immense benefit if it were used for the purposes of science, technology, industry, and for the establishment and maintenance of friendly relations. However, it would also have to be recognized that it could be abused in serious ways. Without speaking of assassinations of individuals or governments, telegraphy could be used in commerce by those who owed its benefits to their good fortune, a privilege, or any other privilege to obtain illicit advantages. Nevertheless, he said, the possibility of abuse did not justify a total prohibition, considering that the advantages accruing to the public and private good from the new means of communication would far outweigh the possible disadvantages, especially if the abuse could be largely avoided by adequate measures by the state. To this end, List proposed the following safeguards:

1. telegraphic communications should be placed under strict police supervision
2. communication must not be in encrypted form
3. general news of interest to trade and industry as a whole should be published immediately
4. less important messages should not be transmitted, especially those whose accuracy has not been verified or at least cannot be easily verified, because such messages blur the lines between admissible and inadmissible communication.

We have comparable challenges today with electronic data transmission, data protection and cybercrime.

Telegraphy is one of the most important inventions of the human mind. It shows how nature is endeavoring to unite or bring all mankind closer together and to what point it is possible for man to overcome the obstacles that distance presents to man's natural needs. A telegraph network spread over the whole globe, Friedrich List was convinced, would enable nations and governments to communicate with each other and transact their business as if they were only a few miles apart. In his 1846 Alliance pamphlet, List wrote, "just think what a tremendous advantage would accrue to England from the laying of an electric telegraph line, by means of which the East Indies could be governed from Downing Street with as much ease as Jersey and Guernsey are now governed," the two British islands in the English Channel.[16]

In the Miscellaneous section of the *Zollvereinsblatt* (ZVB, the customs union newsletter), there are three short reports in which List writes on the latest information on telegraphy:

- The ZVB of 1843 states, "the electric telegraph, called Wheatstone's Messenger, will carry a message from Bristol to Birmingham, on which route it is laid out, in 1/1400 of a second. By this scale, a message would take 1/6 of a second to circle the globe. It is already in operation on several English railways."[17]
- The ZVB of 1846 reported, "the Chester-Holeyhand Railway Company, in conjunction with the government, are erecting an electric telegraph to London and Holeyhand at a distance of 200–300 English miles, by which the principal places of the country, Liverpool, Manchester, and Birmingham, can enter into the fastest communication with London. In their exchanges among themselves, they may communicate with each other in less than a minute, and all questions from one place may receive their answer from others almost without delay. These same results of the telegraphic experiments made on the southwest railway between London and Portsmouth, and on other railways, and indeed on the whole for a distance of 200 English miles, are made in different parts of England. This prompted a new grand plan, the adoption of which should transform the whole correspondence system of the country, and become extremely important to commerce, as well as to government, on account of the lightning rapidity with which dispatches could be conveyed."[18]
- Another ZVB briefing from 1846 reads, "the electric telegraph is doing wonders in America. In another year, the United States will be connected by a complete telegraph system, and the President in the White House in Washington will communicate with several states with the same ease and rapidity as the Lord-Mayor of London with his district superintendents. An American newspaper made the curious remark that a telegraph, were it to exist from the Columbia River (on the west coast) to Washington (D.C., on the east coast), would win the race of the sun by a full five hours. In the reverse case, a message sent from Washington to the Columbia River at 12 o'clock would arrive there at 7 o'clock in the morning of the same day, that is, in a sense, 5 hours earlier than it went out. There is no telling what immeasurable benefits such a lightning-fast means of communication can bring to so vast a system of countries."[19]

These visionary assessments are involuntarily reminiscent of our current global revolution through modern means of communication. What was once telegraphy is now the Internet, the laptop, the i-Phone, teleconferencing and skyping. These technologies are as indispensable for today's globalization as telegraphy was in the 19th and 20th centuries for the "world traffic" and "world trade" of that time.

19.8 The Place of Education in Development Policy

(1) *The intellectual capital (capital of mind)–"The nation's treasure chest".*

For Friedrich List, human capital had the highest priority in the economic development of a country. In the "*National System*", he stated, "the present condition of nations was the result of the accumulation of all the discoveries, inventions, improvements, perfections, and exertions of all the generations that had lived before. They constituted the intellectual capital of living humanity, and each individual nation was productive only in thus far as it had learned to assimilate these achievements of earlier generations and to increase them by its own efforts, in thus far as the natural forces of its territory, its extent and geographical position, its population and political power enabled it to develop all branches of production within its borders as perfectly and equally as possible and to extend its moral, intellectual, industrial, commercial and political influence to other less developed nations and, in general, to cooperate with the whole world.[20]

The more man realizes that he must make provisions for the future, the more his insight and feelings motivate him to secure his future and that of his relatives and to promote their welfare, the more he is accustomed from his youth to reflection and activity, the more his social feelings are cultivated and his body and mind are educated, the more beautiful examples are set before him from his youth, the more he is given the opportunity, the less he is restrained in his efforts, the greater the fruits of his labors remain with him, the more he is able to obtain recognition and respect through governmental order, the less his mind suffers from prejudice, superstition, false opinions, and ignorance, the more he will use his head and limbs to improve his efficiency, and the better he will economize the fruits of his labor.

In all these relations, however, most would depend on the particular condition of the society in which the individual is involved, viz. on whether science and art flourish, state institutions and legislation, religion and morals, intelligence and security of person and property, liberty and law contribute, whether in the nation all the factors of material prosperity, agriculture, industry and commerce, are evenly and harmoniously developed, whether the power of the nation is great enough to secure to individuals progress in prosperity and education from generation to generation, and to enable them not only to use their own powers in all their variety but also to make use of powers of other countries through foreign trade.[21]

In his "*Outlines of American Political Economy*", List already illustrated these theses with the concrete example, postulating that the productive power of a nation is determined mainly by the intellectual abilities and social circumstances of the people, i.e., by what he called intellectual capital (capital of mind). Assuming that ten wool weavers in a country each possess \$1000 of capital; they spin the wool with a spinning wheel, possess very primitive tools and have not mastered the art of dyeing. Each of them manufactures for himself, would have to do all the work himself, and therefore produce no more cloth than for \$1000.00 a year. Now suppose the ten weavers pool their capital and labor, invent a spinning machine and a better loom, are instructed in the art of dyeing, divide the work among themselves, and in this way are able to produce and sell fine cloth worth $10,000 a month. With the same capital to the total value of $10,000, fine cloth with the value of $100,000 would now be produced as a result of improved social and intellectual circumstances, or in other words, as a result of acquired intellectual capital. In the same way, a whole nation, by improving its social and intellectual conditions, could increase its productivity many times over a small amount of financial capital.[22]

This does not mean, however, that the more a country has lawyers, doctors, preachers, judges, politicians, civil servants, writers, teachers, musicians and actors, the greater its productive power. As a negative example List cited Spain, where officials, judges, and lawyers oppress the population, where the priesthood consumes the produce of the land and cultivates the vicious stupidity of the people, where teachers are demotivated and teach young people, at most, elementary skills that do not enable them to become useful members of society. Musicians and actors present there only served to make the idlers inactivity even more pleasant. Even science, he said, was pernicious there because it served not to improve the condition of the people but to make it worse. In this way, intellectual capital, the precious commodity for the people and the government, becomes poison. In the USA, it is quite different, whereby the intellectual professions contribute to the considerable increase of the productive forces, because intellectual capital has helped the United States to enormous power and strength.[23]

In 2001, Arno Mong Daastol, a Norwegian scholar, was awarded a doctorate from the University of Erfurt with a thesis on "*Friedrich List's Heart, Wit and Will–Mental Capital as the Productive Force of Progress*". However, this thesis is very broad and so overloaded with excessive, often very long original quotations, that it misses the point and is also not as light-hearted as the title promises.

In an essay in the Pakistan Development Review entitled, "A Review of Contributions of Friedrich List Commemorating his 225-Year Anniversary", A. M. Daastol summarized his findings, "with his demands for freedom, tolerance, and other immaterial aspects of political economy, List clearly distinguished himself from Western materialism of Smith's type. The mainstream economists of the time, such as Karl Marx, had ignored the creative and cooperative powers of the human mind, and since List had not followed the faith in Galilean-Newtonian physics, he had been dismissed by his opponents as unscientific and unserious." The criticism of this quotation is that List in no way rejected Galilean-Newtonian physics, this thesis was simply false.

Currently, the research findings are different. Among current mainstream economists, terms such as innovation, know-how, learning, communication, human resource management, etc., are to be found in textbooks, albeit not with the same structural coherence and logic as in List´s work. In this respect, his thought system has its unmistakable roots in the philosophy of German idealism or in the so-called German Renaissance. In this context, Daastol criticized Adam Smith for having misjudged the immaterial power of capital and referred, among others, to Chris P. Dialynas, Portfolio Manager of an investment committee of the Pacific Investment Management Co. (PIMCO), who said of Friedrich List, "List's ideas are of great importance today. The global imbalances and wealth transfers that concerned List are most prevalent today."[24]

(2) *The importance of general education and vocational training as a productive force*

In the second Paris Prize competition pamphlet, Friedrich List pointed out in a few sentences the importance of education for individual and national prosperity. He predicted that the new means of communication and transportation would help to make men more perfect, more powerful, and happier. Much of the mental education and the means of instruction, formerly reserved for a small number of people, could now be enjoyed by the whole population.

It is the same with education as with social work. It is necessary to find a certain number of capable people who feel called to take on the difficult business of education. To this end, we need state institutes in which teachers receive solid training before they are entrusted to take part in the great work of general education and vocational training. Vocational education should take place primarily in specialized schools, e.g., polytechnic, agricultural, and veterinary schools, in the form of boarding schools to be able to receive gifted pupils from a large geographic region.[25]

Young people are educated not only through written instruction but also, above all, through oral instruction in personal exchanges with those who are their role models and who impart the relevant knowledge to them on the basis of experience and a better understanding of practice. The knowledge can be learned from books, but the ability can only be learned through practical experience. The talented person benefits more from handling and observing things than from studying books.[26]

From his short teaching career at the Lehrverein in Aarau, Switzerland, we can see how List envisioned the further education and training of the rural population in particular. In this further and continuing education institute in Aarau, a two-part school system was envisaged. On the one hand, the capable preparation of students for university and, on the other hand, the further and continuing education of capable men for industry and well-educated citizens in general. The intended teaching canon of the first group included philosophy, physics, chemistry, logic and mathematics, Greek and Latin, German, French, Italian and English literature as well as political science, state economy and natural law. List justified the necessity of such an educational institution based on his personal experiences at the University of Tübingen, "whoever knows how loosely the study of any science proceeds that does not build on a sound preliminary education, whoever knows the dangers to which students of immature age are exposed at universities, whoever has seen for himself that often the first years of university are frittered away and then in the last period of their academic studies an emptiness is felt that follows them throughout their later professional life, will appreciate the value of such an institution of further and continuing education as is planned here."

The other branch of this educational institution was reserved for the polytechnic education of young boys, who were to be trained as qualified merchants, educated manufacturers, capable farmers and tradesmen, and capable administrators of the commonwealth/government. Their canon of instruction was to consist of philosophy, history, logic, mathematics, political science and state economy, commercial science and commercial law, commercial history and industrial chemistry, agricultural chemistry, botany, accounting, technology and commodity science. In addition, great emphasis should be placed on learning the French language. Furthermore, artistic subjects such as drawing, painting, dancing, horse riding, music and gymnastics as well as religion should be offered.

List also propagated this model during his exile in the United States, which William Notz acknowledged, "it is therefore to be regarded as another of List's merits that he was one of the first to point out to leading circles in America the economic importance of a technical educational system and to make practical suggestions for its development. List's name, therefore, may justly be mentioned in this respect with that of Benjamin Franklin."

In his educational concept for the Lehrverein in Aarau, List had in mind the "École centrale des Trauveaux" in Paris, i.e., the first polytechnic institution in the world, which was founded in 1794, as well as the polytechnic institute in Vienna, which was established in 1814.

At the same time List developed the basic idea of the later known adult education centers and evening academies, even the universities of applied sciences. Compared to the university, he was less concerned with the theoretical instruction of the students, but above all with their practical or, as we would say today, application-oriented education. This concept was to be offered mainly during the quieter winter months to give young men the opportunity to further their education in general education and vocational training. It was also important to him that the pupils should be taught not only by a teacher with a certain general education but also by various specialist teachers who had acquired their specialist knowledge at "Real- und Gelehrtenschulen". These schools would also have the advantage of saving the parents money because the school fees would be incomparably less expensive than at a university and the subsequent studies would be shortened by building up on the previous education, quite apart from the fact that such educational institutions are much better and quicker to reach due to the geographical proximity to the pupils.[27]

In many countries of the Third World, there are still considerable deficiencies in the field of education. There is a lack of qualified teachers, of textbooks and other indispensable teaching aids, of technical equipment, of schoolrooms, to name but a few weak points. There is also the insight that due to the existential and financial constraints of parents, they are not able to have their school aged children receive an adequate formal education. Regrettably, an enormous potential for development is lost. After schooling, widespread unemployment leads to idleness and a lack of prospects for the able-bodied middle generation. The associated social misery then forms the breeding ground for migration and the main reason for the current wave of refugees.

In general, it can be stated that the education system in the countries of the Third World should be oriented much more towards dual training than is the case today. While there is usually no shortage of academicians, the industrial middle class is generally underrepresented.

(3) *The school of reciprocal teaching*

In an essay for the "*National-Magazin*" of 1834 Friedrich List recommended the "school of reciprocal instruction", developed and practiced by the English pedagogues Andrew Bell and Joseph Lancaster, as a teaching method for the education system in Third World countries as just described.[28]

In this method, a qualified teacher teaches a certain number of gifted pupils the subject matter, be it intellectual or practical. When a certain level of knowledge or production is reached by the pupils, they leave and pass on their knowledge to another group of pupils. These teaching students are called monitors. The group of to whom the monitors teach their knowledge should be limited to approximately 8 to 10 students. From their circle, one could then again select the most capable and qualify them again as monitors and entrust them with passing on what they have learned.

While the monitors do their work, those who become free after completing their respective tasks should be further educated by the original teachers and trained with new knowledge and skills. Through this system, as with a snowball system, it is possible to spread intellectual knowledge and practical skills relatively quickly and thus increase the educational level of the lower class. However, this method of teaching is only applicable where the content to be taught is of a mechanical nature or can at least be taught mechanically. In such schools, for example, teaching is limited to reading, writing, arithmetic and religion and now and then also to geography, linguistics, linear drawing or sewing. In the case of some subjects, two-way teaching is limited to the memorization of facts. Therefore, this method is only suitable for teaching elementary knowledge.

Even if one should not find this method very appropriate, it is, as List pointed out, quite useful for millions of people because with this approach a single teacher can teach 6 to 800, even up to 1000 children, and thus contribute in a quick and inexpensive way to raising the educational level of broad classes of the population.

(4) *What proposal would List have to offer to stem the tide of migration from Africa?*

As early as 1835, he criticized the failed colonial policies of England, France, Spain and Portugal on the African continent. He accused the European colonial powers of serious failures because they destroyed the traditional tribal cultures and ruthlessly exploited their colonies. In addition, he said, the African potentates and tribal chiefs were unable to establish economically aspiring democratic states mainly because of ruthless corruption. From this, he feared that if it is not possible to absorb Africa's rapidly growing population through appropriate economic growth, serious social conflicts including migration will be the result.

In this regard, reference may be made to a draft letter of 1826, which he addressed to De Witt Clinton, then Governor of the State of New York, during the early period of his American exile, to call his attention to the problem of youth unemployment and to suggest "how the great mass of a whole nation may be provided with the highest possible degree of education."[29]

Since, when the general population is very poor, only the well-to-do can provide their children with a comprehensive education, both the practical and the intellectual education of the broad mass of young people lie fallow, so that the population becomes increasingly impoverished and the national economies suffer immeasurable damage through the loss of their productive forces. For this reason, the education of youth and men capable of working productively plays a key role in the development of a national economy. To this end, he recommended the establishment of educational institutions that, as we would say today, function according to the dual principle.

In such institutions, one to two thousand pupils between the ages of 13 and 16 were to be admitted with the same educational goal (for example, through an entrance examination). These should then be taught until the age of 21, as well as learning a practical profession. To save school fees, it would be desirable if these boarding school-like institutions were as self-sufficient as possible through an attached farm.

The daily teaching time should be 5 hours in the morning, and the subsequent practical training should be 7 hours in the afternoon. Currently, of course, the total daily time would have to be reduced to 8-9 hours.

With reference to the conditions in Africa today, one could indeed imagine such educational institutions being founded, financed and run, for example, by the Goethe Institutes, the Ministry of Development Aid or by German enterprises, ideally in a joint sponsorship. In this case, the pupils should of course also be taught German as part of the theoretical instruction and be given practical preparation for a particular trade, e.g., as a bricklayer, painter, plasterer, road builder, carpenter or locksmith. One could imagine something similar for the nursing profession and other professions in which qualified young people are desperately sought. At the end of the training, there should be a theoretical, linguistic and technical examination which, if passed, could lead to the right to migrate to Europe or directly to Germany. In this way, German companies could attract qualified migrants who could be integrated into the German labor market relatively easily. For those who do not pass the qualification to migrate, the domestic labor market would be open, where they could build up a decent existence and contribute as productive links to the development of their own economy and no longer have to take the risky flight across the Mediterranean.

(5) *Two opposing concepts*:

The school and vocational education per Adam Smith and Friedrich List

In 1998, Christopher Winch, Professor of Philosophy and Educational Policy at King's College, London, published an article in the Oxford Review of Education entitled "*Two Rival Conceptions of Vocational Education: Adam Smith and Friedrich List*".[30] Winch compares the different educational models of the classic economic school of Adam Smith with the lesser known mastermind of the social market economy Friedrich List, explaining why the UK should pay much more attention to the German economist. As far as Winch could evaluate, List had not spoken at great length about education in his magnum opus, *The National System*. However, his work, Winch found, contained numerous implications about schooling and vocational training. It should be remembered that Germany at that time was in a precapitalist stage with craftsmen guilds, an agrarian economy and strong state regulation of economic activities similar to the level of a developing country today. At that time List had been a reformer who wanted to modernize Germany to achieve intellectual and cultural strength, but not at the price of the inhumane and brutal English style free market.

Adam Smith's economic model consisted of a society of individuals who produced, exchanged and consumed values. In this context, his overarching moral philosophy must also be seen, which, however, appears deficient for explaining economic life because it is based exclusively on the principle of self-interest, i.e., the pursuit of private interests. Somewhat broad, one could say that according to Smith, society consists of a nation of egoists, who are limited in their activities only by social harmony. In this context, C. Winch recalls a famous quotation from Smith, who said, "we do not get our food because of the charity of the butcher, the brewer, and the baker, but because it is in their own interest to do so. So man does not engage himself out of charity, but out of self-interest."

One of the key questions Adam Smith asked himself as a moral philosopher was whether the general welfare of society or personal or individual welfare is more important. Smith responded that the general welfare is maximized by the fact that every economic subject tries to maximize his individual welfare within the framework of social limits. The social limits were what Smith called the "inner judge", i.e., the inner voice or social conscience of man. This natural signal speaks out with every action or decision and determines whether the respective behavior is socially legitimate. Adam Smith thus anticipated a psychological phenomenon that Sigmund Freund later described as the archetypical superego.

According to Smith, an "invisible hand" hovers over the market, regulating prosperity, from which however, not all individuals profit equally. A worker or a farmer does not participate in the blessings of the market to the same extent as a factory owner or a nobleman. Friedrich List's conception of man differs from this in essential points. Both refer to the Enlightenment, but in List's thinking not only does individual freedom play a decisive role, but it is equated with humanity and the common good. His ideas of thought are derived from the nature of things. Natural law forms the basis of his views on the purpose of the state and on the rights and duties of the individual in society. By himself the individual person is nothing. All that he is, all that he can become, he is and becomes only through society. The state forms, as it were, the total power of its individuals, and only in social association can man find his individual satisfaction and fulfillment. The union or confederation of individual forces in pursuit of a common purpose, List said, is alone the source of the individual's happiness. The greater the number of countrymen with whom the individual is linked in social association, the greater is his well-being, so List concludes, "the perfect nation, not perfect humanity is the task to be solved by the present age."

In the industrialization of a country List saw the indispensable prerequisite for the humanization of working and living conditions. He not only saw its advantages but also warned against overemphasizing industrial progress, especially the exploitation of the working classes. The more industry and agriculture flourish in a state, the less the human spirit can be held in chains, that is suppressed, and the more one is compelled to give free space to the spirit of tolerance, morality, and democracy.

Notes

1. Boianovsky, M. (2013): Friedrich List and the Economic Fate of Tropical Countries; In: History of Political Economy, Vol. 45, No., 4, pp. 647–693.
2. List, F.: The national system of political economy; in. W. VI, p. 52 f.
3. Idem: The natural system of political economy; in: W. IV, p. 396 f.
4. Idem: The arable constitution, the dwarf economy and emigration; in: W. V, pp. 418–547; W.V, p. 119, W. VI, p. 49 and W. VII, p.180.
5. P. Sai-wing Ho (2005): Distortions in the trade policy for development debate: A re-examination of Friedrich List; in: Cambridge Journal of Economics, H. 29, p. 742.
6. Weiler, F. (1996): The "Infant-Industry" Argument for Protectionist Measures. Theoretische Einordnung und wirtschaftspolitische Relevanz; Diss. Darmstadt, pp. 245 and 248.
7. Senghaas, D. (2008): Ways out of poverty - What Friedrich List and the history of development teach us; in: Blätter für deutsche und internationale Politik, H. 53, p. 64.
8. Chang, H.-J. (2007): Kicking away the ladder - Development Strategy in Historical Perspective, London, p. 3.
9. Senghaas, D. (2009): World governance and world law in a fractured world; in: United Nations, H. 1, 14.
10. Effenberger, W. (2016): Geo-Imperialismus - Die Zerstörung der Welt, Rottenburg, pp. 185-.
11. List, F. (1837): Railways and Canals, Steam Boats and Steam Carriage; in: Das Staats-Lexikon, 2nd ed., Vierter Band, Altona 1846, p. 228 ff.
12. Patton, S. G.: Friedrich List's Contribution to the Anthracite-Railroad Connection in the United States; in: Canal History and Technology Proceedings, 1990, o.o., pp. 3–19.
13. Wendler, E. (2016): Friedrich List's Exile in the United States, New Findings; Heidelberg 2016, pp. 28–32.
14. Idem (2019): Frederick List and the Little Schuylkill Railroad in Pennsylvania. Friedrich List and the Little-Schuylkill-Railroad in Pennsylvania, Reutlingen.
15. List, F. (1985): Die Welt bewegt sich, Göttingen, pp. 154–59.
16. Idem (1846): The alliance memorandum; in: W. VII, P. 280.
17. Idem (1843): Miszellen des ZVB, p. 543.
18. Idem (1846): Miszellen des ZVB, p: 432.
19. Idem (1846): Miszellen des ZVB, p. 495 f.
20. List, F.: The national system of political economy; in: W. VI, P. 179.
21. Ibid. S. 176.
22. Idem: Outlines of American Political Economy, with a commentary by Michael Liebig, Wiesbaden o. J., p. 62.
23. Ibid, p. 80 ff.
24. Daastol, A. M.: A Review of Contributions of Friedrich List Commemorating his 225-year...
25. List, F. (1837): Die Welt bewegt sich, Göttingen 1985, p. 80 f. and 108 f.
26. Meinungsbild über die Eidgenossenschaft; Diss. Konstanz, pp. 97 ff. as well as Notz, W. (1925): Friedrich List in America; in: Weltwirtschaftliches Archiv, Vol. 21, H. 2, p. 257.
27. Ibid, pp. 80 ff.
28. o. V. (F. List): The school of reciprocal instruction; in: National Magazine, No. 52/11834, p. 414.
29. List, F. (1826): Draft letter to J. De Witt Clinton; in: W. II, p. 295 f.
30. Winch, C.: Two Rival Conceptions of Vocational Education: Adam Smith and Friedrich List; in: Oxford Review of Education, Vol. 24, No. 3, 1998, pp. 365–378.

Chapter 20
Current and Future Core Problems of the World Economy

20.1 The Greatest Global Challenges

In the Global Marshall Plan Initiative lecture, "Die Grenzen des Wachstums—50 Jahre danach: 'Der Bericht des Club of Rom zur Lage der Menschheit'—damals, heute und ein Ausblick" (The Limits to Growth—50 Years Later: 'The Report to the Club of Rome on the Predicament of Mankind'—Back Then, Today and Future Outlook), at the Hospitalhof, Stuttgart in February 2022, Ulrich Sihler summarized in artistic form many of the challenges of "a world in crisis". These are put in the context of the 17 Sustainable Development Goals (SDGs) adopted by all United Nation Member States in 2015, which built upon the predecessor Millenium Development Goals (MDGs) of 2000. Whether in 1972, 2000, 2015, or today, not all that much has changed in the challenges humankind faces, except that the severity in general has intensified further and new dramatic ones have been added to the list, in particular the Covid Pandemic and the war in Ukraine, both with global reach and impact. "Balance the World", in the sense of an Eco-Human-Market Economy has a way to go! (Fig. 20.1).

In their book "*Zukunftsfragen der Entwicklungspolitik*" (Future Issues in Development Policy), Dirk Messner and Imme Scholz summarized the most important global political challenges in eight core topics:

1. The social polarization of the world community and the fight against poverty
2. The explosive growth of the world population
3. Disintegrating states
4. Wars, terrorism, international cartels and warlords
5. The global supply of drinking water and the irrigation of agricultural land
6. Global climate change and limits to world ecosystems
7. The instability of international financial markets
8. Abuse of power and bad governance.

All of these problem areas are closely interwoven and interdependent. They form a dense ball of string wrapped around an enormous core of social explosives and

E. Wendler, *The Political Economy of Friedrich List*, Springer Studies in the History of Economic Thought, https://doi.org/10.1007/978-3-031-24601-2_20

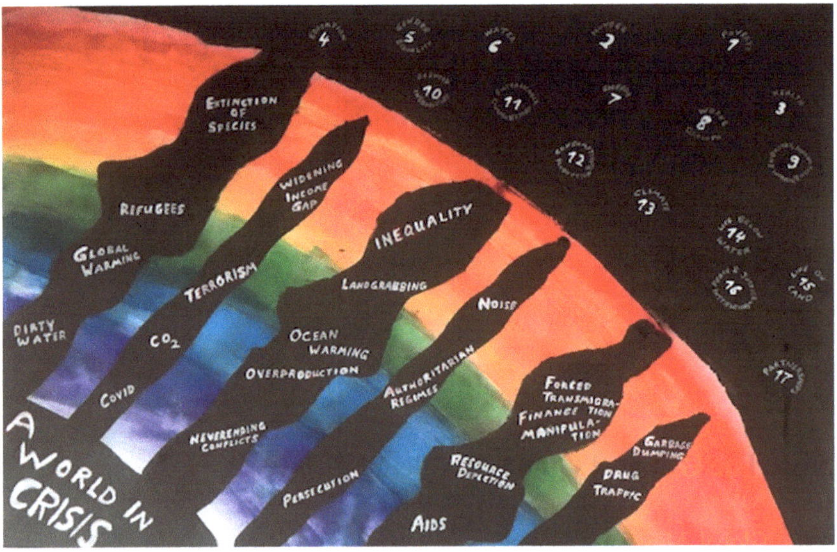

Fig. 20.1 (neu): A World in Crisis: Not much has changed in the challenges…; *Source* Ulrich Sihler, Summer Art Week, Mariaberg, July 2021

equipped with a time fuse. We do not know if and when this will ex- or implode. We only know that this ball is becoming denser and more difficult to untangle and that the challenges it poses to the global community are rapidly increasing, thus creating an urgent need for action. It cannot be appealed often enough that every world citizen should contribute to doing what he or she can to avert the apocalypse.

Our intent here is to summarize the most important aspects of these problem areas and, as far as possible, to enrich them with opinions expressed by Friedrich List to add value in present day analysis. It will also make it clear once again how broad and deep his body of thought is and how senseless it is to reduce the discussion of this ingenious and pragmatic economist to the keyword protectionism. We will also propose potential solutions, contenting ourselves with List's remarks. We certainly would not venture to produce a recipe book that goes beyond these approaches. At the same time, we are convinced that if one were to take its recommendations for action seriously and act accordingly, a great deal would be achieved.

20.2 Social Polarization in the World Community and the Fight Against Poverty

In the second Paris Prize competition, Friedrich List commented on the state's duty of caring for its citizens. Throughout modern times, the care for those who belong to the poor, the weak and the sick has rightly been considered one of the main obligations of the government. In the face of globalization we must apply this duty of care to the entire community of states.[1]

The more nations progress with the help of industrialization, the more important it becomes to exercise great effort to the living conditions of the poor. In doing so, one must take into account the fact that, for obvious reasons, a large part of the poor are concentrated in large cities, where their living conditions are even less favorable than in the countryside.

According to research by French economist Abhijit Banerjee and his fellow researchers, the richest one percent of the world's population has more than doubled its income since 1980. In terms of income disparities, they note serious differences. The gap is smallest in Europe, where 10% of the population has 37% of national income, compared with 47% in North America and 61% in the Middle East.

The aid organization Oxfam complains that the gap between the rich and poor is widening. In 2017, 1% of the world's population was able to secure 82% of the increase in wealth. The 42 richest people in the world owned as much as the entire poorer half of humanity. The 3.7 billion people who make up this poorer half have experienced virtually no growth in wealth. According to Oxfam, 2043 people worldwide have at least $1 billion in wealth (2017), with a new billionaire added every day. Oxfam denounced the tax tricks of the rich, who as a result save about $200 billion annually. Developing countries lose at least $170 billion in revenue this way, more than the entire $145 billion in development aid.

The term "poverty" as a mass phenomenon in the Third World is difficult to define and measure. The most common benchmarks are the average per capita income of a country's population, the daily availability of funds, the minimum wage or the annual gross national product compared to the size of the population. However, these measures are only statistical averages that inadequately describe the complex phenomenon of mass poverty. The Nobel Prize winner Esther Duflo, who dealt with this problem in detail, did not find a patent solution to measure poverty in her "fighting against poverty" research either but contented herself with the description of four central poverty problems: education, health care, the fight against corruption and the need to drive self-initiative through small loans. The economics professor and banker Muhammad Yunus, who as head of the Grameen Bank in Bangladesh was awarded the Nobel Prize in 2006 for providing microcredits to the poorest people and especially women in his country so that they could become self-employed and start their own businesses, moves in the same direction. The secret of Yunus ' success lies in mobilizing the personal initiative and drive of these people. Even if such examples are only small in effect, as is the case with international state development policy and charitable development aid from NGOs, these are certainly hopeful approaches.

The World Hunger Index of 2014 shows that while the problem of hunger has eased since 1990, this should not hide the fact that it is still a major issue in many African countries, India, Pakistan and Bangladesh. Additionally, there is the phenomenon of "hidden hunger", which refers to malnutrition, for example, the diet lacking in vitamins and protein. According to the latest surveys by the Federal Statistical Office, 821 million people worldwide were chronically malnourished in 2017, that is, 11% of the world's population went hungry. In view of the war against Ukraine, the world's famine is expected to worsen, and food prices are expected to rise in an inflationary manner.

Hunger means chronic malnutrition and undernourishment. According to estimates, about 30 million people die every year from this plague of the twenty-first century. According to the FAO, the Food and Agriculture Organization of the United Nations, approximately 30% of children under the age of five are malnourished worldwide.

Friedrich List was touched by this phenomenon can be seen, for example, in a short article in the "*Reading Eagle*" of 1826. Under the heading "*News from Europe*", he reported on the poverty and famine in Great Britain at that time, "the condition of England has not yet improved. Whole families live on boiled nettle leaves. A laborer, if so fortunate as to find work, receives six pennies a day. Poisoning from impure flour is common. The philanthropist's heart breaks on reading these ghastly accounts."[2]

To break the vicious circle of hunger and poverty, List pinned his hopes, as already mentioned, on the modernization of agriculture, on the successes of agricultural chemistry, and on innovations in agricultural technology.

For List, Justus v. Liebig was a messenger of a new age. In the unlimited division of land ownership List saw, as described, one of the main evils in that farm workers become "walking skeletons". While the grandfather was still working with four beautiful horses and had enough cattle and food to feed his large family, the grandson was starving year in and year out. If his children now also want to follow in their father's footsteps and participate in the poor land ownership, where, List asked himself, should the people for industrial production be found?[3]

Under such poor conditions, even the spiritual forces in the common worker could not be awakened. List comments, "the talents do not develop and find no opportunity to show themselves to advantage. Physical efforts alone are rewarded and this quite poorly, since the landlords with their fields monopolize the workers." This is especially true in Latin American countries where the proportion of propertyless agricultural workers still account for one third of the population. They work on the plantations of the large landowners, who either cultivate their land extensively or leave it fallow as an object of speculation. The situation is particularly serious in Brazil, where a considerable part of the tropical rainforest falls victim to clearing every day and is permanently lost as a source of climate protection.

There have also been frequent attempts to link the dwarf economy with industrial work. Friedrich List, however, did not think much of this, noting that "half a farmer and half a tradesman is a miserable position in between." We see it differently. After World War II, part-time farmers contributed significantly to the food supply and reconstruction, and during the financial crisis, Greeks who still owned agricultural land and were self-sufficient were at an advantage. In Russia and the Eastern European countries of the Balkans but also in Italy, Spain, Portugal and France, self-sufficiency continues to play an important role in securing livelihoods.

Friedrich List very much recognized the hard labor of factory work. Nevertheless, he thought that the hardest factory work was still better than when farm workers and small farmers, often very poorly nourished, had to carry heavy loads uphill and down, so that they were crippled in body and soul.

For List agricultural chemistry was a major source of hope. In 1844, he forecasted that "chemistry would ally itself with agriculture, and that artificial-, bone-, mineral, and chemical fertilizers as well as imported guano would not be too costly to find abundant use with a satisfactory financial profit. Capital, mechanization and labor would also be used in agriculture, and it would pay to convert swampy, sandy and dusty lands into fertile arable land by drainage or irrigation, soil improvement and fertilization.[4]

Agricultural chemistry, together with the use of agricultural machinery, has made enormous progress over the last 180 years, making giant monocultures possible. The flip side of the coin, however, is that soils are increasingly being depleted, and as a result increasingly more fertilizers, pesticides and fungicides are being used to maintain the crop yield. As well known this, however, causes equally enormous damage to the environment, the ecosystem and the chemical balance of the water.

The agricultural economy is not the only loser from globalization. The same applies to pasture farming, forestry, fishing and mining. Agricultural land can hardly be expanded by cultivating natural areas. Even in countries where dense tropical rainforests have extended over large areas, deforestation has already reached such an extent that hardly any new usable land can be gained. In 1950, 0.23 hectares (0.6 acres) of arable land was available to every person in the world, currently it is 0.13 hectares, and in 2030 it will be only 0.08 hectares. In the course of 80 years, the arable land available per capita of the world's population has shrunk by two-thirds. Therefore, there is no need to be surprised about increasingly fierce land distribution struggles.

An additional enormous problem arises from the growing importance of biofuel production. Five percent of the world's available arable land is already used to produce "green gold". If emobility does not progress quickly enough, a further sharp increase can be expected. According to Franz Nuscheler, "the renaissance of sugar cane for the production of ethanol strengthens the political power of the old land oligarchy, which forms a blocking force against the necessary agrarian reform in Latin America. It also promotes the continuation of exploitative and quite slave-like working conditions on the plantations. Ecologists worry about the loss of biodiversity in view of monocultures. The soya boom in Latin America, which supplies livestock farms in North America and Europe with a nutrient-rich feed, is leaving behind major ecological damage. This extends to rivers contaminated by pesticides and landscapes in which biodiversity can no longer survive. At the same time only a few jobs are created due to the "modern" industrial production methods.

The burning of palm oil as biodiesel as well as its use as a raw material in the production of cosmetics and food accelerate the growth of oil palm plantations in former tropical forests, which have been destroyed by slash-and-burn methods, and from which the rich diversity of fauna also disappear. Beneficiaries are national and international agribusinesses, international trade groups, the producers of fertilizers and pesticides, the governments with the foreign exchange earnings and the customers in the western consumer markets. At the same time urban slums are filled with landless and unemployed agricultural workers, as well as former small farmers who can no longer feed their families from the crop yields of their fields."[5]

The World Hunger Index (WHI) rates the situation in 52 countries of the world as serious or very serious. For example, the Central African Republic is at the bottom of the Index. In 2012 a civil war broke out in the country, with militias from the Christian majority and the Muslim minority fighting each other. The situation stabilized only following a French military intervention, which was followed by a UN peacekeeping mission. However, new fighting broke out again in 2017. The head of the UN World Food Program (WFP), David Beasley, also called for more international efforts.

The war in Syria and the mass exodus of civilians is an example of the high price to be paid for neglecting the hunger problem. Feeding a Syrian in Syria costs approximately 50 cents a day, Beasley notes, but feeding him in Berlin or Munich would cost €50 a day. He comments, "for every one percent increase in hunger, there is a two percent increase in migration." List expected that the new means of transport and communication to do wonders in the fight against poverty. Day laborers, small farmers, workers in villages and market towns, who often lacked work for many weeks, would no longer pass their time in idleness but would go to distant cities or regions where there was a demand for labor.

A large proportion of the food consumed in Europe is produced in the poorer regions of the world, and its exportation means that it is lost as a basis for subsistence in the producing country. Due to the decreasing fertility of the soil, the situation is dramatically exacerbated, with desertification on the rise in the Sahel and other arid regions.

The new magic word is genetic engineering. However, the development and cultivation of genetically modified plants that are more resistant to drought and pests is highly controversial. Monsanto, the former American company, is the absolute market leader in this field as it holds 90% of the patents for genetically modified plants. In this respect, Bayer AG, as the new owner now has a key role to play, which means a great deal of responsibility. How serious this responsibility is can easily be demonstrated by the extremely high risks in terms of lawsuits and damage claims in relation to glyphosate, the former Monsanto Roundup herbicide, which is strongly affecting Bayer. As a nonexpert, I cannot pass judgement on whether genetic engineering will be the blessing or the curse of the twenty-first century, but all the efforts that are being made to explore the possible applications of this technology and to carry out risk assessments are very welcome.

Nevertheless, it is to be feared that the already serious division of the world into the "haves" and the "have-nots", as recognized by Friedrich List long ago, will remain and even increase significantly. The gap between the rich and poor will continue to widen, and the social gradient will become ever steeper. However, this phenomenon not only refers to the North–South problem but also affects every single country on Earth in terms of its social structure.

In this context it is helpful to recall the French Revolution. Today we are again experiencing that there are considerable explosive tensions between the first and the third social classes, which thus far can be felt "only" in the mass exodus of migrants. Whether and to what extent it will intensify and possibly come to a head in the form of violent protests and even revolution in the course of this century is not foreseeable. What seems certain, however, is that the global struggle for wealth distribution will become significantly more intense.

List already knew what the consequence of unprofitable farms is when he wrote, "if the farmers lack work, they devastate the forests." What is needed is a change in agricultural policy of the kind already envisaged by him. Of course it is not possible to provide a patent remedy for this issue because the starting position, including the cultural and social conditions, is different in every country, and individual solutions must therefore be sought. In doing so, the latest findings of agricultural science, -chemistry and -technology should be used for the benefit of each country's own population as well as for the entire world population.

The situation is similarly disastrous in fisheries. Worldwide, two-thirds of fish stocks are already overfished. The ruinous fishing methods contribute to the fact that 20 million tonnes of bycatch are caught every year, most of which is dead when it is disposed of overboard. The depleted fish stocks could only recover if fishing quotas were reduced by at least one-third. To achieve this, globally binding catch quotas similar to those within the EU would have to be agreed upon. However, these apply not only to European waters but also to the maritime zones in West Africa, the Arctic and Antarctica. It is feared that overfishing of the seas will continue to increase and that in the medium term, there will be supply shortages for the endemic population. In addition, seafood will become so expensive that the poor will hardly be able to afford it, and only the wealthy will consume it as a delicacy.

The magic word is "sustainability", which means that even more aquacultures, shrimp farms, mussel beds, etc., are being set up in coastal regions to protect marine fisheries, although these farms have by no means only advantages and in some cases are also questionable from an ecological standpoint.

In this context, the enormous pollution of the world's oceans, especially with plastic waste, should be mentioned. Presently, several young inventors are testing high-tech "vacuum cleaners", which are supposed to catch and recycle the unimaginably large "seas" of waste. One can only hope that these devices will prove suitable for mass use, although even if they succeed in capturing plastic objects, the problem of water pollution with microplastics still remains unsolved.

20.3 The Explosive Growth of the World Population

(1) *Population forecasts*

Of the numerous attempts to forecast the development of the world population up to the end of this century, we selected the one undertaken in 2012 by the United Nations Foundation on World Population, which Franz Nuscheler also used as a basis for his comments.[6] According to this analysis, the world population in 1800 was about one billion people. In the following 125 years to 1925, it doubled to 2 billion. Between 1925 and 1975, i.e., in a period of only 50 years, it doubled again to 4 billion. For the period from 1975 to 2025, i.e., in another 50 years, a further doubling is expected, so that the world population should amount to approx. 8 billion people by 2025. All further forecasts assume that the maximum growth rate will then have been reached and will decline from then on.

Friedrich List also ventured some population forecasts. His prediction for North America, which he made at a time when the USA had only approximately 17 million inhabitants, is particularly accurate. He predicted rapid growth for the end of the twentieth century, with a population of 300 million rather than 180 million. At approximately 280 million, his estimate was entirely correct. He put the population capacity of North America at 450–500 million. This figure corresponds fairly closely to the expectations of the German Foundation for World Population (DSW) in 2008.

The development of the world population until the end of this century is referred to as the "demographic transition", that is it is expected that absolute population growth will slow down and that the world population will increase to approximately 10 billion by the year 2100. This expectation is based on the assumption of a declining fertility rate, higher levels of education, people's growing needs in terms of standard of living, sexual education and increased use of contraceptives, and higher mortality from HIV disease and later age at marriage. All these factors contribute to the birth rate converging towards the replacement rate.

However, it should not be concealed that there are other forecasts that predict a much stronger growth of the world population which is also due to the average age of people rising due to better medical care, while at the same time infant mortality is falling. Despite the slowdown in population growth, this demographic transition is frightening.

Approximately half of the world's population is under the age of 25 and thus in prime fertility age with 87% of these young people living in developing countries, where they contribute to the strongest population growth. The African continent has by far the highest fertility rate, with 4.7 births per woman. That is why the risk of population explosion is greatest there.

In Japan and China, but also in Germany, Austria and Italy, the older age groups are growing as the respective population pyramids are constricted in the middle due to low birth rates, the one-child policy and the abortion of female fetus, so that the working life generation has to cope with ever greater "burdens of the past".

Globally, the threat is not so much a food trap as it is a sociopolitical and ecological trap. World political stability is threatened not only by the uprising of the poor but also at least as much by the disproportionate consumption of resources and energy, environmental pollution and global warming, for which the wealthy are responsible. Cities, especially megacities with more than 10 million people, harbor significant social unrest. There, ever larger slums are emerging where the police and the judiciary can hardly do anything. Violence, drug trafficking, crime and sexual exploitation prevail there, not to mention poor hygiene, a lack of sewage systems, dignified housing and poor water and electricity supplies. There is often merciless competition among the inhabitants for the few odd jobs.

Of course, it is impossible to offer patent remedies for solving these manifold problems. The only certainty is that no one is served by warning of horror scenarios and then throwing up one's hands and giving up. First, it is the task of national governments to take the necessary and feasible measures to create the conditions in their own countries that serve to de-escalate the situation. Second, the world community of the wealthy, through international, national and charitable development aid, must literally provide the most humanly possible assistance to curb population growth and improve the social situation in the respective states so that the haves and have-nots no longer seek their salvation in migration.

Again, we can refer to List, where in his "*Politics of the Future*", he appealed to the politicians and wealthy classes in the industrialized nations. In view of the growing problems they must look far into the future to come to understand the penalties for their inactivity and carelessness, to gain the high degree of moral strength which is necessary to overcome all those formidable obstacles that existing interests and prejudices, craftiness, inertia, short-sightedness and the like everywhere that stand in the way of strong measures aimed at long-term goals.[7]

(2) *The rejection of the population theory of Thomas R. Malthus by Friedrich List*

In 1798, Malthus published a study in which he developed a horror scenario with regard to the population explosion. His core thesis is that the world population will reproduce in a geometric series. The food supply, on the other hand, will only increase as an arithmetic series. Shortage of food, famine, epidemics and wars were inevitable if population growth was not slowed down by birth restrictions and sexual abstinence. Malthus himself did not believe that it was possible to achieve this balance. He firmly reckoned that the population trap would lead to a demographic apocalypse.

Already in the second Paris Prize competition pamphlet of 1837, Friedrich List strongly contradicted this theory. Based on his expectations regarding the blessings of the new means of transport and communication and the progress in the agricultural economy through improved cultivation methods and increasing mechanization, he expressed the conviction that Malthus' theory trampled on all natural laws and emotions as well as morality and religion.[8]

In the "*National System*",[9] List further elaborated his concerns, "it was only through a misunderstanding of the cosmopolitan tendency of the productive forces that Malthus could have been led into the error of wanting to limit the increase of population. The theory here resembles Saturn devouring its own children. It is not true that the population increases on a greater scale than the production of subsistence means. At least it is folly to suppose such a disproportion, or to attempt to prove it by artificial calculations and sophisticated arguments, while the globe has a mass of natural forces whereby ten and perhaps a hundred times more people than now might be fed, (taking a look at) the mass destruction of fruits and vegetables in the industrial countries."

List continues, "it is narrow sightedness to take the present capacity of the productive forces at all as a measure of how many people can feed themselves on a given stretch of land. The savage, the hunter and fisherman, according to the calculation of Malthus, would not have room for even one million, the herdsman not for ten millions, the crude cultivator not for one hundred million on earth, and yet two hundred million now live in Europe alone. The culture of the potato and edible plants and the new improvements in agriculture have increased the productive power of mankind to increase the food supply tenfold."

Looking at the development, List notes that, "in the Middle Ages, the wheat yield of an acre in England was four times what it is today ten to twenty times, and five times more land was cultivated in the process. In many European countries, whose soil has the same natural fertility as that of England, the yield is now less than four times as much. Who would wish to stop the discoveries, inventions, and improvements of the human race? Agricultural chemistry is still in its infancy so who can predict that tomorrow, by some new invention or discovery, the productive capacity of land will not be increased five- or tenfold? Artesian wells are already a means of transforming barren deserts into rich fields of fruit."

Optimistically, List asks, "what powers may still slumber in the bowels of the earth? Suppose a new discovery were to enable us, without the aid of the fuels now known, to produce heat everywhere in a convenient manner. What stretches of country could be cultivated with it, and in what incalculable manner could the productive capacity of a given country be increased? If the Malthusian doctrine appears to us in its tendency as a limited one, it presents itself as a horrible one as it is one that is contrary to nature, as one that kills morality and strength. It seeks to kill the instinct which nature makes use of as the most effective means of stimulating men by the exertion of their minds and bodies and of awakening and nourishing their nobler feelings. An instinct for which the human race can thank the greater part of its progress. It (the doctrine) wants to make law of the most heartless selfishness. It wants us to close our hearts against the starving, because if we give them food and drink, another might have to starve in thirty years time instead of him. It seeks to substitute a calculation for compassion. This doctrine would turn men's hearts into stones. However, what in the end could be expected of a nation whose citizens carried stones instead of hearts in their bosoms? Nothing but the utter ruin of all morality, and consequently of all productive powers, and consequently of all the wealth and civilization and power of nations?

List continues, "when in a nation the population rises higher than the production of food, when in the end capital accumulates in such a way that it can no longer find accommodation (i.e., be invested) in its own country, when machinery renders numerous workers unemployed and factories abound, this is only proof that nature will not accept that industry, civilization, wealth and power should benefit only a few countries but must be distributed among all the cultivated regions of the earth to free the human race from crudeness, ignorance and poverty."

Developments to date have proven Friedrich List right. Food supply has by and large kept pace with population growth. However, it would be irresponsible to be satisfied with this finding and to trust that this parallelism will also prove to be viable in the future. Agricultural yields can certainly be assumed to be increased. However, the supply problem shifts to the settlement problem and to the creation of jobs in the commercial and service sectors. The population agglomeration of cities is taking on ever greater dimensions, the metropolises with millions of inhabitants bursting at the seams, with the same appling to traffic density, housing shortages, environmental pollution and social infrastructure. It is above all in these areas that we must see whether we can avert the impending catastrophe of the population explosion in this century.

(3) *The dependence of fertility on wealth and educational attainment*

Friedrich List already knew that a woman's fertility depends on her age at marriage, wealth and level of education and decreases as these increase.[10] In this connection, he stated that, "in the North American free states, the population doubles every 30 years because it is easy to set up a household and support a large family, so that a high number of children is a blessing rather than a burden to the parents. The greatest increase in population is recorded in the newly cultivated countries among the peasantry. An unmarried person over 25 years of age or a family man in his thirties with at least half a dozen children are rare exceptions in these nations.

The more capital that is required to establish a household, the greater the demands of working life for the preservation of family and social class, the later marriage takes place and the smaller the number of children. That is why in the American southern states the large landowners, the merchants, and learned circles are less blessed with children than are the country people in the west.

While population growth keeps pace with the increase in prosperity in the USA, Ireland teaches the opposite. In Ireland, people marry easily because it is easy to rent a potato field as people there have no special demands on life other than to live on potatoes, living in miserable mud huts and dressed in rags. Many children that are born there are fed potatoes and their parents do not care for their welfare.

In developed countries, on the other hand, population growth among the wealthy is slower because it is more difficult to maintain a certain standard of living, to find decent housing, and even more difficult to provide it for their children.

Among the workers in England, List noted that the daily wages of laborers are so high that they can marry at a young age. As they have little motivation to move up in the social classes and have no ambition in educating their offspring, they have many children. When the parents lose their jobs and then fall into hardship, they console themselves with the fact that in such cases, the welfare systems steps in. However, this relief is only temporary. The incessant inventions of new machinery, of improvements in older inventions, of new methods of production, and the growing demands upon the standard of living give hope that in the course of time, a decrease in the population growth rate may also be expected among the working classes.

20.4 Disintegrating States

Thirty years ago, we saw East Germany (the DDR, Deutsche Demokratische Republik) unifying with West Germany, as the former Soviet Union broke up. As a result, the three Baltic countries Estonia, Latvia and Lithuania, as well as Belarus, Ukraine, Moldova, Georgia, Azerbaijan, Kazakhstan, Kyrgyzstan and Turkmenistan gained their independence. Soon after, Yugoslavia broke apart with Slovenia, Croatia, Serbia, Bosnia-Herzegovina, Montenegro, Kosovo and Macedonia emerging as independent states. In Spain the Catalans are seeking independence, and in the aftermath of the Brexit, the existence of the United Kingdom may be at risk.

In Africa, Sudan has broken in two. The Arab Spring uprising in the north of the continent has brought great political instability to Tunisia, but especially to Libya and Egypt. In Libya, several rival powers are fighting each other. In further African countries including Zaire, Nigeria, the Ivory Coast, Mali and Chad, as well as in Eritrea, Somalia and Burkina Faso, civil war-like conditions prevail.

Similar conditions have prevailed and continue to prevail in South America, especially in Colombia, Mexico and Nicaragua, where separatists and opposition activists are fighting against the respective governments. Conditions are particularly bad in Venezuela, but there is also great discontent in Argentina because of political and economic misery.

The situation is particularly fragile in the Middle East, where Iraq in particular is threatening to break apart. The catastrophic conditions in Syria and Yemen reveal the destructiveness of proxy wars and the helplessness of the global community. Even more serious appears the conflict between Israel and the Palestinians, which seems to become increasingly unsolvable. The situation in Afghanistan and Pakistan is equally difficult. The Kashmir problem between India and Pakistan also remains an unresolved flashpoint. In the South Pacific, the Bougainville archipelago separated from New Guinea in 2019 and constituted itself as the latest independent state.

Such tensions and potential for conflict were also not alien to Friedrich List and he would provide his opinion and statements on such subjects. The key words for understanding List's constitution of the state are liberty and national unity.[11] Freedom, he argued, was the most important prerequisite for the development of a nation's productive forces and prosperity. The lack of free institutions, he said, could not be replaced by anything else. As long as there are nations that subjugate the national interests of one's own country, it is foolish to speak of free competition and trade between nations. For this reason, he also spoke out against national fragmentation on principle. He likened a fragmented nation to the glass splitters of a jar, which is why he spoke of the splittered nation. Current examples are North and South Sudan, North and South Korea or the Kurdish region.

The national interests are often very different from the private interests of the individual citizen. The individual is not usually concerned with the common good and national sovereignty but is primarily concerned with his own advantage and that of his descendants. Therefore, private interests must be subordinated to national interests.

In this connection, List left no doubt that he was a born republican. He wanted every national community to be a republic, free from anarchy and despotism. The essence of the state, he said, was that sovereignty should emanate from the people. Without this principle, neither the duty of the authorities to form a legitimate government, nor the right of the people to have a say and control in legislation, nor any reasonable social condition of society could be derived.[12] At the same time this state sovereignty emanating from the people could not be exercised by them as a mass directly but only in the form of representative democracy. Here, the overall interest is above the will of the individual.

List always advocated peaceful reforms which is why he also rejected civil wars, noting that, "civil wars are the predecessors of subjugation by an external enemy" because hostile parties also attract "foreign powers to their soil." One need only think of the Orange Revolution in Ukraine, which resulted in the Russian occupation of Crimea and the Donbass, or Georgia, with the same effect.

Among the countries for which List wished national unity, Italy, Germany, Hungary, and Ireland stand out. He criticized Italy for the fact that the Italian cities and oligarchs did not feel themselves to be members of a common body. The internal discord, he said, was further nourished and intensified by foreign invaders and the native priesthood, who divided the people into two hostile camps with their banishment activities. The decay of the Italian republics, the internal rivalry and resentment were symptomatic of the fact that there were no large, strong and united nation states on the European continent at that time.[13]

List had particular sympathies for the national independence of Hungary. The Hungarians had to revive their nationality and national language in their own well-understood self-interest. Only a Magyar nationality that bears the stamp of its own character at the basis is capable of forming a large, flourishing state on its soil. This noble Hungarian nation is also in close friendship with Germany.

Similarly, he argued for Irish independence to break away from colonial exploitation by Britain. List complained that the large English landowners were treating the Irish small tenants like slaves and were downright starving them to death. The social misery he said was so pitiful that only national independence could provide a remedy. Therefore, Ireland must shake off this yoke and strive to improve its situation through a state of its own.

With regard to the disintegrating states, he expected an imminent collapse of the Ottoman Empire, which was so rotten that it could no longer sustain itself with its own strength and was inevitably heading for dissolution. As mentioned, List feared that after the fall of the Ottoman Empire, a new power struggle would break out as to who would gain the greatest possible political influence on the Bosporus. These considerations are valid up to the present day where, after all, we are witnessing President Vladimir Putin massively pushing Russian influence in Turkey and the West being pushed back accordingly. Moreover, Recep Erdogan seems to be reviving the Ottoman dream, judging by his current policies in Syria and Libya.

20.5 Wars, Terrorism, International Cartels and War Lords

Since 11. September 2001, the global potential for violence has become much more dangerous and severe. There are not only the "classic" military conflicts in the form of wars and battle grounds such as in Afghanistan, Iraq, Syria and Yemen, revolutions and revolts as in the Arab Spring, in Egypt, Ukraine, Zimbabwe and Catalonia, as well as permanent conflicts such as the Kashmir region between India and Pakistan,

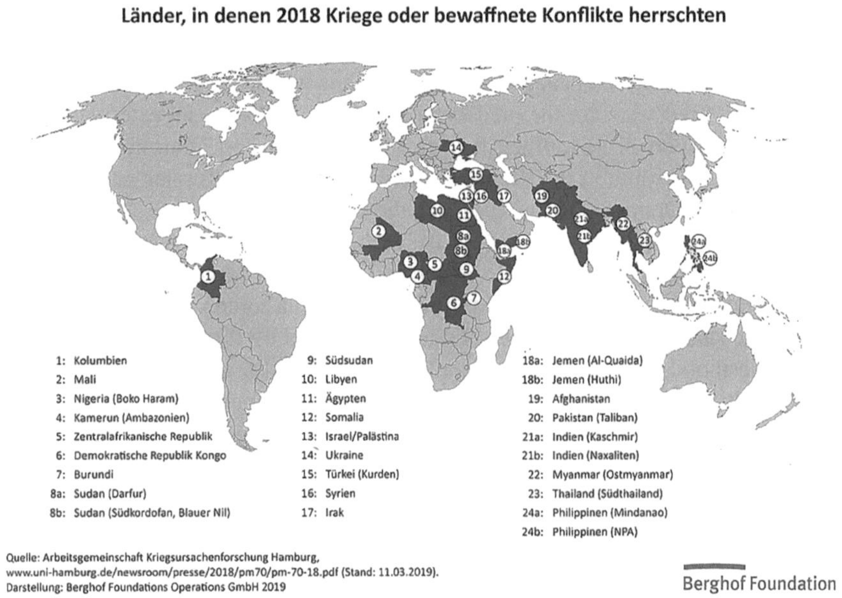

Fig. 20.2 Countries where wars or armed conflicts prevailed in 2018; *source* Berghof Foundation

between Israel and the Palestinians, between North and South Korea and between Turkey and the Kurds, but entirely new forms of violent extremes have emerged.

First and foremost, there is international terrorism. We need only recall the recent terrorist attacks in France, Belgium, Great Britain, Norway, Sweden, Germany and Spain but also in Indonesia, India, Pakistan and Afghanistan, and above all in Iraq, to which countless people have fallen victim in recent years Fig. 20.2.

Civil war-like violence carried out by warlords is rampant in African countries including Zaire, Nigeria, Mali, Eritrea and Somalia, as well as in Afghanistan, Iraq and Colombia. These agitators do not recognize the respective governments and have conquered a lawless space in which they destabilize their own state and tyrannize the population with their own militias, often recruiting child soldiers.

Another major potential threat is posed by the international cartels involved in trafficking in human beings, drugs and weapons, as well as the illegal trade in ivory and wild animals subject to species protection. This also includes the army of smugglers who help African migrants flee to Europe, collecting huge sums of money in the process.

Another aspect which Friedrich List reveals is the back side of the honorable merchant. The merchant is indifferent to the effect that the goods he sells have on the morals, prosperity and power of nations. As mentioned, he imports and sells poisons such as medicinal substances. Whole nations are weakened by opium and distilled spirits. It is indifferent to him whether, through his importation and smuggling, hundreds of thousands find employment and subsistence or are reduced to begging. As a businessman, he was only interested in whether he made a profit. If the breadless then try to escape the misery in their homeland by emigrating, the merchant gains again from their "deportation" abroad. In war, the merchant often supplied the enemy with weapons and ammunition. He would even, to the degree possible, sell land and property abroad, until the last one was sold and then would embark on a ship and set off abroad himself.[14]

Among the few visions in which Frederick List completely miscalculated was his conclusion that the new means of transportation and traffic, including telegraphy, the expansion of international trade into world commerce, and the advancing world spirit will help to avert the danger of war. The more industry develops and the more evenly it spreads to all the countries of the world, the less wars would be possible, as two nations that are industrially about equally developed, would do each other greater damage in a week than they could repair in a whole human lifetime. Examples include the immense destruction in Syria, Iraq, Yemen, and Ukraine, that is so great that a human lifetime probably would hardly suffice to repair the damage. The culturally valuable bazaars and many sacred works of art are irretrievably lost.

With the trade congresses, the great European powers would have the basis for future national congresses at their disposal. Even now, List said, there was a discernible desire to settle political and economic differences by treaty rather than to seek justice by force of arms. The more the civilized countries come to realize that international agreements promise them incomparably richer and more secure fruits than mutual hostilities and wars, the greater their overall progress and prosperity. It can be assumed that industrialization and a higher level of education are contributing to the gradual disarmament of standing armies and citizens, as part of a national army reserve, have their rifles at home, as is the case in Switzerland.

He believed that the second generation would no longer want to destroy what the first had laboriously built up and that the third would then have to make a fresh start to repair what had been destroyed. It is rather in the interest of the succession of generations that the following generation continues to work not only to maintain what has been achieved but also to increase that level.

List, as mentioned, felt that the mere existence of the new means of transport and communication would deter people and governments from war. The more industrialization expands and the greater the investment required for driving progress, the more costly, expensive and devastating war will become. Not only do governments and nations run out of time to fight wars, but war becomes such a nuisance that nations can no longer justify the sacrifices it causes, so that it becomes increasingly difficult to fight wars and finally more and more impossible and ridiculous. The governments and the nations of the civilized world would thus have to renounce war and turn to improving the living conditions of their citizens. In this way, they would eliminate in themselves the seeds of unrest and revolution.[15]

List felt that this restraint was called for not only in land wars but also in naval wars, which were equally foolish. Instead, he wisely advocated the establishment of an international maritime police force that would resolutely combat all hostile differences as well as piracy.

Unfortunately, all these visions have remained pipe dreams to this day, with no improvement in sight. In contrast, it is to be expected that the distribution struggles will increase in the further course of the twenty-first century, and we are currently experiencing a global arms race again. The weapons exports of the world's largest arms producers are reaching new highs from year to year, and it is to be feared that these weapons will not rust away but will be used at some point.

20.6 The Global Supply of Drinking Water and Irrigation of Agricultural Land

The United Nations estimates that between 30 and 40% of the world's population will not have access to clean water by 2030. This large supply problem has many causes. Many large cities, especially megacities, are growing so fast that the supply system of the municipalities is reaching its limits in terms of water and electricity supply and even more so in terms of sewage, wastewater treatment and recycling, in turn overtaxing their capabilities. In many cases, streams and rivers have become stinking cesspools that are nothing more than dead bodies of water. The silting up of rivers and inland lakes is also a major problem. In many regions of the world, the groundwater level is sinking, with the result that palm groves in India, for example, are dying over large land areas. Water shortages lead to crop failures as well as to political conflicts, not the least due to expanding population growth.

In view of global warming, water is likely to become a scarce commodity in the coming decades. Its price will then rise with the danger that the poorest people in the world will no longer be able to afford this most precious commodity. More than 80 countries in the world, home to nearly four billion people, are struggling to supply their populations with drinking water. Moreover, drinking water is more than unequally distributed. While in the rich northern hemisphere it bubbles away and is often wasted, where in the Sahel region, for example, there is no end to the years of drought, and two-thirds of Africa's rivers are ecologically endangered drylands or deserts. The semiarid and arid land areas are expanding more and more.

The problem of water supply leads to both internal and an external political explosiveness in water-scarce regions. In many developing countries, corporations monopolize the drinking water supply and wealthy citizens in Mexico City, for example, water their gardens and fill their swimming pools with almost free water, while the poor are not connected to the supply mains and must buy expensive bottled drinking water. Not acceptable is the sad reality that the poor of this world often only have access to more or less polluted water, not to mention insufficient hygiene and adequate disposal of waste water.

Heavy metals and wastewater from industrial and private households, as well as fertilizers and toxins from agriculture, end up in rivers, lakes and groundwater. Seventy percent of the world's water consumption is used in agriculture, and it is precisely in this sector that much water is also wasted. Only approximately 2.5% of the water on earth is fresh water, and only a fraction of this is potable for use by humans. In view of the growing world population, there is a threat of hunger and environmental crises as well as political conflicts due to the lack of water.

Although no wars have yet been fought over the water supply, they cannot be ruled out in the future. The conflict hotspots mainly concern dam projects with transnational impacts. In northwestern Ethiopia, Africa's largest dam is currently being built on the Blue Nile. The construction is causing tensions with Sudan and Egypt, which are concerned about their share of the Nile water flow. Turkey is damming the Euphrates and Tigris Rivers to the great dissatisfaction of Syria and Iraq. There is also constant wrangling between Israel and the Palestinians over their share of the Jordan River water supply, where Israel claims 80% of the volume. Pakistan's agriculture depends on a single river, the Indus. That is why the government in Islamabad is trying hard to prevent its arch enemy India from building hydroelectric dams upstream.

Further east, China could become an international problem case. The country is home to 20% of the world's population but has only 8% of its freshwater resources. To supply its rapidly growing industry with sufficient electricity, the Chinese government is pursuing extensive dam projects. Its southern neighbors view this with concern. Vietnam fears that China's new dams will affect the flow of the Mekong River, India sees the same threat to the Brahmaputra. The USA is using the Rio Grande so intensively that there is hardly any river flow left for Mexico.

These and other cross-border conflicts can only be resolved through international negotiations. Angola, for example, provides an encouraging example. After the end of the civil war in 2004, the country intended to build large dams and irrigation facilities at the expense of Botswana. The resulting conflict was then peacefully resolved through a joint agreement. However, such agreements are rare. Therefore, much sharper international tensions over water supply are to be feared in the future.

List had already recognized that the more man wants to develop his agricultural and manufacturing power, the more urgently he is dependent on the use of natural resources. By this he understood all kinds of raw materials that nature provides, including the soil that is transformed into arable land, the stones that are needed to build houses, the seas that serve fishing, the fuels that are necessary for the new means of transport and industry, or the water that is needed for drinking and for irrigation in agriculture. Important to note is that at that time List could still assume that water was abundant.

At the sixth annual conference of German farmers and foresters in Stuttgart in September 1842, List gave a lecture on the importance of field irrigation for livestock farming. In it he not only substantiated with some practical examples the advantages in increasing livestock feed yields, he also presented a financing proposal in which he brought the model of share associations into play. Basically, this was the archaic form of a cooperative, in which each participant acquires a claim to the water right through his financial participation.

20.7 Global Climate Change and Ecosystem Limits

Since the beginning of the twenty-first century, the effects of climate change have been clearly felt. Summers are getting longer and warmer, winters shorter and milder. At the same time, climate extremes are increasing in frequency and intensity. Hurricanes, cyclones and tornadoes are becoming more frequent. This increases the risk of catastrophic floods with widespread destruction, major casualties and enormous property damage. If the monsoon is weaker or fails completely in tropical regions, there is a risk of drought damage and even drought catastrophes. The melting of glaciers in the Arctic and Antarctic as well as in the high mountain ranges is being measured and observed with concern. By the end of this century, sea levels are expected to rise significantly, threatening the existence of coastal regions and island states that lie just above sea level.

The main causes of climate change can undoubtedly be traced to the industrial nations, which contribute by far the largest share to the greenhouse effect, especially with CO_2 emissions and the burning of climate-damaging coal. It is doubtful whether it will be possible to keep to the "two-degree Celsius guard rail" or whether, if this is exceeded, a climatic apocalypse threatens.

In the Autumn of 2018, the Intergovernmental Panel on Climate Change (IPCC) published its global climate report. In it climate researchers sound the alarm for the umpteenth time. Their findings are based on the analysis of over 6000 empirical studies. They warn that the 2° limit is basically no longer sufficient to avert climate catastrophe, calling most emphatically for a reduction to the 1.5° mark. In the latest calculations by the World Meteorological Organisation (WMO), it is feared that the 1.5° mark will already be reached in the period 2022–2026, which would have dramatic consequences for the global economy. Droughts, water shortages and crop failures would be the result. Therefore, every effort should be made to make the switch from fossil to renewable energy as quickly as possible.

The Nile Delta and other river deltas are already experiencing major losses of arable land due to seawater intrusion. An ice-free Arctic Ocean in summer is likely to occur only once per century if the 1.5° target is met but once per decade if the 2° target is met. The report exhorts all governments to make enormous efforts to act and calls for highly ambitious and rapid action. No more time should be lost.

According to a report published at the same time by the German government, about 200 million people currently live in coastal areas that are only 5 m or less above sea level. By the end of the century, the number will rise to between 400 and 500 million. Without coastal protection, a global rise in sea level of between 0.5 and 2 m by the turn of the century would affect the livelihoods of between 72 and 187 million people.

At the same time the impoverishment of species, namely biodiversity, is also feared, with unforeseeable consequences. These hit and affect the developing countries in particular, 90% of which have to bear the consequences of the extinction of species, soil erosion and forest elimination. "The biosphere, which includes all living creatures and plant species on land and water, as well as their genetic blueprints, is in crisis. The loss of species and genes threatens the future of the world's food supply and weighs heavily above all because what is lost remains lost. Biodiversity loss diminishes humanity's natural heritage and damages the planet's ecological capacity." The FAO estimates that three-quarters of genetic diversity has already been lost in crops since the beginning of the twentieth century. The success story of modern agriculture is based on the use of fewer species. However, there is a danger in that as crops are reduced, ever larger monocultures will be grown that are more susceptible to disease and pests, requiring ever higher doses of pesticides and fungicides.

The loss of biodiversity accompanies the destruction of tropical rainforests. Japan alone imports more tropical timber than the entire EU. The commercially exploitable tree population accounts for barely 10% in Africa and Latin America and approximately 25% in Asia. Large areas in the Philippines, Indonesia, Thailand and Malaysia have already fallen victim to overexploitation. The situation is not much better in Central Africa and Brazil. "Humanity has learned nothing from past eco-disasters. We know that the deforestation of North Africa and Sicily by the Romans turned former granaries into deserts and that the treeless area of the (former) Yugoslav coast was due to the overexploitation of coastal forests by Venetian shipbuilders. Today, the destruction of the environment, especially tropical forests, is progressing even faster. Satellite images document the work of destruction but do not stop governments and multinational timber companies from continuing, even under the pretext of using a development resource. In the meantime, there is already talk of 'eco-crimes', i.e., crimes against the environment. Such crimes take place every day."

That List had an intimate relationship with nature even in the few happy hours of his life may be illustrated by a poem entitled "*Feeling in Spring*," which he wrote while in exile in America and working at the Reading Eagle. The last two paragraphs read:

> What excites the senses will never bind the mind.
> In nature's temple, in her meadows
> where with heaven's ray the sun shines;
> Where to look like Elysium the corridor,
> With most beautiful ornaments, tree and flower wreathes themselves.
> Where we trust only the holiest feeling,
> There the spirit feels God; for pure and even
> Truth is before him and life everlasting.
> In her sanctuary, I will kneel -
> Balsamic breathes the scent of ether blossoms,
> Lively singer of tender melodies
> Ring my bell for the service!
> Where streams run gently through plains
> And in the forest's shadowy tomb -
> There alone is the home only of the spirits,
> And there in silence I honor the great master!

List was convinced that nature provides everything in abundance that man needs for life and that it is good what nature itself forms in its orderly course. For this, he said, she had irrefutable reasons, and science had no choice but to detect them and incorporate them into her own system. The transgression of the laws of nature has fatal consequences for man.

20.8 The Instability of the International Financial Markets

More than ten years ago, following the collapse of Lehman Brothers, the global economy experienced a collapse in the international financial markets, the effects of which are still being felt today. The experience at the time demonstrated the inherent instability of the global financial system. The leading economist who warned of this crisis was Hyman Minsky (1919–1996). During his lifetime, however, his fears were not taken seriously by mainstream economists because they were sworn to the theory of neoclassicism. This is based on the fundamental axiom of homeostasis. At its core, this theory states that the goods and money markets form an equilibrium. For this reason, the international financial sector was often ignored and considered irrelevant.

Minsky saw in this a perversion of the teachings of John Maynard Keynes, who in Chap. 12 of his famous work, "*The General Theory of Employment*", dealt with the role of speculation and in this context analyzed the phenomenon of mass psychosis and herd instinct. Minsky reproached the neoclassical followers for criminally neglecting the concept of uncertainty, which Keynes considered particularly important. Minsky disputed the equilibrium axiom and instead put forward the opposite thesis that "stability leads to instability". As a result of the unbridled money creation of the banks, speculation is fuelled, and the international debt volume grows fast. In the phase of perceived stability, the economy becomes increasingly risk averse and therefore takes out an increasing number of loans to realize promising investment projects. In this phase of economic boom, credit creation is by no means cut back, but on the contrary, it is vigorously fuelled. At some point, the peak is reached, and the mood suddenly changes. Then, the debtors can neither pay the interest nor pay back the financial obligation. Banks would then cut back on lending, prices for products and assets start to slide, distress sales pile up, dragging the entire economy into a downwards spiral.

Minsky saw only one way out of this dilemma. To bring the extreme imbalance back into some semblance of equilibrium, the state would have to step in with monetary policy support measures. In addition, he demanded that the banks have a much higher equity capital coverage than was customary during his lifetime. The state must not allow unbridled capitalism and must keep a tight rein on the financial system.

In the 1980s, neo-Keynesians, neoclassicists, monetarists and adherents of the Austrian school dominated economic doctrine. It was a time of high intellectual and rational expectations about the efficiency of financial markets, underpinned by sophisticated mathematical models. Then, at the beginning of this century, the real estate bubble inflated in the USA, but it was also oversized in other regions, especially in Europe, and led to unhealthy development. Finally, there was the bang in 2007/2008 that was so strong that the international financial system almost crashed.

The late American economist and Nobel Prize Laureate James Tobin had already praised Hyman Minsky in 1987 as the most convincing contemporary economist because he had recognized that excessive debt policy was the Achilles heel of capitalism. In view of the current perceived stability of the global economy, many experts again fear monetary overheating, which could lead to another global financial crisis.

Global debt is greater today than it was at the start of the financial crisis 10 + years ago. Two-thirds of global debt is accounted for by the private sector, i.e., households and companies, and one-third by local and national government debt. Developed countries, led by the USA, account for the largest share of the global debt volume. However, the largest debtor has been China, although the official figures do not reflect the full extent of China's debt problem. Financial experts assess the situation as a ticking time bomb.

In the context of the EU, Italy's high level of debt is a particular cause for concern. Italy's public debt currently amounts to 132% of GDP. However, Italy is not alone in this respect as Japan's mountain of debt is much higher and other countries such as Greece, Portugal, Belgium, France and Canada also have above average debt levels.

While the EU as a whole is trying to meet the Maastricht Criteria, the Trump Administration opted for the opposite. Despite a good economy, a higher national debt ratio must be accepted to finance tax giveaways. While the EU wants to reduce the debt ratio to 72% by 2023, an increase to 117% is expected in the USA.

The current global debt volume in absolute terms amounts to the unimaginable sum of USD 215 trillion. This sum corresponds to more than three times the annual global value added. The largest increase in debt is in emerging markets. With interest rates expected to rise in the foreseeable future, concerns are growing about another financial collapse. Of course, the bulk of this is due to the developed world, which has a total of USD 160 trillion, almost four times the Annual GDP. If there is another financial collapse, developing countries will be the main victims, as they were during the financial crisis.

The Financial Stability Report published at the Joint Annual Meeting of the International Monetary Fund (IMF) and the World Bank in Bali in Autumn 2018 warned of increasing monetary policy risks and abrupt turbulence on the financial markets. An escalation of trade conflicts and growing geopolitical risks are fuelling fears of a new financial crisis.

In contrast to Adam Smith, Friedrich List recognized the importance of the balance of trade for the wealth and prosperity of nations. In doing so, he spoke out against both the monetary theory of mercantilism and liberalism. In this connection, he urged the theorists that they should always support their theories with practical examples. Then they would see for themselves whether they were right in their views. He said that there was nothing wrong with reproducing macroeconomic problems on a small scale to present one's theoretical views in an understandable way and to check their validity.

No one would deny that the wealth and prosperity of a nation is based on the same principles as the prosperity of a single province, a single city, a single family or a single person. Wealth, they say, can only be attained by producing quite a lot of exchange values and by producing more than one consumes. If an economic entity does not produce exchange values, it has no choice but to consume its available capital.

Instead of objects of exchange, most producers and service providers would demand money as a means of compensation for value. Should the buyer not have sufficient monetary funds, he would have to pledge or sell his real estate, tangible assets or his valuables. It would be false to conclude from this situation that since the economic subject could still offer money in exchange, he would not become impoverished.

These examples should convince those who hold to the fundamentally false thesis that whoever trades money for goods must know the exchange value of the goods and thus cannot suffer a loss because he receives the equivalent value of the money in the form of goods. The same applies to states that, like individuals, consume money that they have not previously earned but received from foreign investors.

The common theory maintains that in the national as well as in the international trade of goods, it depends only on the reciprocal relation of prices whether a commodity is cheap or expensive. The respective exchange rate would then automatically lead to an equilibrium between imports and exports and thus to a mutual balance of trade. So the economic relations of a nation would be most surely and best regulated by the nature of things, or in other words, brought about by the free interplay of forces. This argument is perfectly correct in internal trade but contradicts the experiences in foreign trade.[16]

If we look at the world conditions we find that if there is unrestricted trade between a manufacturing nation and an agricultural nation, the latter is always in debt to the former. These imbalances could then give rise to trade crises of greater or lesser magnitude. This is exactly the reason why so many demonstrators go to the barricades at the G20 Summits.

This was also Friedrich List's explanation for the severe financial crisis during the Van Buren administration, who was American President from 1837 to 1841, and under whose reign the American national bank was dissolved, causing a severe economic crisis. This List explained in that capital rich England, which had reached the highest stage of development, had been anxious to throw as many goods as possible into the American market, granting more and more credit to importers to encourage them to make purchases and to flood the American market with their manufactured goods. Further on, the importers and retailers would have persuaded the farmers to buy as many products as possible on credit. The farmers would then have tried to compensate for the overconsumption by continually increasing their own production and increasing their exports. However, as demand for their agricultural products fell far short of keeping pace with imports, their prices fell rapidly. When the loans came due, the farmers were no longer able to meet the debts they had incurred. This then led to payment difficulties for the traders, who in turn were no longer able to service the loans from the importers or the English manufacturers. At the same time, sales plummeted, and much of the existing stock proved unsaleable. "Unworthiness of manufactured goods and unworthiness of fruit, the claims of foreign countries and the inability of domestic countries to pay met in the great market, and a general stagnation, cessation of all credit, and general bankruptcy ensued."[17] According to

List, this crisis could have been prevented with the help of a protective tariff system because such a system would have been able to neutralize the trade balance and bring it into equilibrium.

Wealth theory, he argued, was of the mistaken view that international trade would only benefit each nation. Here List alluded to David Ricardo's Theory of Comparative Costs. On the other hand, the example of Portugal proved that a nation could lose not only important branches of its national prosperity but also its entire manufacturing power through foreign trade, that is, it could be degraded from an agrarian manufacturing nation to a mere agrarian nation. If an agrarian nation does not succeed with the help of its trade policy in bringing its imports into equilibrium with its exports, "terrible crises" could result.

Privately, what mattered was not necessarily the possession of liquid means of payment but the power of disposition of the available cash and tangible assets. A wealthy man might have only a little cash at his disposal but could have a much larger overdraft facility (for example, letters of credit) than a less well-off man.

At the public level, the dispositional power of a nation results from an extended and balanced relationship between domestic and foreign trade, and the latter in turn from a manufacturing power that is developed in all directions. There are only two ways to deal with international imbalances in the balance of trade, either stopping the flow, whatever specifically that may be, through which too many currency reserves are draining away or making an effort to increase exports. From this point to a pragmatic tariff system would be only a stone's throw away. Since it would not be so easy to increase exports in a developing country if no exportable products were available, only a protective tariff system for certain manufactured goods against the onslaught of foreign products and services would come into consideration.

Not so long ago, the mercantilists would have held the erroneous view that national wealth consisted of the availability of precious metals and therefore prohibited their export. It is just as wrong, however, if one now pays no attention at all to the export of precious metals and completely overlooks the existence of a possible passive trade. The reality is that gold and silver must be regarded as commodities that, like all other goods, must be traded and exported. As with other goods, there is asset and liability trade. Passive trade arises when, due to excessive imports, more financial assets flow out than flow back through exports, and thus national capital in the order of magnitude of the gap (or delta) must be expended, as was the case with the German territorial states during List's lifetime. Since too little gold and silver could be produced domestically, it would be necessary to temporarily attack one's savings. However, gold and silver money would subsequently flow back in the form of bonds, which would open up the possibility of spending it again then receive it back in this form.

20.9 Abuse of Power and Bad Governance

The core problem of development politics concerns the control centers of political power, therefore the respective state of the three parts, government, parliament and the judiciary. In many countries of the world, and not only in developing countries, their condition is criticized to a greater or lesser extent. One only has to think of the current catastrophic conditions in Venezuela, which despite its oil wealth is a broken state.

In many nations the abuse of power, bad governance, political instability and elite bureaucracy prevail. "*The Bertelsmann Transformation Index*" of 2014 declares 54 of the 129 countries studied to be autocracies and 42 to be 'defective democracies.' New York's Freedom House infers a 'retreat of democracy' based on its empirical data research.

In its "*Democracy Index 2013*", the Economist Intelligence Unit was able to identify only one truly functioning democracy in the whole of Africa, namely, the island state of Mauritius, which has worked its way up from an ailing sugar monoculture, a colonial legacy, to a flourishing emerging market. Rapid structural change is thus possible if steered by a smart, not corrupt, elite. "Mauritius has practiced good governance in its democratic version and Rwanda in its autocratic version and succeeded" Fig. 20.3.

Rwanda, whose authoritarian president Paul Kagame has managed to turn a country traumatized by civil war into something like a'model African country' supported by considerable international reconstruction aid, which has been able to be used wisely for reconciliation and cooperation between formerly hostile large ethnic groups. So Rwanda is a notable, albeit very rare, limited exception. Regrettably, this model country ends outside the showcase of the capital Kigali, where the scars of genocide have not yet healed. 148

Fig. 20.3 Abuse of power and bad governance; cartoon by Ajinkya Ghadge

Africa expert Robert Kappel commented on the current situation on the African continent in a 2015 interview with Macro host Eva Schmidt, "for approximately 10 years, most African countries have shown positive economic growth. However, it is largely based on China's increased demand for commodities and higher prices for oil, minerals and agricultural products, rather than on domestic market dynamics. As a result, growth has had no employment effect, and the number of unemployed and underemployed has risen despite the boom. In addition, approximately 40% of African countries are politically unstable or ruled by dictators. Especially in the countries in the Sahel belt but also in countries such as Burundi, Congo, Malawi, Somalia and Eritrea, people have little hope for the future. People are fleeing to the north from these fragile countries as well as from regions marked by civil wars."

Africa has made some progress. After the lost decades of the 1980s and 1990s, many countries have implemented economic and political reforms. However, in almost all respects, the continent lags behind those of the other world regions. The main objective, per the Millennium Development Goal, has been clearly missed since the absolute number of poor people has continued to rise. This was foreseeable, despite the high input of funds and experts. Where there have been successes, as in the improvement of the education system, the 'lower-hanging fruit' have been reaped by increasing the enrollment rate of children while at the same time neglecting the quality of the education system and the educational opportunities for girls. The main problem is that the African state elites, who agreed and signed off the development goals with the international community, are hardly willing to eradicate poverty and bring about development. They were only interested in the inflow of financial development aid.

The extremely high population growth is undoing all the progress that has been made. A high number of children is still considered as insurance for the future. There are two general mistakes that have been made in recent decades. One is the neglect of the education system for large parts of Africa, especially for women. For example, just 25% of girls in Muslim northern Nigeria go to school. Second, birth control and family planning are not at all on the agenda of governments. In contrast, many states speak proudly of their growing populations and the youth who are supposed to be the future of Africa. This is an absolute fallacy. Unfortunately, the churches also contribute to the marginalization of this issue.

If the high population growth continues, even more young people in Africa will be unable to find jobs because the economies are only agriculturally oriented and/or based on the production of raw materials but do not create any significant jobs in the process. Numerous concepts are known but await implementation including promotion of vocational training in conjunction with the development of small and medium-sized enterprises, as well as support for the development of industrial clusters through tax incentives and financing systems for small and medium-sized enterprises. In parallel, the integration of local producers into regional and global value chains should be realized.

Above all, it is important that the economic and political elites in Africa finally bring about a push for modernization. More far-reaching goals create new expectations that cannot be met in most African countries. What Africa needs is not so much an increase in development aid and new agendas but responsible elites who create trust and strive through good governance to promote the prosperity of their countries and fight poverty. That this can be achieved in individual sectors if the will is there is shown by the example of Ethiopia, where the current government has settled the decade-long political dispute with Eritrea over access to the Red Sea through negotiations and has substantially improved the health system by setting up a large number of stationary and mobile health clinics."[18] On the other hand, the country is shaken by the civil war in Tigrai, which puts the gains made at risk again.

Botswana, which has only been an independent state since 1966, is a shining example of how things can be done differently. Although it is a purely landlocked country and only one percent of its land area can be used for agriculture, Botswana has the highest per capita income in all of Africa. The country ranks 34th in the *Corruption Perception Index*, ahead of Poland, Spain and Italy. More than 90% of children attend school. In the health care sector and the democracy index, the country is ahead of France, Belgium and Italy. The basis for relative prosperity is mineral resources, especially diamond deposits. The proceeds from the diamond industry are invested wisely and effectively in education and health care, as well as in the expansion of other infrastructure. As a result, Botswana has managed to build a peaceful and relatively balanced social structure. Therefore, it would be desirable if the other African countries would follow this example based on their own specific circumstances.

Ethiopia is an important coffee producer. However, until now, the green beans were exported. Only recently have there been three or four roasting plants built where green coffee is processed and only then exported. Since the price of roasted coffee is more than double that of green coffee and jobs are being created in the roasting plants that are relatively well paid, the country is benefiting from this new added value. This is a fine example that should set a precedent in all African countries.

Notes

1. List, F. (1837): Die Welt bewegt sich, Göttingen 1985, p. 106 f.
2. Idem: W. II, p. 240.
3. Idem: W. I/2, pp. 580–584.
4. Idem: W. IV, p. 238 ff. and W. V, p. 294.
5. Stockmann, R., Menzel, U., Nuscheler, F. (2016): Entwicklungspolitik; 2nd ed., Berlin, pp. 285–333.
6. Idem: pp. 337–357.
7. List, F.: W. VII, p. 484.
8. Idem (1837): Die Welt bewegt sich, Göttingen 1985, p. 105.
9. Idem: W. VI, p. 168 f.
10. Idem: W. VII, p. 374 f.
11. Idem: W. VI, p. 37 f.
12. Idem: W. I/1, p. 103 and 359.
13. Idem: W. VI, p. 68 and p. 409.
14. Idem: W. VI, p. 280.
15. List, F.: Die Welt bewegt sich, Göttingen 1985, p. 153.

16. List, F.: Die Welt bewegt sich, Göttingen 1985, p. 153.
17. Wendler, E. (2016): Friedrich List: The Politics of the Future, Wiesbaden, pp. 308 ff.
18. Stockmann, R., Menzel, Nuscheler, F.: Entwicklungspolitik, 2nd ed., Berlin 2016, p. 406.

Chapter 21
Epilog

List understood the term "politics" to mean "the statesmanship of leading a people standing on a low level of culture towards its maturity, of gradually curing the infirmities of the state without shock and violent measures, of improving its organism, and of helping the principle of right to recognition."[1] He was aware that this description differed substantially from the common definition of the term. Going further into details, List states, "the highest aim of rational politics is the union of nations under the law of rights. An aim which can only be attained by the widest possible equality of the nations of the earth in culture, wealth, industry, and power, and by the transformation of the antipathies and conflicts existing between them, into sympathy and harmony. The solution of this task, however, is a work of infinitely slow progress."[2]

The most common causes of such antipathies, he said, were territorial conflicts, opposing trade interests, conflicting interests in shipping, naval power, and colonial possessions, different levels of culture, religious struggles, and different power relations. The less powerful allied against the stronger, the oppressed against the conquerors, the land powers against the sea powers, the industrialized countries against the agricultural countries, the culturally advanced against the less developed countries, the dictatorships against the democracies. Coalitions and alliances would be forged to protect opposing interests to be armed against adversaries. Such alliances are changeable, so what are friends today can be enemies tomorrow and vice versa.

Politics had long felt that the equality of nations was a task that could hardly be solved. What is called the preservation of European equilibrium has always been nothing other than the effort to stop the inferior from encroaching on the superior. Politics has not rarely confused the obvious goal with the more distant goal, and vice versa.

The true profession of the politician and national economist in its highest significance is providing for the inevitable and necessary needs of the state and the nation, today as well as for the near future, making possible the progress of the future, sowing the seeds daily for the best fruits, which may not come to full maturity for centuries. Nevertheless, it is no less true that a nation may possess in abundance high public servants, diplomats, legislators, administrators, and financiers, with the

E. Wendler, *The Political Economy of Friedrich List*, Springer Studies in the History of Economic Thought, https://doi.org/10.1007/978-3-031-24601-2_21

greatest expertise in their area, and yet run the risk of meeting its doom if it does not possess statesmen capable of foreseeing the future course of world affairs, and thereby prescribing the aim and direction towards which present policy is to be directed. This clear vision speaks for itself. We content ourselves with List's statement which to us seems to be of great importance with regard to current world politics:

21.1 Democracy and Industrialization Are Synonymous, They Are Inseparable![3]

His years spent living in the United States proved to be the training ground for the national economy and political life for Friedrich List and prepared him for his later life. Here, he reached the great spiritual horizon that broke his nationalistic attitude and made him a cosmopolitian. In his travels through the Atlantic coastal states, he became acquainted with the most important regions and most influential politicians in the U.S. These impressions and encounters brought to his national economic and political ideas an abundance of new impulses. Contrasting the economic life of the Old World and the New World was indispensable in finalizing List´s major work on economics. "*The National System of Political Economy*" is counted among the works that, in the five centuries of the printed book in the Western world, have helped shape its history.

Through his time in America, Friedrich List became a notable intermediary between Germany and the United States and a citizen of both countries. He earned the respect and recognition of both. The profound gratitude that List felt toward his temporarily adopted country is nowhere more clearly expressed than in the poem he wrote about the Fourth of July in 1776, the day of the U.S. Declaration of Independence. He set it to the Beethoven melody "*Ode of Joy*" and published it on 29. July 1830, in the Reading Eagle.[4]

With a happy jubilant sound.
Toast the glasses full.
And with cheerful rounds of song.
Cry: "Hail to every man!".
Let the heroes‘ names ring out.
To whom this day is dedicated:
Those in the halls of heaven.
To whom this happy scene is shown.
As their wonderful work accomplished,
So divine, as well, their wage:
From the judge‘s throne in the afterworld.
Their names will be sung on high.
Which joy do we yet lack?
Freedom, peace, wealth, glory.
Why we call the grace of God -

Is already ours to have;
However, still one thing, many lack:
Something you still must strive for,
That which our wisemen teach us -
Brothers!—cosmopolitan consciousness.
Let it echo once again;
Pure cosmopolitan spirit!
As God is called the Father.
So are all men brothers.
What Washington has given us;
What Jefferson has taught us;
Our freedom, our entire lives,
Our lives‘ entire value;
Not only to the few millions.
Was this great spirit endeared.
To all citizens of the universe.
It imparted its cosmopolitan consciousness.
The heart must raise itself higher,
Brothers! By the great spirit.
Extolled in happy cheer,
All people should live.
Cold selfishness will not.
Desecreate our happiness.
which all around the earth.
Is gladly cradled in brotherly hands;
He who gives his all for freedom.
Has brought magic to his homeland.
Every child in every zone.
Greetings, cosmopolitan spirit!
Give not bitter anguish.
To prejudices instead of a good turn;
No! There beats only a single heart,
In freedom‘s beautiful land.
And united in heart and soul.
Echo our jubilant sound.
Through the air of the sweeping halls.
To the universal judge‘s throne -
Those who fought this day for us!
What a heavenly benefit:
Thousands have joined together.
In cosmopolitan consciousness.
Let the choirs ring merrier;
Our happy jubilation.
Our hearts resounding.
Should be heard unto the stars.

Notes

1. List, F.: I/1, P. 437.
2. Ders.: W. VI, p. 406 and W.VII, p. 485 f.
3. Ders.: W. IV, p. 207.
4. Wendler, E. (1989): Friedrich List/1789–1846): An Historical Figure and Pioneer in German-American Relations, Munich, p. 113 f.